Lecture Notes in Computer Science   2249

Edited by G. Goos, J. Hartmanis, and J. van Leeuwen

DATE DUE FOR RETURN

Springer

Berlin
Heidelberg
New York
Barcelona
Hong Kong
London
Milan
Paris
Tokyo

Khaled Nagi

Transactional Agents

Towards a Robust Multi-Agent System

 Springer

Series Editors

Gerhard Goos, Karlsruhe University, Germany
Juris Hartmanis, Cornell University, NY, USA
Jan van Leeuwen, Utrecht University, The Netherlands

Author

Khaled Nagi
University of Karlsruhe, Institute for Program Structures and Data Organization
Am Fasanengarten 5, 76131 Karlsruhe, Germany
E-mail: nagi@ira.uka.de

This is the doctoral thesis of Khaled Nagi, born in Karlsruhe.
The thesis was accepted by the Faculty of Computer Science of the Fridericiana
University of Karlsruhe and the author was granted the academic degree "Doctor of
Engineering" (Doktor der Ingenieurwissenschaften) based on this work.
Date of the oral examination: July 6th, 2001
First advisor: Prof. Dr.-Ing. Peter C. Lockemann
Second advisor: Prof. Dr.rer.nat. Peter Deussen

Cataloging-in-Publication Data applied for

Die Deutsche Bibliothek - CIP-Einheitsaufnahme

Nagi, Khaled:
Transactional agents : towards a robust multi-agent system / Khaled Nagi. -
Berlin ; Heidelberg ; New York ; Barcelona ; Hong Kong ; London ; Milan ;
Paris ; Tokyo : Springer, 2001
  (Lecture notes in computer science ; Vol. 2249)
  Zugl.: Karlsruhe, Univ., Diss., 2001
  ISBN 3-540-43046-6

CR Subject Classification (1998): H.2.4, I.2.11, C.2.4, D.2.12, H.3, H.4

ISSN 0302-9743
ISBN 3-540-43046-6 Springer-Verlag Berlin Heidelberg New York

Springer-Verlag Berlin Heidelberg New York
a member of BertelsmannSpringer Science+Business Media GmbH

http://www.springer.de

© Springer-Verlag Berlin Heidelberg 2001
Printed in Germany

Typesetting: Camera-ready by author, data conversion by Steingräber Satztechnik GmbH, Heidelberg
Printed on acid-free paper   SPIN: 10845957   06/3142   5 4 3 2 1 0

To my parents

Foreword

The term "agent" is one of those catchwords that mean widely differing things to different people. To telecommunications people it is little more than a mobile piece of code that may be executed at any place. At the other extreme, AI people often associate with agents human-like traits such as social behavior. In between, software people view agents as fairly self-contained pieces of software that, at the low end, pretty much act like objects and, at the high end, more or less autonomously decide when and how to react to stimuli or proactively initiate effects that can be observed from their environment.

Software agents are particularly important when it comes to distributed environments. There, much of the communication takes place asynchronously, that is the sequence of events cannot be planned ahead in all detail. Instead, agents are given rules as to how to interpret the current situation and, given a common goal, so that they adjust their response accordingly.

Surprisingly enough, few researchers seem to ponder the question what happens in the case of unexpected – and hence entirely unplanned for – situations such as disturbances or failures in the underlying technical system, or unforeseen demands in the real world that the agents are supposed to serve. Such exceptions may affect just a single agent, or they may inflict wounds on a number of collaborating agents. It is the author's intent to leave a first imprint on the all too important issue of robust multi-agent systems.

But what is a promising approach to robustness in multi-agent systems? With his background in database technology, it is only natural for the author to rely on transactions with their well-defined failure semantics. These have proven their worth in both centralized and distributed databases, and have become an essential part of all of today's middleware systems.

Now, is there any meaningful connection between database and agent technologies? There is – so the author claims – if there are data to be shared asynchronously between agents. Indeed, the basic assumption underlying this thesis is that the agents share a world model whose current state is reflected in a common database. Consequently, by relying on this assumption the work is indeed a first step, though just a first step, in the direction of robust multi-agent systems.

If this still sounds too general, it is. And indeed, the author further narrows down his choices. He restricts the agent architecture to the BDI paradigm, and he argues that a variant of open nested transactions is the natural counterpart to the paradigm. Much of the work revolves around the issue of how to tie these two together. What's more, the author aims for an orthogonal solution, that is one in which robustness to any desired degree can be added to agents with only very little need for modifications to the agents themselves.

Much of today's progress in information technology is due to interdisciplinary approaches – or to changing viewpoints on a particular problem. The thesis is a beautiful example of such an interdisciplinary approach that brings together database knowledge that rarely cares about agents, and agent techniques that have little in mind with databases.

What I hope for is that this monograph will stimulate others into seeking interdisciplinary collaboration to lead to further progress in the vital area of distributed multi-agent systems.

Prof. Dr. Peter Lockemann

Preface

The ever-growing complexity of modern distributed Information Systems (IS) and the difficulty to foresee all potentially arising disturbances make the applicability of Multi-Agent Systems (MAS) in this important domain very appealing. Despite many research efforts in the last decade, this technology is slow to find its way into large-scale information-rich applications such as Enterprise Resource Planning (ERP) and Production Planning and Controlling (PPC) systems. This can be largely attributed to technical challenges facing the introduction of MAS to such mission critical core applications. The most pressing technical issue is the *lack of robustness* in existing MAS architectures.

The aim of this work is to increase the robustness of MAS applied in IS domains through an underlying middleware. The middleware will be able to provide formal guarantees on the robustness of the system by itself and independently from the original structure of the MAS architecture. We define the robustness provided by the middleware in terms of guarantees given on a technical basis, which is guaranteeing the *correctness* in normal operation and *recoverability* of the system in case of disturbances. In order to fulfill these robustness requirements, we capture both agent plans and their contingency behavior in an extended transaction model that we developed during the course of this work. To execute this transaction model, we add an Execution Agent that is responsible for guaranteeing the robustness of execution of agent actions and define its interactions with the other components of a generic MAS architecture.

Although robustness is a deciding factor in the application of MAS in large-scale IS applications, any robustness guaranteeing solution is not allowed to decrease the overall system performance or its scalability. In order to evaluate the performance of our proposed solution, we develop an extensive simulation model that represents the operation of MAS in an IS environment. By conducting many simulation runs under various workloads and system settings, we prove the system to be scalable. The simulator serves also to enhance the predictability of the MAS and reveals the insights of their complex behavior in the system.

Acknowledgment

Since 1998 I have been a member of the Database Group of the Institute for Program Structures and Data Organization in Karlsruhe. I am most grateful to Prof. Dr. P.C. Lockemann, the head of this group, for the continual advice and support. I have learned so much from his wide spectrum of scientific experience and have always treasured his views and sound scientific advice.

A former version of this book has been submitted and accepted as a thesis for obtaining the degree of Doctor Engineer at the Fakultät für Informatik, Universität Fridericiana zu Karlsruhe (TH), in Karlsruhe, Germany. I am very grateful to the German Academic Exchange Service (DAAD) for awarding me a Ph.D. scholarship in Germany and the German Research Foundation (DFG) for funding the research project KRASH, which delivered the necessary test bed for this work.

I deeply appreciate the cooperation and support of my colleagues and students in the Database Group. My special thanks go to Dr. G. Hillebrand and J. Nimis for their valuable discussions and contributions. I also appreciate the comments of Prof. Dr. P. Deussen during the final stage of this work. My thanks to private individuals have been expressed personally.

Khaled Nagi

August 2001

List of Abbreviations

2PC	Two-Phase Commit protocol
ACA	Avoids Cascading Aborts
ACC	Agent Communication Channel
ACL	Agent Communication Language
ACP	Atomic Commit Protocol
AMS	Agent Management Service
AOP	Agent Oriented Programming
APG	Agent Plan Generator
ATM	Agent Transaction Manager
BDI	Beliefs, Desires, Intentions
BOT	Begin Of Transaction
CAD	Computer-Aided Design
CIM	Computer Integrated Manufacturing
CIS	Cooperative Information Systems
CM	Cache Manager
CP	Commit Projection
CSR	Conflict Serializable history
DAI	Distributed Artificial Intelligence
DBMS	Database Management System
DDBMS	Distributed Database Management System
DF	Directory Facilitator
DG	Disturbance Generator
ECA	Event, Condition, Action
EOT	End Of Transaction

ERP	Enterprise Resource Planning
FIPA	Foundation for Intelligent Physical Agents
GCSR	Globally Conflict Serializable history
GPG	Global Precedence Graph
GTM	Global Transaction Manager
IS	Information Systems
JDBC	Java Database Connectivity
KIF	Knowledge Interchange Format
KQML	Knowledge Query and Manipulation Language
KSE	Knowledge Sharing Effort
LDBMS	Local Database Management System
LTM	Local Transaction Manager
MAS	Multi-Agent System
MEG	Merged Execution Graph
MGPG	Modified Global Serialization Graph
MGSG	Modified Global Serialization Graph
PG	Precedence Graph
PPC	Production Planning and Controlling
RC	Recoverable history
RM	Recovery Manager
SG	Serialization Graph
SR	Serializable history
ST	Strict history
TID	Transaction node Identifier
TM	Transaction Manager
VSR	View Serializable history
XML	Extended Markup Language

Table of Contents

1 Introduction

1.1 General

Multi-Agent Systems (MAS) emerged from the domain of *Distributed Artificial Intelligence* (DAI). Early MAS were designed to solve highly abstracted complex distributed planning problems. Simultaneously, MAS were used in the *robotic* domain to control production machines performing repetitious work in a world full of disturbances. Today, MAS technology is increasingly applied to *Information Systems* (IS). The ever-growing complexity of modern IS and the difficulty to foresee all potentially arising disturbances makes them an inviting test bed for MAS.

Over the last decade, many research efforts were dedicated to deploying this emerging technology in the field of distributed IS. Yet, this technology is slow to find its way into large-scale information-rich applications such as *Enterprise Resource Planning* (ERP) and *Production Planning and Controlling* (PPC) systems. This can be largely attributed to technical challenges facing the introduction of MAS to such mission critical core applications. One of the most pressing technical issue is the lack of *robustness* in existing MAS.

1.2 Motivation of the Work

Leaving their traditional domains, MAS show their very strong potential in their new fields of intelligent information retrieval, web assistants, information trading, matchmaking, etc. Common to all these information systems areas is that they are of a decision support nature. In general, they only *read* the IS and return valuable suggestions to the user, who is actually in the decision making position. Accuracy and relevance of the MAS results are the deciding factors in these applications. In case of failure, their operations can be arbitrarily retried since they do not involve actions that change the state of the IS. Here, robustness comes in the second place.

On the contrary, robustness is a basic requirement if MAS are to be applied to large-scale information-rich applications, e.g., PPC. In these domains, it is expected that MAS automatically *execute* actions that read from and *write* to the IS and hence change their state instead of just providing decision support services. By robustness, we mean that both individual agents and the MAS as a whole correctly execute their actions in normal operation and reach well-defined states in case of disturbances, failure, or uncontrolled interactions between the various

K. Nagi: Transactional Agents, LNCS 2249, pp. 1–4, 2001.
© Springer-Verlag Berlin Heidelberg 2001

components of the systems. Here, MAS have a long way to go to increase their robustness in order to make themselves candidates for the application in their mission critical large-scale IS.

1.3 Scope of the Work

1.3.1 Objectives

The aim of this work is to increase the robustness of MAS applied in IS domains through an underlying middleware. The middleware will be able to provide some formal guarantees on the robustness of the system by itself and independently from the original structure of the MAS architecture. Separating the robustness guaranteeing aspect from the development of the MAS itself eases the portability of MAS from one application to the other and lets the MAS designers concentrate on their original assignment, namely, designing the MAS that solves the planning problem.

Since the middleware cannot encapsulate the whole semantic of the application, we define the robustness provided by the middleware in terms of guarantees given on a *technical basis*, which is guaranteeing the *correctness* and *recoverability* of the system. By correctness, it is meant that, in normal operation modes, the agent plans are executed in a way that guarantees the absence of any undesired side effects that might result from the concurrent execution of agent actions in the multi-agent environment. By recoverability, it is meant that, in case of disturbances, the system reaches a well-defined consistent state. In view of this technical definition of robustness, we should be able to provide necessary guarantees on the robust *execution* of agent actions. In other words, this definition of robustness fulfills the requirements of applications that both *read* from and *write* to the IS.

1.3.2 Approach

In order to fulfill these robustness requirements by the middleware, we obviously need a structure that captures the semantic of the plan of each agent. We choose this structure on the basis of the *open-nested transaction* model introduced in the 80s in the database environments. The reason for choosing an advanced transactions model to represent the structure is twofold. Transactions have been the means for achieving robustness in databases environments over the past 25 years. The traditional flat ACID transactions are the understandable form of submitting actions to the underlying IS. They established themselves as the standard transaction model in almost commercially available *Database Management Systems* (DBMS). This is mainly due to their simplicity, their strong theoretical foundation, and the great potential to optimize their performance. The open-nested transaction model builds on these flat transactions to capture a more semantically rich model.

Nevertheless, the open-nested transaction model must be extended to be integrated in the MAS paradigm and to form its basic execution structure. For this purpose, we develop a transaction model that supports the high *reactivity* of agents by allowing more flexibility in its definition. It also supports automatic execution of several standard patterns of error handling in case of failure. At the same time, the transaction model supports the *proactive* nature of agents. For example, in case of disturbances, it is able to independently choose the appropriate contingency behavior that makes the agent reach a consistent and well-defined state. Central to MAS is their *social* aspect. The transaction model supports cooperation between agents executing a common shared plan through the implementation of various coordination primitives between the transaction trees of the transaction model.

To execute this transaction model, we divide each agent into two physical entities: a *Planning Agent* and an *Execution Agent*. The Planning Agent perceives the IS and develops the logical plan to achieve its goal. In other words, it only reads the IS, and hence its actions do not change its state. Then, the Planning Agent delegates the execution of its plan to a peer Execution Agent after formulating it into a transaction tree. The Execution Agent is responsible for all write operations performed on the IS. The actions of the Execution Agent run under transactional protection to achieve the robustness guarantees on the execution. In order to successfully accomplish its role, the Execution Agent must interact with its peer Planning Agent to couple the planning process with the execution process. Moreover, it coordinates its execution with other Execution Agents to reflect the cooperation between their peer Planning Agents, thus supporting the social aspect of MAS.

1.3.3 System Evaluation

Although robustness is a deciding factor in the application of MAS in large-scale IS applications, any robustness guaranteeing solution is not allowed to decrease the overall system *performance* or its *scalability*.

Unfortunately, simple analytical tools, such as mathematical models, seldom succeed in modeling the MAS with all its complexity and the variety of input parameters and system settings. Therefore, we develop an extensive simulation model that represents the operation of MAS in a heterogeneous IS environment. By conducting many simulation runs under various workloads and system settings, the performance of the introduced solution is analyzed and proven to be scalable. The simulator serves also to enhance the *predictability* of the MAS. One of the main problems of MAS is their unpredictable nature. Simulation helps us a lot to gain insight about the behavior of MAS under the operational workload.

1.4 Organization of the Thesis

The rest of the thesis is organized as follows. In Chap. 2, we present an application scenario drawn from the field of Production Planning and Controlling. We believe this field to be a rich environment for illustrating the importance of robustness in MAS when applied to an information-rich environment. In Chap. 3, we present an overview of agent technology with a special focus on their application in IS domains. Since our solution is based on an extension of an advanced transaction model, we give an overview of transaction processing in databases in Chap. 4. We present both the theoretical aspects, as we will need them in proving the correctness of our model, and the existing transaction models, as we extend them.

In Chap. 5, we present our approach of having transactional agents for increasing robustness in MAS applications. In this chapter, we motivate the choice of the open-nested transaction model as a basis of our transaction model and introduce the Execution Agent, which is the actual transactional agent in the system. In the following three chapters we go into each aspect of our approach in details. In Chap. 6, we present the transaction model and explain its operation using several examples from the application scenario. The proof of correctness for the transaction model is also given in this chapter. Then, we describe the internal operation of the Execution Agent by showing how it executes the transaction model and gives formal guarantees on the robust execution of the agent actions in Chap. 7. Finally, Chap. 8 illustrates the interaction of the Execution Agent with the other components of the MAS.

The simulation study is a very important part of the thesis. Chaps. 9 and 10 are dedicated to describe the simulation model and the experimental results. In Chap. 9, the simulation model is presented. The performance indices and typical parameter setting are also explained. In Chap. 10, we describe the conducted experiments and analyze the obtained results.

Chap. 11 summarizes the thesis and presents an outlook in the future work. At the end, we present a brief description of a prototype implementation of the proposed solution in a separate appendix.

2 Application Scenario

In this thesis, we choose the field of *Production Planning* and *Controlling* (PPC) as an application domain for our proposed architecture. *This choice is by no means restrictive.* The technology can be applied to any information-rich environment, in which actions, involving database write operations, are to be carried out under hard requirements for robustness. This could be any application such as enterprise resource planning, supply chain management, e-commerce, travel assistants, etc. However, we choose this particular domain, as we believe it to be a rich environment for illustrating the importance of the tackled problem, namely, *robustness in MAS*. In this chapter, we provide a brief overview of the PPC domain and motivate the need for a MAS approach. We surely present a simplified and highly abstracted application scenario. Nevertheless, the scenario possesses sufficient illustrative power, without falling into much detail, to accompany the reader through the thesis in form of various examples. We end the chapter with a categorization of disturbances that might occur during the operation of the MAS and an intuitive requirement analysis for any solution trying to face them and conclude the chapter with a basic requirement analysis for a robust MAS in PPC.

2.1 Overview of the PPC Domain

There is no canonical definition for Production Planning and Controlling. A generic definition is given by Scheer [99].

Definition 2.1

> "PPC is the primary managerial and planning component of a
> Computer Integrated Manufacturing (CIM)-model covering
> order flow, requirement planning, time planning, production
> controlling, collection of operational data, till the final ship-
> ping process".

The job of the PPC is to make the necessary decisions defining the way to produce parts, their quantities and their production dates as well as the resources they utilize [107]. These decisions must be optimized to maximize the profit as a top goal [123]. However, this goal is hard to model. It is often broken down into several primary and secondary goals. Kernler [59] identifies four basic goals for PPC:

- high stock availability,
- low work-in-progress,

K. Nagi: Transactional Agents, LNCS 2249, pp. 5–19, 2001.
© Springer-Verlag Berlin Heidelberg 2001

- high utilization of capital equipment, and
- short manufacturing time for a specific product from start to finish.

Other goals include: optimal flow of material through the production process, diversity of supported products, high adaptation to fluctuation in demand, high adaptation to disturbances in resource availability. Obviously, these goals are in conflict with each other. The PPC must compromise between these goals. However, the relative importance of each goal is dependent on the nature of the product and its market.

Because of its importance, PPC systems were one of the early domains for the application of information technology. Already in the 60s, several algorithms were developed and implemented for mainframes. One of the early systems was implemented in the USA by Wight [64]. It was a pure Material Requirement Planning and worked according to the *Push* scheduling concept. The system created the basis for the widely spread MRP II systems, that are still in use today. Other methods for implementing push strategies included constraint-based problem solving, with its long tradition in artificial intelligence, and numerical programming [89]. These methods were relatively simple to implement and were able to adapt to new products with small batches. However, under these systems, lead-time and inventory size grow geometrically with utilization. Meanwhile, a *Pull* strategy was beginning to emerge. This manifested itself in the Kanban [53] system that first appeared in Japan. Kanban means "card" and refers to the identification card, located at each production unit. This card has a double function. It serves:

- as an order card, if the buffer at the production unit is exhausted, and
- as an identification card for the produced unit.

This strategy has the advantage of having low work-in-process, and a high visibility of production problems. However, it is only suitable for stable production demand and is slow to adapt to new products.

2.2 The Need for Multi-agent Systems in PPC

According to a classification given within the AARIA project [90], illustrated in Fig. 2.1, *pull* scheduling strategies reside in the upper right corner of the chart, as they are highly constrained by commitment as well as by demand; whereas *push* strategies have a low constraint on commitment as well as on demand and, hence, reside in the opposite part of the chart.

Nowadays, both strategies cannot cope with the new changes in the emerging manufacturing landscape. Globalization, increasing decentralization and the high autonomy of production units consolidating in loosely coupled virtual organizations make it impossible to use centralized monolithic PPC systems anymore [127]. This decentralization and high autonomy paved the way for the holonic manufacturing approach. The Holonic Manufacturing Systems (HMS) initiative is one of five programs of the Intelligent Manufacturing Systems (IMS) consortium.

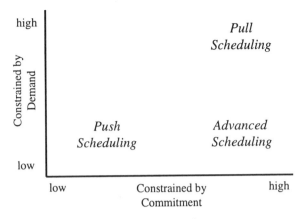

Fig. 2.1. Possible Scheduling modalities

It is based on representing the production unit a single holon[1]. A holon is an autonomous and cooperative building block of a manufacturing system for transforming, transporting, storing and/or validating information and physical objects [17]. The holon consists of an information processing part and often a physical processing part. A holon can be part of another holon. The Holonic Manufacturing System would hence be a holarchy that integrates the entire range of manufacturing activities from order booking through design, production, and marketing to realize the agile manufacturing enterprise. Intuitively, it makes sense to represent the information processing part of the holon as a software agent, such as in [38].

On the product side, the demand for customization is increasing enormously. Products tailored according to the wishes of their buyers make them almost individual, thus leaving no chance for the manufacturing of large batches and waiting for them to be sold. Under these circumstances, the importance of the time-to-market and just-in-time manufacturing is by far higher than that of the traditional goal of optimizing the utilization of production units. Altogether, this poses many challenges to the existing centralized PPC systems with either push or pull strate-

---

[1] Holon is a combination of the Greek word *holos*, meaning whole, and the suffix *on* meaning particle or part. Thirty-three years ago, the Hungarian author and philosopher Arthur Koestler proposed the word "holon" to describe a basic unit of organization in biological and social systems [61]. A holon, as Koestler devised the term, is an identifiable part of a system that has a unique identity, yet is made up of sub-ordinate parts and in turn is part of a larger whole. The strength of holonic organization, or *holarchy*, is that it enables the construction of very complex systems that are nonetheless efficient in the use of resources, highly resilient to disturbances (both internal and external), and adaptable to changes in the environment in which they exist. All these characteristics can be observed in biological and social systems. The stability of holons and holarchies stems from holons being self-reliant units, which have a degree of independence and handle circumstances and problems on their particular level of existence without asking higher level holons for assistance.

gies. Here, it makes also much sense to represent each product or production lot as an autonomous agent in a MAS and let it interact with the agents representing the holons in an open virtual marketplace.

This is the core philosophy behind the several research efforts that took place in the last decade towards porting traditional PPC concepts to the open market paradigm and to let agents interact with each other to perform the production planning and scheduling process in a completely decentralized and competitive way. Several prototypes, based on Contract Nets [106] were developed, such as the Yet Another Manufacturing System (YAMS) [88]. Several other prototypes were based on pure bidding mechanisms, with the first attempts dating back to the 1983 by Shaw and Whinston [101]. In year 1999, the German Research Foundation (DFG) decided to launch a six-year priority program on "Intelligent Agents and Realistic Commercial Application Scenarios". This program brings together researchers from management science, information systems, and computer science. Its long-term aim is to provide significant new insights into the theoretical and methodological foundations of agent technology in the particular context of large, and inherently complex real-world business applications. The main challenge of the program is to identify, and to successfully implement those real-world cases in which agent technology has provable benefits, compared to conventional information systems approaches [25].

The Institute for Program Structures and Data Organization, at the Faculty of Computer Science of the Universität Karlsruhe, is involved in this priority program with its project KRASH. KRASH stands for Karlsruhe Robust Agent SHell and is motivated by the observation that the acceptance of MAS into the PPC market is slow to non-existent. We believe that the market success of multi-agent-based PPC systems hinges on their ability to function reliably and with a result quality comparable to established centralized systems [127].

To increase system reliability, a test bed and runtime environment for MAS are developed with KRASH. On the one hand, KRASH allows an extensive simulation and evaluation of the system in real-world production scenarios and, on the other hand, provides a robust, transaction-based infrastructure for executing agent actions in a resilient way. Both the simulation environment and the transaction layer are designed to fit into the standard FIPA agent platform architecture, thus making their services easily accessible to FIPA-compliant multi-agent systems. Much of the work presented in this thesis is done within this project. In the next section, we present a simplified scenario - abstracted from KRASH - of a MAS-based scenario for the PPC domain.

2.3 The Scenario

Within the manufacturing process, MAS can be incorporated in any of the three levels of the manufacturing process [13].

- *The manufacturing organization level.* This includes enterprise integration services, and supply chain management systems based on agents.

- *The within-the-factory planning and controlling level.*
- *The physical units level.* In this level, agents control the production units, such as robots, pick-and-place machines, NC machines, etc.

In our scenario, we are interested in the middle level, i.e., the automation of the planning layer and its automatic adaptation to the Controlling layer. Fig. 2.2 illustrates the information flow between these layers [113]. We do not concentrate on how to achieve the production goals, such as leveraging the utilization of capital equipment. We assume that the process of optimizing the production plan results from the dynamics of the MAS, i.e., the organizational structure of the agents, the applied negotiation protocols, and the collaboration algorithms. Designing and improving these aspects are beyond our competences and interests. That's why we will always assume that the agents will do some sort of contracting based on a generic bidding mechanism for task allocation without restricting ourselves to a specific combination. However, implementing them and being able to provide formal guarantees for the robustness of their execution constitute the focus of our work.

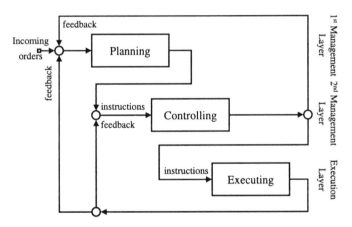

Fig. 2.2. Information flow in PPC [113]

In the scenario, the manufacturing enterprise is represented by a federation of autonomous and heterogeneous databases. Information stored in these databases is logically divided into *four* groups.

- *Production Units Master Data*: contains information about the production units, such as machine configuration, capacity, the capability of producing specific products, time needed for producing them including setup times, the associated costs, the economical utilization level, optimal batch sizes, etc.
- *Product Master Data*: contains general description of the products as well as a listing of the properties to be defined for customizing each single product. This master data also contains the production steps needed to manufacture the product, the bill of materials, and the construction dependencies between the single production steps. Construction dependencies are necessary for defining a partial

order between the manufacturing dates of the various production steps. Example 2.1 is a simple example of construction dependencies.

- *Production Schedule Data*: contains the time schedule for each production unit. Using a production scheduling software, each production step of a product is allocated to a time slot of a production unit. In this time schedule, setup and shutdown procedures as well as regular maintenance are scheduled. Fig. 2.4 is a sketch of a time schedule for a drilling production unit.
- *Production Control Data*: is one level below the production schedule data. It represents what actually occurs on the shop floor level. The data is directly extracted from the production units, such as NC-machines. Ideally, this data is consistent with the production schedule data. However, due to machine failures and various sources of disturbances, there is always a deviation from the production schedule data, which requires adjustments on the side of the scheduling software.

Example 2.1. Construction dependency

An example of construction dependency is the production sequence for the part illustrated in Fig. 2.3. "The channel must be drilled first, then it must be milled or else the placement and the diameter of the drilled holes will never be exact".

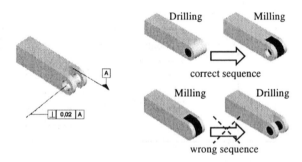

Fig. 2.3. Drilling and milling sequence as a construction dependency

Definition 2.2. The role of the Multi-Agent System in this application scenario is:

to populate the production schedule databases by fulfilling the incoming orders and to readjust the existing schedules accordingly to meet the actual production control data. The operation of the MAS must guarantee the robust execution of agent actions in the face of both *technical* and *operational* disturbances. In their processing, the agents materialize the main goals of the entities they represent, such as high utilization of capital equipment and low waiting time during the manufacturing of the single products.

Time slot		Order ID	Prod. Step	Price	...
...		...	...	...	...
15.10.00	8^{00}-15^{00}	415	Drilling of shaft A	20	
16.10.00	9^{30}-14^{00}	628	Drilling of shaft B	30	

Fig. 2.4. A time schedule for a drilling machine

In our scenario, the agents represent the two main entities in the system: *the production units* and *the products*. Each production unit (or holon) is represented by exactly one agent. Of course, if the production units can be broken down into smaller autonomous units (in a holarchy) their representing agents can correspondingly be broken down into finer grains while preserving the one-to-one relationship between agents and holons. This class of agents represents the interests of the production units during the allocation of time slots in the production schedule databases. It is responsible for ensuring the presence of the necessary setup and shutdown times, the presence of maintenance operations, the feasibility of the resulting production schedule with respect to material and tool flows, while trying to optimize the schedule as much as possible to achieve the local goals of this production unit (e.g., maximizing machine utilization). The agent passes this schedule to the shop floor control and observes the progress through the production control data. It checks this data against the production schedule and, in case of discrepancies often resulting from machine failures, notifies the affected parties to readjust the schedule in order to meet the emerging situation. Fig. 2.5 is an illustration of the operation of such an agent.

On the other side, a group of product agents are created with each incoming production order. Since the domain is that of low-volume, just-in-time, customized products, it is feasible and also useful to represent each single product (or each single lot) by at least one agent, sometimes referred to as *order holon* [9]. We will not use the latter term in the course of this thesis for readability. Fig. 2.6 illustrates an outline of the life cycle of product agents.

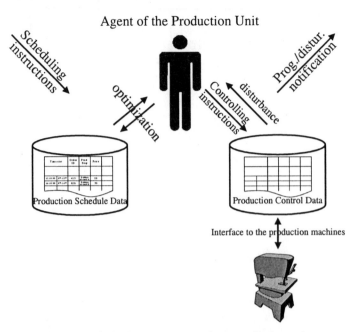

Fig. 2.5. A holonic agent representing a production unit

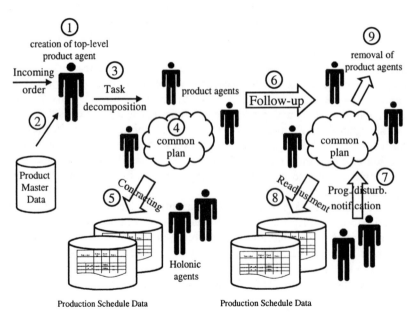

Fig. 2.6. Life-cycle of product agents

The top-level product agent is created upon the receipt of the production order (step 1). It is then fed with the information from the product master database and the personalized customer setting (step 2). Its job is to *identify the production steps needed to manufacture this particular product* and to *develop a plan to allocate time slots for the various production steps*. Example 2.2 shows an abstract identification of the production steps for a robot gripper. This plan must respect the construction dependencies between the production steps defined in the product master database as in Example 2.1. The agent might develop this plan alone or might engage other agents following a distributed problem solving approach (steps 3 and 4), thus developing a distributed common plan. Cooperation between these agents is often in a master/slave form, such as task delegation illustrated in Example 2.3, or as collaboration, as in Example 2.4, in which some key production steps are to be synchronized according to some milestone constraints during the manufacturing process.

Example 2.2. Task Decomposition

> After analyzing the product master data and the customer requirements, the production steps for a tailored robot gripper, illustrated in Fig. 2.7 can be decomposed in three major steps, shown in Fig. 2.8: the production of the chassis unit, the actuator, and the gripper unit. The chassis unit can, in turn, be broken down into the production of the chassis and the flange.

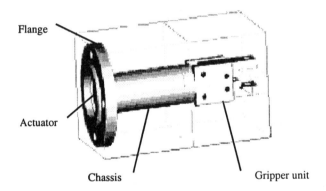

Fig. 2.7. A tailored robot gripper

Example 2.3. Task delegation

> Based on the previous example, the top-level agent for the robot gripper delegates each of the three major production steps to three independent agents. It might do this for several reasons. One reason is the use of domain expertise of a certain agent, such as it ability to access a knowledge base about the hydraulic systems for actuators. Another reason might be motivated by the distributed nature of the

underlying information system: an agent might do the job simply because it has a faster access to a specific database.

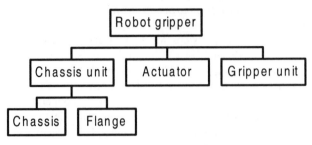

Fig. 2.8. Production steps for a tailored robot gripper

Example 2.4. Task coordination

As can be seen in Fig. 2.7, the actuator is situated inside the chassis of the robot gripper. This means that the three agents cannot allocate all the necessary production time slots completely independent from each other. At the latest, they must coordinate their actions at the assembling phase. First, a synchronization point must be set between the agent of the chassis unit and the agent of the actuator for allocating a time slot for the production step of installing the actuator into the chassis. This must *precede* the synchronization point needed for mounting the gripper unit onto the chassis. After adhering to these synchronization points, each agent can progress with the allocation of other time slots for independent production steps, such as fixing the flange to an external tube.

Having developed the distributed plan, the production agents start executing it by finding the appropriate time slots for each production step. Based on the information in the production master data, they try to contract an appropriate machine for each production step (step 5 in Fig. 2.6). We assume that this will occur within a bidding procedure. The details of this procedure are irrelevant to this scenario. *The execution of the plan must respect construction dependencies between the production steps and hence temporal dependencies in time slot allocation.* Through the implementation of coordination primitives the execution also respects the cooperation rules between the agents that developed the distributed plan.

Now that each production step has its allocated time slot in the production schedule data, the agents enter a follow-up phase till the completion of the product manufacture (step 6). This phase spans several days or weeks. In case of machine failure, the corresponding holon agent notices this disturbance and notifies the affected product agents (step 7). This can be easily tracked using the data in the production schedule. Nevertheless it is unnecessary to re-compute the whole plan for these products. It is often sufficient to readjust the existing schedule while maintaining the construction dependencies. The agent would de-allocate some time slots and would try to find free time slots for each step that is left unscheduled due to this disturbance (step 8). Having manufactured the product, its corresponding agent(s) have achieved their goals and can be removed from the system (step 9).

2.4 Sources of Disturbances

As mentioned in Definition 2.2, the operation of the MAS must guarantee the robust execution of agent plans in the face of disturbances. In fact, robustness of MAS is the focus of this thesis (refer to Chap. 1). Before thinking of increasing the robustness of the MAS, the sources of disturbances must be identified and a requirement analysis for the desired behavior of the MAS in such cases must be made. There are many sources of disturbances, but they all fall into *two* coarse categories:

- *Technical disturbances* occurring due to problems in the IT-infrastructure, and
- *Operational disturbances* occurring due to problems in the environment, in this case, the production domain.

In this section, we elaborate on these two categories by identifying the various sources for disturbances and we give an elementary list of requirements for the system behavior. Our aim is to provide a solution that guarantees the robustness in the face of technical disturbances. This solution should be powerful enough to extend its effect to cover the higher level, namely, the operational disturbances.

2.4.1 Technical Disturbances

Technical disturbances occur due to failure in the IT-infrastructure. This covers the whole infrastructure starting from hardware, communication devices, operating systems, database management systems, runtime environment (e.g., the Java virtual machine), service middleware (e.g., the CORBA bus), and hosting agent platforms, down to the individual agents. The effects of these failures can be divided into three groups.

Disturbance in the Operation of the Databases

System failures (either software or hardware) or *media failure* can put a database out of service. Furthermore, a communication failure between the nodes of the federated database can isolate one or more of these nodes causing the same effect as a down database. These failures affect all agents trying to perform their actions against this database. Another source of disturbances affecting databases results as a side effect of the DBMS trying to preserve the consistency of the database. Almost all modern DBMS support the notion of transactions to encapsulate a group of data operations in a single unit of work. The DBMS has no idea about the internal semantic of these transactions and hence assumes the inner consistency of the transactions. However, since these transactions are executed concurrently, they must appear equivalent to some sort of a serial order to guarantee the so-called outer consistency. In Chap. 4, the notion of equivalence and serialization will be exposed in depth. The job of the DBMS is to ensure this outer consistency. It does this by reordering the incoming database operations and sometimes rejecting whole transactions. This affects only the agent trying to execute its actions within this rejected transaction. In all cases, the operation of the MAS should not be interrupted by such disturbances. An intuitive reaction is to retry the affected transaction whenever the DBMS is ready to process it again.

Disturbance Due to Agent Failure

Agents may crash because of programming errors, failures in the hosting agent platform, runtime environment, service middleware, operation system or even hardware failures. In this case, the agent must be re-instantiated and its status before the crash must recovered in order to resume the execution. However, recovering the whole agent status is not feasible, since it requires logging the whole agent trace in persistent storage. Moreover, it might also not be desirable, since changes in the real world during the down time of the agent might outdate much of its internal knowledge. Therefore, it is wise to identify the parts of the agent mental states that must be recovered. It is reasonable to assume that the plan development process itself is *idempotent* and can be restarted any time. However, it is vital to know which actions were already performed by the agent against the database and which messages were interchanged with the other agents before the crash. It is also desirable to automatically undo the effects of any incomplete actions. Automatically providing these services through the infrastructure certainly eases the recovery process after a crash. The agent would know about its accomplished task. It does not have to do any cleanup for incomplete actions. It only has to rebuild its plan in view of the new world model and the accomplished tasks and then resume the execution of the plan.

Disturbance Due to Failure in the Communication Channel

Sporadic failures in the communication channel connecting the agents can lead to a possible loss of messages. More persistent failures can lead to network partitioning and the isolation of some agents. With the increasing tendency for distribution over the last decade, several approaches were developed to reduce the effect of such failures. On the implementation level, many commercial products, such as IBM's MQSeries [57], guarantee the delivery of exactly one copy of a sent message through the so-called *persistent transactional message queues*; thus overcoming the problem of loss of single messages. On the level of the cooperation protocols, several mechanisms were developed to avoid blocking the agents in the case of network partitioning. A typical example of such protocols is the extension of the famous *two-phase commit* protocol in databases with a third phase to avoid the blocking of database nodes involved in a distributed transaction [8]. However, the agents must be able to interact with theses services. Agents operate autonomously, often leading to an asynchronous behavior. This requires a special handling of delayed or out-of-context messages. The agent must register its incoming and outgoing messages for recovering from agent crashes. It must also make its current state within a communication protocol persistent for recoverability. Again, automatically providing these services through the infrastructure certainly eases the recovery process after a crash.

2.4.2 Operational Disturbances

Operational disturbances occur as a result of problems on the production shop floor. Typical problems arise because of resource scarceness, over-constrained requirements, machine failures, and missing material, tools or personnel. This all is reflected into the MAS. Agents are then forced to retract some previous made agreements. These agreements could be between the agents representing the production units and the product agents or between the product agents themselves. Again, the effects of these problems could be divided into three groups of disturbances.

Disturbance Due to Resource Unavailability

A product agent executes its plan by acquiring the necessary time slots for its production steps. As execution progresses, the agent acquires more and more free slots in the production schedule database. However, all the necessary resources, i.e., free time slots, might not always be available. Reasons include resource scarceness in case of high demand or an over-constrained deadline requirement by the customer. The agent could certainly not foresee such situations before begin of execution. It discovers them during the execution of one or more of its actions. In this case, it must stop the execution of the affected actions and undo their effects. Then, according to the emerging situation, it might be forced to withdraw its whole plan or at least backtrack parts of it. It can then change some details in the plan, such as the input constraints, and retry the execution once more. For such situations, it is highly desirable that the underlying infrastructure provides an automatic cleanup service for the interrupted actions and the possibility for a multi-level recovery to predefined save points within the original plan.

Disturbance in Agreements between the Environment and the Agents

During the normal operation of the organization, a production unit can temporarily be made unavailable due to an unforeseeable machine failure. The holon agent responsible for this production unit will notice this failure through its observation of the production control data. Through the production schedule data, it finds out the affected products and notifies their agents of the unfeasibility of their previously made agreements. These agents are waiting in their follow-up phase, step 6 of Fig. 2.6. More generally, *a long executing agent plan might be invalidated before the completion of its execution in the database model of the world through unexpected changes in the real world.* Unlike the previous subsection, a backtracking is too expensive. After all, the plan execution of the product agent is completed in the database. Moreover, backtracking and retrying might cause the agent losing all already acquired time slots, since retrial would be within a much tighter deadline constraint. This should be the last resort for the product agent. It is much wiser to first assess the damage caused by the broken agreement and then to try allocating an alternative time slot for the affected production steps, while preserving the original plan. However, all time slots for the productions steps with construction dependencies must be reassessed. With some luck, it might be possible to find an alternative time slot that would only affect a small subset of the depending steps. Such a recovery in the forward direction is certainly very desirable as an automatic feature provided by the agent infrastructure, if the overhead associated with defining the required behavior during the plan development process remains minor.

Disturbance in Agreements between the Agents

In this case, agents do not hold to agreements made as part of a coordinated execution of a distributed common plan. Even if the agents are assumed to be good-willing and cooperative, breaking the agreements can be a consequence of any sort of disturbance, either technical or operational. Consider the following example.

Example 2.5. Example of breaking agreements between production agents.

> Referring to Example 2.4, of p. 14, concerning task coordination, the agent responsible for the chassis unit as well as the agent responsible for manufacturing of the actuator are finished with acquiring time slots for the manufacturing their parts. Now, they reach the first synchronization point and progress to acquire the time slot for the assembling step. Having done this, each agent carries on with the execution of its local plan. The agent responsible for the chassis unit acquires a time slots for fixing the flange to the external pipe. Due to a machine failure in a production unit needed for manufacturing the actuator, its agent gets a later time slot and thus misses the scheduled synchronization point. It notifies the agent of the chassis unit about the broken agreement; but the latter has already acquired the time slot for fixing the flange. The newly rescheduled synchronization point now invalidates this time slot allocation.

As in the previous subsection, backtracking and retrying might cause the agent losing all already acquired time slots. The desirable procedure is to assess the damage caused by the broken agreement and then try allocating an alternative time slot for the affected production steps. Again, providing this functionality by the agent infrastructure is certainly desirable.

2.5 Conclusion

The application scenario, presented in this chapter, is an illustrative example for employing MAS in an information rich environment. In this application domain, the basic functions of MAS are needed. Their ability to develop abstract plans and execute them on the underlying IS, their ability to divide the development of the solution of the given problem among them and to cooperate together to devise a common shared plan, and their competitive nature through the organizational structure of a MAS help breaking the monolithic nature of traditional PPC.

Nevertheless, MAS need supplementary guarantees on the robustness of execution. This is crucial to their application in such domains. First, they must guarantee the correctness of execution in presence of uncoordinated concurrent actions from the side of other agents in the system. Second, they must recover to a well-defined and desirable status in the case of disturbances. These disturbances can be of technical or operational nature. In Sect. 2.4, we identified these disturbances and gave a list of requirements for the system behavior in face of these disturbances. The key behind a successful implementation is to allow the definition of this contingency behavior beside the normal behavior in the original plan. Only then, it is relatively easy to design a robust MAS architecture that uses the intelligent qualities of MAS to autonomously execute the appropriate behavior in face of disturbances.

In the next chapter, we present an overview of agent technology. In the course of the presentation, we try to judge how well MAS research efforts did in fulfilling these robustness requirements.

3 Overview of Agent Technology

Since the early 80s, huge advances have been made in the field of MAS. Today, it is no longer a small research subordinate of the Distributed Artificial Intelligence domain. MAS is now a basic part of robotics, Information Systems (IS), network management, traffic control, mobile computing, e-business, etc. In this chapter, we certainly cannot give a complete overview of the whole MAS technology. We concentrate on the most relevant parts to our work, which is MAS in IS.

First, we start by giving the basic definitions and theory to build a common ground with the reader. Then, we give an overview of planning strategies employed by agents, since we want our transaction model to capture the semantic of the agent plans. Then, we investigate the means of increasing the robustness of the MAS in three well-established agent frameworks with application domains in IS. Finally, since we want our proposed solution to be open for all agents regardless of their internal architecture, it must obey the open standards in the agents' world. That is why we give an overview of the agent standardization efforts followed by a concluding section to end the chapter.

3.1 Definitions

3.1.1 What Is an Agent?

There is no standard definition for agents that all researchers in the MAS can agree upon. This is mainly due the variety in the application domains of MAS and the variety in the background of MAS researchers. A good overview of the notion of agenthood is found in [40, 126]. Since IS is the domain of MAS in this thesis, we borrow the definitions of the glossary of the AOIS community [118].

Definition 3.1. Agent

> An Agent is any system that is capable of perceiving events in its environment, or representing information about the current state of affairs and of acting in its environment guided by perceptions and stored information.

This definition applies to any agent. Here, an agent can be a human being, a dog, a robot, or a computer program. Hence, a more precise and yet very general definition is provided for software agents in [118].

K. Nagi: Transactional Agents, LNCS 2249, pp. 21–39, 2001.
© Springer-Verlag Berlin Heidelberg 2001

Definition 3.2. Software agent

> A software agent is a computer program that can accept tasks from its human user, can figure out which actions to perform in order to solve these tasks and can actually perform these task actions without user supervision.

3.1.2 Agent Properties

In the weak notion of agents, found in [58], the behavior of the agent must have at least the following four properties.

- *Autonomy*: related to control; although an agent may interact with its environment, the processes performed by an agent are in full control of the agent itself.
- *Reactivity*: leading the agent to rapidly respond to new information perceived from its environment.
- *Proactivity*: According to [58], agents should not simply act in response to their environment; they should be able to exhibit opportunistic, goal-directed behavior and take their initiative where appropriate.
- *Social ability*: is the central property in *multi*-agent systems. Agents must be able to communicate and cooperate with other agents and humans to complete their own problem solving and help others with their activities.

Other non-mandatory properties of agents include *adaptability*, *mobility*, *ability to learn*, and *intelligence*. Although the term software agents is sometimes used as a synonym for intelligent software systems, software agents do not have to be intelligent. In software engineering, for instance, the ability of an agent to communicate and cooperate with other systems in a flexible manner, and the ability of a mobile agent to migrate to another computer providing resources via suitable network links are considered more fundamental than any form of intelligence.

3.1.3 Formal Representation of Agents

Almost all agent models assume that agents maintain an internal representation of their world and that there is an explicit mental state, which can be modified by some form of symbolic reasoning [78]. A very elegant model that established itself in the formal representation agents is the *Belief, Desire, Intension* (BDI) architecture, whose notion dates back to 1987 in [10]. The architecture has its roots in the philosophical tradition of understanding *practical reasoning*.

The basic idea of the BDI approach is to describe the internal processing state of an agent by means of a set of mental categories, and to define a control architecture by which the agent rationally selects its course of action based on their representation. The mental categories are:

- *Beliefs*: They express the agent expectations about the current state of the world. Beliefs can be *environmental* beliefs that reflect the state of the environment, *social* beliefs that relate to the role and the functions of the other agents in the society, *relational* beliefs that are concerned about the skills, intentions, plans, etc. of the other agents, or *personal* beliefs that include beliefs of the agent about itself.

- *Desire*: is an abstract notion that specifies preferences over future world states or courses of action. An agent is allowed to have inconsistent desires. It does not have to believe that its desires are achievable.
- *Intention*: Since an agent is resource-bounded, it must concentrate on a subset of its desires and intend to materialize them.

In more practical BDI approaches, such as [71] or [94], BDI is often supplemented by the notion of *goals* and *plans*:

- *Goals*: are stronger notions of desires. Goals must be believed by the agent to be achievable. The agent, thus, selects a consistent subset of its goals to pursue. The commitment of an agent to a certain goal describes the transition from goals to intentions.
- *Plans*: are very important for the programmatic implementation of intentions. In fact, intentions can be viewed as partial plans of actions that the agent is committed to execute to achieve its goals. Plan development is a central point in MAS that occupied the AI community for a long time and will be handled separately in this chapter.

Later, Rao and Georgeff [93] formalized the BDI model, including the definition of the underlying logics, the description of beliefs, desires and intentions as modal operators, the definition of possible worlds semantics for these operators, and an axiomatization defining the interrelationship and properties of the BDI operators. In [94], they provide the first BDI interpreter.

The popularity of the BDI theory paved the way for the development of a new programming paradigm, namely the *Agent-Oriented Programming* (AOP), that was proposed by Shoham [104]. The key behind this approach is to directly program agents in terms of mentalistic notions (i.e., beliefs, desire, and intentions). The first implementation of the AOP paradigm is the AGENT0 programming language [104].

3.1.4 Layered Agents

As seen in the BDI theory, an agent can have several goals that it simultaneously pursues. Some of them require a proactive behavior, while others simply react to the change in their environment. This also goes with the weak notion of agenthood mentioned in Sect. 3.1.2. An intuitive approach for supporting these different types of behavior involves creating separate subsystems in so-called hybrid or *layered* agents. Layering can be done either *horizontally* or *vertically*.

In *horizontally* layered architectures, the software layers are each directly connected to the sensory input and action input. In effect, each layer itself acts like an agent, producing suggestions as to what to perform [125]. The great advantage of this type of layering is its conceptual simplicity: if we need an agent to exhibit *n* different types of behavior, then we implement *n* different layers. The real problem in that approach is that the overall behavior of that agent may not be coherent because the layers are always competing to generate action suggestions. Therefore, we always need a mediator function to pick up the right suggestion.

The touring machines architecture of Ferguson [34] is an example of such layering. The architecture describes layered control architecture for autonomous, mobile agents performing constrained navigation tasks in a dynamic environment. As illustrated in Fig. 3.1, the Touring Machines consist of three layers:

- A *reactive* layer: is designed to compute hard-wired action responses to specific environmental stimulus,
- A *planning* layer: is responsible for the generating and executing plans for the achievement of the longer-term relocation tasks that the agent has to perform, and
- A *modeling* layer: provides the agent capability of modifying plans based on changes in its environment.

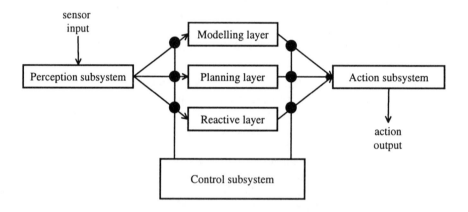

Fig. 3.1. Touring Machines: a horizontally layered agent architecture

In *vertically* layered architectures, sensory input and action output are each dealt with by at most one layer each. They avoid the disadvantages of horizontal layering using their hierarchical structure. A well-known example of this architecture is the INTERRAP architecture designed by J. Müller [71]. INTERRAP stands for <u>INTE</u>gration of <u>Re</u>active behavior and <u>RA</u>tional <u>P</u>lanning. It is based on the BDI theory. The architecture is an approach to modeling resource-bounded, interacting agents by combining reactivity with deliberation and cooperation capabilities [39]. As illustrated in Fig. 3.2, an agent is described by a world interface, a knowledge base, and a control unit.

Agent   Agent
knowledge base   control unit

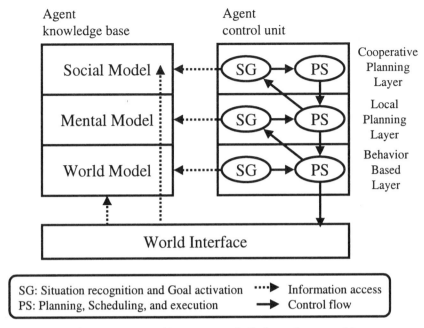

Fig. 3.2. INTERRAP architecture: a vertically layered agent architecture

The agent control unit consists of the following three layers:

- The *behavior-based* layer: responsible for the reactive behavior of the agent.
- The *local planning* layer: responsible for the deliberative behavior of the agent.
- The *cooperative planning* layer: responsible for the social behavior of the agent.

Accordingly the agent knowledge base is hierarchically structured into corresponding models: the world model, the mental model, and the social model. Each model is a higher level abstraction of the one in the directly underlying layer. It represents beliefs of a layer about the layer directly underneath it. The world interface is sensed by the world model by the means of sensors. The new world status is reflected upwards to the appropriate knowledge base layer. Conversely, the behavior-based layer carries out the agent actions by means of actors. At each level of the control unit two modules exist:

- The *Situation recognition and Goal activation process* (SG): recognizes situations relevant to the layer and activates the appropriate goal. Source for the situation recognition is the directly underlying layer (or the world interface in case of the Behavior-Based Layer).
- The *Planning and Scheduling process* (PS): receives the (Situation, Goal) pair from the SG and implements the mapping from goals to intentions (and hence actions). It executes the corresponding plan and schedules it within the current intentions of the agent.

These modules operate on a hierarchical competence-based control mechanism [39]. This mechanism consists of an upward activation request, and a downward commitment posting. By upward activation request it is meant that an incompetent PS at one layer reports this new situation to the SG of the layer above. So, the SG module recognizes its new situation either from its corresponding model in the knowledge base or from the PS of the underlying layer. As for the downward commitment posting, the PS of one layer communicates its commitment to the underlying PS, which results in activation requests for the underlying layer.

3.1.5 Agent Taxonomy

In light of the various characteristics of agents, several attempts have been made to build an agent taxonomy. In [85] the ongoing research on agent technology is classified into the following seven categories of agents:

- *Collaborative agents*: their major characteristics are that they cooperate with other agents,
- *Interface agents*: they act mainly as personal assistants to human users,
- *Mobile agents*: they can migrate between hosting systems to enhance the efficiency of computation and reduce the network traffic,
- *Information agents*: they play the role of managing, manipulating, or collating information from many distributed sources,
- *Reactive agents*: they respond in a stimulus-response manner to the present state of the environment in which they are embedded,
- *Hybrid agents*: They are a combination of two or more agent categories within a single agent, and
- *Smart agents*: They are capable of learning from their actions.

Franklin and Graesser [40] identify a more general taxonomy of agents involving biological agents, robotic agents, software agents, and artificial life agents. A slight variation of this taxonomy is illustrated in Fig. 3.3. An extension to the classification of Franklin and Graesser is made by Klusch and can be found in [60]. It elaborates more on the various types of information agents.

3.2 Planning in Agents

Agent planning has been the focus of interest in the AI community since the early 70s. Planning tries to find the right sequence of applying agent actions in order to achieve the desired goal. Over the past decade, this research area has radically expanded in many areas. In this section, we present a brief overview of the theory behind planning and outline the most relevant parts to our work.

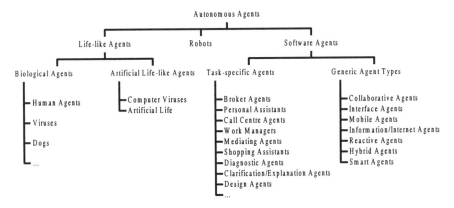

Fig. 3.3. A taxonomy of agent types

3.2.1 Planning Theory

An agent uses its perception to build a *complete* and *correct* model of the current world state. Then, given a goal, it calls a suitable planning algorithm, called *Ideal Planner*, to generate a plan of action to be executed [97]. Planning algorithms usually use *first-order* logic or a subset thereof to describe the main parts of the problem, namely:

- *Initial* state: is a logical sentence describing the current world situation.
- *Goal* state: is a logical query asking for suitable situations.
- *Operators*: is a set of descriptions of actions.

The classical approach that most planners use is the STRIPS language [35] or one of its extensions. The STRIPS language lends itself to efficient planning algorithms, while retaining much of the expressiveness of situation calculus representations. Using this language, the initial state of a product agent seeking a time slot for manufacturing the flange of the robot gripper might look like this:

$$\neg Have(allocatedTimeSlot) \wedge MoneyInPossession(100)$$

Its goal will then be:

$$AtMachine(x) \wedge MachineProduces(x, Flange) \wedge MachineHas(x, freeTimeSlot)$$

Definition 3.3. Agent action

An action, expressed in the STRIPS language, consists of three components:

- The *action* description is what an agent returns to the environment in order to do something.
- The *precondition* is a conjunction of atoms that say what must be true before the action can be applied.

- The *effect* of an action is a conjunction of literals (positive or negative) that describes how the situation changes when the action is applied.

So, the agent action to reserve a time slot can be formulated in STRIPS as follows:

ACTION: *ReserveTimeSlot(T)*
PRECONDITION: $\neg Have(allocatedTimeSlot) \wedge HaveEnoughMoney()$
EFFECT: $Have(allocatedTimeSlot) \wedge MoneyInPossession(100 - Price)$

A plan can thus be formally defined as follows.

Definition 3.4. Plan

A plan is a data structure consisting of the following four components:

1. A set of plan actions, each action is one of the operators for the problem,
2. A set of action ordering constraints. Each ordering constraint is of the form $S_i < S_j$, which means that step S_i must occur sometime before S_j. This yields to a partial order over the actions of the plan.
3. A set of variable binding constraints. Each variable constraint is of the form $v = x$, where v is a variable in some action and x is either a constant or another variable. This corresponds to parameter passing in conventional programming languages.
4. A set of causal links. A causal link documents the purpose of actions in the action set.

Clearly, only the first *three* components are needed for the execution of the plan.

Definition 3.5. Solution

A solution is a *complete* and *consistent* plan.

A complete plan is one in which every precondition of every action is achieved by some other action. An action achieves a condition if the condition is one of the effects of the action, and if no other action can possibly cancel out the condition. A consistent plan is one in which there are no contradictions in the ordering or binding constraints. A contradiction occurs when both $S_i < S_j$ and $S_j < S_i$ hold or both $v = A$ and $v = B$ hold, where $A \neq B$.

Starting from the definition of the plan, the planning problem is converted to a normal search problem to reach the goal situation starting from the initial situation. The first option is to search in the situation space. The search could be done in the *forward* direction, i.e., from the initial situation to the goal situation. In this case we have a *progression* planner. The main problem with this approach is the high branching factor and thus the huge size of the search space. The other option is to start from the goal situation and search *backwards* down to the initial situation. This *regression* planner is a way to cut the branching factor. Nevertheless, this approach has also its drawbacks. A very appealing approach is the use of means-ends strategies [77]. It tries to find an intermediate situation, which the agent knows it certainly leads to the goal situation and it sets this situation to its temporary goal situation and recursively starts the planning algorithm. The second option is to search in the plan space. In this case, the planner has a library of plans. It searches this library for a plan that seems to lead to the goal situation. This plan is then refined to develop the solution. It can then be added to the planning library for later reuse.

3.2.2 Practical Aspects of Planning

The planning theory, presented above is too restrictive for handling complex and realistic domains. Fortunately, it can be easily extended in several ways. In face of complex problems, planners cannot cope with the exploding search space using simple problem solvers, or sometimes called *theorem provers*. That is why almost all the practical planners nowadays adopt the idea of hierarchical decomposition of the problem.

In this approach, an *abstract action* can be decomposed into a group of actions that forms the plan. These actions can, in turn, be further decomposed to less abstract actions or *simple actions* at the bottom level. These decompositions can be stored in a library of plans and retrieved as needed. Now, a planner can easily develop an abstract plan consisting of abstract actions. Then, it can refine them by developing partial plans for each of the abstract actions. The means-ends strategies and the search in the plan space are obvious applications of this hierarchical decomposition of tasks.

Furthermore, the STRIPS language can be made closer to situation calculus by allowing *conditional* effects, in which the effect of an action depends on what is true when it starts executing. This corresponds to the branching in conventional programming languages. Also allowing for universal quantification, in which the precondition and effect of actions can refer to all objects of a certain class, adds more expressing power to the planning language.

Typical to realistic domains is that actions consume resources. In the time slot allocation example, the agent action *consumes* money to acquire a free time slot from the production unit. It is convenient to treat these resources as numeric measures in a pool, as we did in the example and as modeled in the DESIRE system [70], instead of trying to reason about them. Simple actions are thus capable of generating and consuming resources. It is usually effective to check partial plans for satisfaction of resource constraints before attempting further refinement [97].

There is no unbounded resource in the real world. This automatically leads to conflicts between agents trying to acquire their needed resources. Philosophically, conflicts over resources, in all types, are the sources of disturbance in the execution. Alone due to their existence in the real world, there must be a link between plan *development* and plan *execution*. But before getting into the details of plan and execution in Sect. 3.2.4, we first investigate a central problem in planning in

MAS, namely *distribution*. Distributed planning is the direct consequence of hierarchical decomposition.

3.2.3 Distributed Planning

Distributed problem solving is the original name applied to the field of distributed AI in which the emphasis is on getting agents to work together well to solve problems that require collective efforts [28]. Solving distributed problems requires the *willingness of agents to work together* and *the heterogeneity of their competence*.

All planning processes among multiple agents involve three stages: making plans, synchronizing and coordinating plans, and executing plans [33]. As one or more agents can be used in each of these stages, it is possible to obtain a large number of different agent organizations. In general, distribution falls in three main classic modes of organization in MAS planning.

- *Centralized planning for distributed plans*: In this category, plans are developed by a centralized agent using techniques mentioned in Sect. 3.2. These plans are then executed in distributed fashion through several agents. In this case, the centralized coordinator agent must break this plan into separate threads of execution. It then introduces synchronization nodes to coordinate their execution.
- *Distributed planning for centralized plans*: Here, the problem is so complicated that the competence of several agents is required in order to find a solution. In such systems, each agent develops a part of the whole plan and communicates its developed part to its counterparts. Examples of this category include [22] and [122]. Often, blackboard systems are used as medium for exchanging the partial plans for further improvement by the agents in the group. Once the plan is finalized, it is executed by a single agent.
- *Distributed planning for distributed plans*: This is the most general case, where both the planning process and its execution are distributed. The literature is rich in this category. We adopt a classification of this category from [28]. *Plan merging* is when multiple agents formulate plans for themselves as individuals and then must ensure that their separate plans can be executed without conflict. Centralized plan coordination approaches fall under this classification. It suggests the presence of centralized agent that collects the partial plans, detects and tries to resolve the conflicts between them. *Negotiation* tries to solve the conflict through direct negotiation between the agents involved. *Iterative plan formation* addresses the problem that local decisions are dependent on the decisions of others. One way of tempering proposed local plans based on global constraints is to require agents to construct the set of all feasible plans for accomplishing their own local goals. The distributed planning process then consists of a search through how subsets of agents' plans can fit together.

3.2.4 Planning and Execution

Due to the presence of disturbances in the real world and the incomplete and incorrect information perceived by the agent, planning and execution should not be handled separately. The relationships between planning and execution are an important topic in AI with work dating back to the early 80s. There are two different ways to deal with this problem.

- *Contingency planning*: It deals with incomplete information by constructing a conditional plan that accounts for each possible situation that could arise. The agent finds out which part of the plan to execute by including sensing actions in the plan to test for the appropriate conditions. This corresponds to exception handling in conventional programming languages.
- *Execution monitoring*: The planning agent can monitor what is happening, while it is executing the plan to follow that its actions produce the desired effect specified in its original plan. If it discovers an inconsistency, the plan execution is stopped and *replanning* takes place from the current situation to achieve the original goal. In a world full of disturbances, the goal becomes some sort of objective function and the plan is to move towards the local optimum.

This altogether leads to strong interleaving of planning and execution. Such interleaving is suggested in early theoretical works such as [2, 47] and is present in almost all agent frameworks that do some sort of planning and execution. Examples spread from early works such as AGENT0 [104] to recent work such as DESIRE [70] and INTERRAP [71].

3.3 Robustness of MAS in IS Domains

Because of their huge potential, MAS has been more and more applied to IS domains. Mainly, they are applied in information discovery and information managers [60]. Sources for the information are either enterprise databases or the Internet. Almost all MAS come in three major layers:

- A *provider* layer containing the information sources. They are usually accessed through *wrapper agents* that try to provide a unified access interface to these sources.
- A *requester* layer containing the *user agents*. They consume the information obtained from the provider layer and present it to the user.
- A *matchmaking* layer containing broker or *mediator* agents. They enable a mutually beneficial collaboration between the provider and the requester layers and enable the interoperability between the various sources of the provider layer [121].

Several of these mediators may be coordinated by a *facilitator* agent. The DARPA *Intelligent Integration of Information* (I3) project [23] is based on this three layers architecture and allows federations among the facilitators.

Today, there are a very large number of research prototypes that follow this architecture. This resulted in a number of general MAS frameworks that can be configured for direct application in their specific IS scenarios. However, almost all concentrate on reading the information systems. Their added value is providing a better view of the world to the user. In fact, only a few of these frameworks are actually used to write to the IS. In the rest of this section, we present three of these frameworks that are capable of writing to the databases of the underlying IS and investigate how they achieve robustness in their operation.

3.3.1 RETSINA

The RETSINA (REusable Task Structure-based Intelligent Network Agents) multi agent framework is being developed at the Carnegie Mellon University [110]. It consists of a system of reusable agent types that can be adapted to address a variety of different domain-specific problems. In harmony with the above-mentioned general I3 architecture, RETSINA contains three agent types: *interface* agents, *task agents* that formulate user requests in problem solving plans and execute them, and *information agents* that wrap the information sources. The interactions between these types of agents are illustrated in Fig. 3.4.

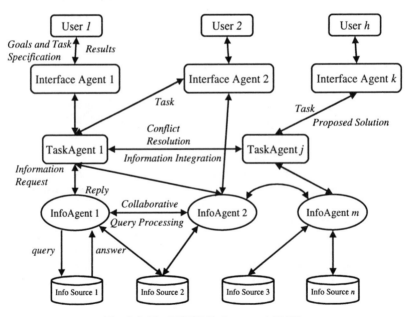

Fig. 3.4. The RETSINA framework [108]

The architecture of each single RETSINA agent is based on several reusable modules [110]:

- A communicator that receives and parses messages in the agent KQML language [102],
- A planner that performs domain specific problem solving,
- A scheduler that schedules executable actions, and
- An execution monitor that initiates replanning if needed.

The collection of RETSINA agents forms an open society of reusable agents that self organize and cooperate in response to task requirements. The framework was used to develop various domain-specific applications. For example, WARREN is a system developed using the RETSINA framework that provides an integrated financial picture for portfolio management [111]. PLEIADES is an intelligent agent system that provides automated calendar coordination for visitors to a department [109]. Matchmaker and WebMate provide customized browsing, searching, and general brokerage services in the Internet [16].

3.3.2 InfoSleuth

The InfoSleuth, developed at MCC, aims at integrating information from the World Wide Web [4]. It is the successor of the Carnot project [54], which tried to integrate heterogeneous database sources. In contrast to the database world, this environment is *dynamic* in the sense that information sources arbitrarily join and leave the system without any control. Furthermore, the environment has no consistent and global schema definition.

The architecture is comprised of a network of cooperating agents communicating by exchanging KQML messages [36]. The architecture contains the usual *user* agents, *broker* agents, and *resource* agents. The architecture can be also equipped with a *data analysis* agent that supplements each of the resource agents and that provides data analysis methods. Additionally, the architecture has *ontology*[2] agents that provide an overall knowledge of ontologies and answers queries about them to bridge the semantic gab between the metadata of the various information sources.

A *task execution* agent coordinates the execution of high-level information gathering subtasks and a *monitor* agent tracks the agent interactions and the execution steps. It reports the progress of the submitted queries to the user.

This agent framework has been used in a wide range of knowledge discovery applications, such as [66].

---

[2] An ontology may be defined as the specification of a representational vocabulary for a shared domain of discourse, which may include definitions of classes, relations, functions, and other objects [51].

3.3.3 Social Abstractions Using Agents

In the work of Singh and Huhns, essential functionality found in multi-databases technologies are ported to the domain of *Cooperative Information Systems* (CIS). These systems are distinguished by the fact of having networked and interrelated, but heterogeneous, information resources [105]. To make it more complicated, CIS are extremely autonomous and they are free to join in and leave the system. This is the typical environment expected to be found in e-commerce and virtual enterprises applications.

CIS have increased expectations over robustness, especially guarantees on the atomicity, durability and recoverability of agent actions. Traditional work in the distributed database technology usually coordinate the execution of actions spanning more than one database using low-level infrastructural techniques, namely *distributed transactions*, as will be seen in the next chapter. Despite their strong theoretical foundation and their performance success, these techniques are not capable of coping with the new domain of highly autonomous information sources, which are not necessarily of a database nature.

In this work, it is argued that addressing the issues of coordination using a high level of abstraction is more natural. In [105], the authors propose that agents can use their capability of capturing the semantical constraints and apply them in order to execute their actions in a robust manner. Under this assumption, the agents, when contracted to perform an action, must be committed to performing it and preserving the integrity of the manipulated data. It is the responsibility of the agent under commitment to take all the possible measures to execute the action or else it must completely undo its effect. It may employ any of the low-level techniques found in distributed databases. Since agents may recursively contain other agents, we have *spheres of commitment*.

3.3.4 Approaches for Robustness

Taking RETSINA and InfoSleuth as typical examples for agent frameworks, it is clear that they can carry out actions that write to the database. Within an action, they might use database transactions to guarantee the robustness of the single actions. However, there is no clear structure that preserves the execution dependency between their actions.

In both frameworks, the MAS designers must ensure that the agent actions are *correctly* executed in the presence of conflicts resulting from the concurrent execution of actions. These conflicts over resources must be resolved within the internal implementation of the agent and the interaction protocol governing the agents in the system. As for the *recoverability*, the system must seek refuge in redundantly distributing information and control to allow a graceful degradation of the system in the case of disturbances leading to the loss of one or more agents. Recoverability is then achieved through the reconstruction of the recovered agent from the redundantly stored information in the other agents. Unfortunately, execution robustness is not automatically guaranteed by the frameworks. It must be implemented by MAS designers that use the frameworks. This is a huge overhead in the design and the implementation process and, moreover, robustness guarantees must be proven from scratch each time the framework is applied due to the absence of a formal model defining the concurrency model, the redundancy scheme, and the recovery model.

The last approach, in Sect. 3.3.3, tries to address the issue of preserving the execution dependency between the actions across the agent boundaries. Nevertheless, the model presents only a formal abstraction of the commitments and does not specify how each agent can keep up to its own commitments. In fact, there is no means of verifying whether the agent is over- or under-committing itself. In contrast to the first two frameworks, this model lacks a ready-made agent architecture implementing the concept of spheres of commitment that can be directly used.

3.4 Agent Standardization Efforts

No agent is an island. In a multi agent environment, agents must be able to interact with each other. For this, they need communication protocols to enable the exchange of messages and interaction protocols to enable the conversations with their counterparts. Therefore, standardizing the interaction between the agents has occupied the mind of MAS researches since its infancy in order to promote the open MAS paradigm.

To date, almost all communication between agents is based on the *speech act theory* [3]. Speech act has its origins in human communications. It views natural human language as actions. A speech act has *three* aspects:

- *Locution*: which is the physical utterance by the speaker.
- *Illocution*: which is the intended meaning of the locution.
- *Perlocution*: which is the action resulting from the locution.

A lot of research efforts aimed at developing agent frameworks that are capable of implementing the speech act based MAS. The JAva-based Framework for Multi-Agent Systems (JAFMAS) is one of these frameworks [15]. The framework supports both directed communication and subject-based broadcast communication. It is actually used in several existing projects, such as the AARIA project [90] (please refer to Sect. 2.2)

Nevertheless, the main challenge is enabling the sharing of knowledge among the agents through communication rather than providing an implementation framework. In this section, we present two standardization efforts sharing knowledge in a MAS: the *Knowledge Sharing Effort* (KSE) and the *Foundation of Intelligent Physical Agents* (FIPA).

3.4.1 The Knowledge Sharing Effort

The *Knowledge Sharing Effort* (KSE) was initiated by DARPA in the early 90s with the participation of dozens of researchers in the academic field as well as in the industry. Its aims are developing techniques, methodologies, and software tools for knowledge sharing and knowledge reuse. There are several components in this standardization effort [91]. The most important components are:

- The *Knowledge Interchange Format* (KIF), and
- The *Knowledge Query and Manipulation Language* (KQML).

The Knowledge Interchange Format (KIF) is on a *syntactical* level. It is intended to be a core language for representing and interchanging knowledge. KIF is an extended version of the first order predicate logic with the following features [91]:

- Simple list-based ASCII syntax.
- Model-theoretic semantic with axiomatic characterization of a large vocabulary of object, function, and relation constants.
- Function and relation vocabulary for numbers, sets, and lists.
- Support for expression of knowledge about the properties of functions and relations.
- A sub-language for defining objects, *n*-ary relations, and *n*-ary functions that enables the augmentation of the representational vocabulary and specification of domain ontologies.
- Support for expression of knowledge about knowledge.
- A sub-language for stating both monotonic and non-monotonic inference rules.

The *Knowledge Query and Manipulation Language* (KQML) lies in the *pragmatics* level of agent communication. It is a high-level, message-oriented, Agent Communication Language (ACL). The language is independent of the transport mechanism used to transmit the message (e.g., tcp/ip sockets, CORBA objects, or even simple email, etc.). It is independent of the content language (e.g., KIF) and also independent of the ontology assumed by the content. A KQML message represents a single speech act [36], as illustrated in Fig. 3.5 with the *tell* performative and its parameters.

```
(tell    :sender          senderAgent
         :receiver        receiverAgent
         :in-reply-to     id7.24.97.1504
         :ontology        books
         :language        Prolog
         :content
    "price(ISBN12345,49.99)")
```

Fig. 3.5. A KQML message

Over the period of four years, the number of KQML performatives exploded with its application in the various domains. At the first glance, KQML seems only about syntax. However, *semantics* and *protocols* can be associated with the message through the parameters of the message [63].

Both RESTINA and InfoSleuth, presented in Sects. 3.3.1 and 3.3.2, respectively, used KQML as their ACL. Unfortunately, there are many dialects of the KQML use by the existing agent frameworks, which requires the introduction of special adapter agents to integrate agents coming from different agent frameworks, originally supporting KQML. An adapter agent is described in [48].

3.4.2 The Foundation of Intelligent Physical Agents

The Foundation for Intelligent Physical Agents (FIPA)[3] is a non-profit association [37]. It was formed in 1996 to produce software standards for heterogeneous and interacting agent and agent-based systems. FIPA operates through more than 60 international organizations including leading companies, universities, research institutes, and government agencies.

FIPA can informally be viewed as the successor of KSE. Its goal is pursued by making available, in a *timely* manner, internationally agreed specifications that maximize interoperability across agent-based applications, services, and equipment. Its work goes far beyond defining an ACL. It defines standards in agent management, communication, including message format, semantic, and interaction protocols, human/agent interaction, agent/software interaction, agent mobility, security, and ontology services. Fig. 3.6 illustrates the hierarchy of its specifications [37].

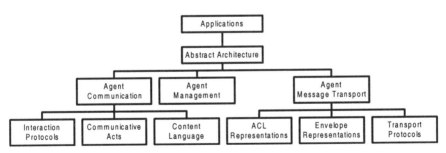

Fig. 3.6. The hierarchy of the FIPA specifications

The FIPA ACL is also based on speech acts, whose message has a similar syntax to KQML as seen in the example of Fig. 3.7. However, the FIPA ACL is more powerful with composing new primitives. Furthermore, its real power stems from the binding of the message with a *Semantic Language* serving as a content language, which is a logical framework to define the mental attitudes of the agents, such as belief, uncertainty, and choice. The semantic language can also express

---

[3] The word Physical in FIPA is due to historical reasons.

propositions, objects, and actions. This is the main difference to KQML with its lack of commitment to a content language.

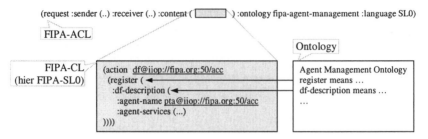

Fig. 3.7. A FIPA message [80]

FIPA agents can belong to one or more agent platforms, all providing the same basic services. A FIPA agent platform is illustrated in Fig. 3.8. The *Agent Management System* (AMS) provides services that manage the lifecycle of the agents in the platform, such as creation, deletion, suspending, authentications, etc. The *Directory Facilitator* (DF) provides yellow pages services, which describe the attributes and capabilities of agents in the platform. The *Agent Communication Channel* (ACC) accepts and delivers messages between agents on different platforms. They also provide store and forward facilities for messages and firewall functionalities. The internal platform message transport is responsible for the message exchange within the platform. Inter-platform communications can be done using any transport protocol provided by the hosting systems. However, for initialization purposes, the platform must use IIOP.

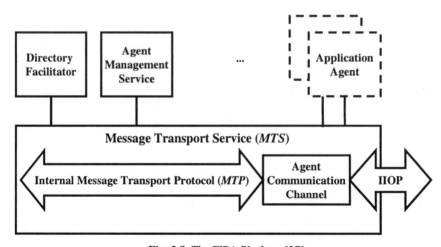

Fig. 3.8. The FIPA Platform [37]

To date, there are a good number of implementations of the FIPA platform. Some of the most well known implementations include FIPA-OS, originally developed at Nortel Networks [92], the JADE platform of CSELT [5], and Zeus, which is developed at the labs of the British Telecom [131].

3.5 Conclusion

The MAS paradigm enjoys very strong theoretical foundations especially in abstract logical architectures, planning strategies, and plan representation. Accompanied with standardization efforts through strong international bodies, MAS have made their march into the world of IS.

Over the last decade, dozens of agent frameworks were developed to be applied for build MAS applications. These frameworks are guided by the principles of the agent theory and try to follow the agent standardization efforts in the field of agent communication. This certainly shortens the development time as compared to building the MAS from scratch. However, taking a deeper look into these frameworks, one notices the absence of any predefined framework for robustness. Robustness aspects must be explicitly implemented by MAS designers. This is a huge overhead in the design and the implementation process. Moreover, robustness guarantees must be proven from scratch by the designers due to the absence of a formal model defining the correctness and the recovery models.

4 Overview of Transaction Processing

As mentioned in Chap. 1, the focus of this thesis is increasing the robustness of MAS by providing a means for the correct execution of agent actions even in the presence of disturbances. We seek for a solution to this problem in the database world. Over the past 25 years, database technology has learned to deal with failures by developing a suitable technology, namely *transactions*.

This chapter is an overview of transaction processing. We first present a formal definition of transactions and introduce the theory that formally guarantees their robust execution. Then, we present the approaches to extend the theory for the case of multi-databases. Multiple heterogeneous and highly autonomous databases are expected to be the underlying infrastructure for any MAS operating in a data-intensive environment. The second part of this chapter is dedicated to extended transaction models that emerged in the early 90s to adapt the traditional transaction model to the requirements of advanced applications. We cast light over the models, which we believe to be most related to our proposed transaction model for MAS.

4.1 Transactions

Informally, a transaction is an execution of a program that accesses a shared database [8]. This access can be in the form of a read operation, denoted by $r[x]$, where x is a database object, or a write operation, denoted by $w[x]$. This is called the read/write (r/w) database model. The transaction boundary is defined by a begin transaction operation, denoted by b, and end transaction or commit, denoted by c, or abort, denoted by a. More formally,

Definition 4.1. A transaction T_i is a partial order with ordering relation $<_i$ where

1. $T_i \subseteq \{r_i[x], w_i[x] \mid x \text{ ist a data object}\} \cup \{a_i, c_i\}$;
2. $a_i \in T_i$ iff $c_i \notin T_i$;
3. $\forall t \in T_i \ \ t = c_i \vee t = a_i \succ (\forall s \in T_i \ \ s <_i t)$; and
4. if $r_i[x], w_i[x] \in T_i$, then either $r_i[x] <_i w_i[x]$ or $w_i[x] <_i r_i[x]$.

K. Nagi: Transactional Agents, LNCS 2249, pp. 41–61, 2001.

4.1 Robustness of Transactions

To formally guarantee the correctness of execution, all transaction models are considered using two orthogonal dimensions: *serializability* and *reliability* [31]. Serializability is supported by a concurrency control mechanism that ensures each user is treated as the only one currently in the system. Well established concurrency control mechanisms are based on database object locking, such as the famous two-phase locking protocol, with its proof of correctness dating back to the early 80s [115]. Reliability, often referred to as *recoverability*, guarantees that users' queries are executed to completion, and the effects of their activities are either reflected in the database, if the transaction is committed, or any indication that the query existed is obliterated, if the transaction is aborted. We will use the term *recoverability* for the remaining of the thesis.

These properties are supported by conformance to criteria represented by the ACID acronym [50]:

- *Atomicity*: The transaction is executed as a single atomic unit, where all of the operations are executed or none of them affect the database.
- *Consistency*: The transaction views are maintained so that part of the transaction sees the precise snapshot of the database at the end of the transaction's execution that it would have seen if the same access has been made earlier.
- *Isolation*: Transactions should not interfere with the activities of other transactions, nor should they affect the execution of any other system activities.
- *Durability*: The system guarantees that the effects of committed transactions on the database persist after the transaction is completed or another validly executed transaction changes these values.

These criteria apply to the so-called *flat transactions* and form a solid basis for defining formal guarantees for transaction robustness. However, in several advanced applications, such as Computer-Aided Design (CAD) applications or other collaborative activities, these criteria are too restrictive. Later in this chapter, we introduce some advanced transaction models that relax these criteria to provide more flexibility, however at the cost of being no longer able to completely provide formal guarantees of correctness solely based on the underlying database management system.

4.3 Serializability

4.3.1 Theory

Serializability theory is the mathematical tool that allows proving whether or not a database scheduler works correctly. In the theory, a concurrent execution of a set of transactions is represented by a *history*. The theory gives precise properties that a history must satisfy to be serializable [8]. A history is called *serializable* if it is *equivalent* to a *serial* history. By implementing a correct concurrency control mechanism, the database management system is able to assure that all resulting histories are serializable. In this section, we provide an overview of the basic definitions needed for the serializability theory in centralized databases.

Definition 4.2. Conflicting operations

> In the r/w database model, two operations p and q are said to be in conflict, denoted $p \, \mathbb{V} \, q$, iff they access the same data object and at least one of them is a write.

Definition 4.3. Complete history

> Let $T = \{T_1, T_2, ..., T_n\}$ be a set of transactions. A complete history H over T is a partial order with ordering relation $<_H$ where:
>
> 1. $H = \bigcup_{i=1}^{n} T_i$;
>
> 2. $<_H \supseteq \bigcup_{i=1}^{n} <_i$; and
>
> 3. For any two conflicting operations $p, q \in H$, either $p <_H q$ or $q <_H p$.

A *history* is a prefix of a complete history[4].

Definition 4.4. Schedule

> A schedule is a history with a *total* order of operations.

Definition 4.5. The Commit projection

> A commit projection of a history H, written $CP(H)$, is a complete history containing the operations of all committed transactions of H.

Definition 4.6. Serial history

> A complete history H_s is a *serial* history if, for every two transactions T_i and T_j that appear in H, either all operations of T_i appear before all operations of T_j or vice versa.

Thus, a serial history represents an execution in which there is no interleaving of the operations of different transactions. Definitively, this sort of history is important for the serializability theory, since it guarantees both consistency and isolation properties and is intuitively considered as correct.

---

[4] Given a partial order $L = (\Sigma, <)$, a partial order $L' = (\Sigma', <')$ is a *restriction* of L on domain Σ' if $\Sigma' \subseteq \Sigma$ and for $a, b \in \Sigma'$, $a <' b$ iff $a < b$. L' is a *prefix* of L, written $L' \subseteq L$, if L' is a restriction of L and for each $a \in \Sigma'$, all predecessors of a in L (i.e., all elements $b \in \Sigma$ such that $b < a$) are also in Σ'.

Definition 4.7. Serializable history

> A history H is *serializable*, denoted by SR, if its commit projection, $CP(H)$, is equivalent to a serial history H_s.

Serializable histories are very important, since they represent correct concurrent execution of transactions, which are to be expected to occur during the operation of the database. However, we must agree on a definition for *equivalence*.

4.3.2 Equivalence of Histories and Schedules

Alone the notion of equivalence is complicated. In [116], equivalence is defined in relation to schedules, whereas in [8], it is defined for histories. In the course of this thesis, we will stick to the second definitions. In both works, there are several degrees of equivalence. The first level is the so-called *final-state* equivalence. According to this notion of equivalence, two histories are equivalent if they include the same set of transactions and the final value of each database object is the same in both histories. However, this is a too simple notion of equivalence to be used for correctness. It is only applicable for batch processing, in which only the end result is the one that counts. The most appealing and intuitive definition of equivalence is the *view* equivalence. Informally, view equivalence requires that each transaction in both histories always produce the same results. This means that having a view serializable history maintains a consistent view of the database at each instance of time. Unfortunately, this definition for equivalence cannot be applied as a correctness criterion for the practical operation of databases, because finding out whether a schedule is view serializable (VSR) or not is an NP-complete problem. That's why we must be satisfied with a subset of the view serializable histories, namely, the *conflict* serializable (CSR) one, since they can be determined in polynomial time. Following is the formal definition of conflict equivalence.

Definition 4.8. Conflict equivalence

> Two histories H and H' are conflict equivalent, denoted $H \equiv_c H'$, if:
> 1. they are defined over the same set of transactions and have the same operations; and
> 2. they order conflicting operations of non-aborted transactions in the same way; that is, for any conflicting operations p_i and q_j belonging to transactions T_i and T_j respectively where $a_i, a_j \notin H$, if $p_i <_H q_j$ then $p_i <_{H'} q_j$.

4.3.3 Serialization Graph

The graph theory offers a useful tool for verifying the serializability of histories. We can determine whether a history is serializable by analyzing a graph derived from the history called the *serialization graph*. Let H be a history over $T = \{T_1, T_2, ..., T_n\}$, the *serialization graph* (SG) for H, denoted $SG(H)$, is a directed graph whose nodes are the transactions in $CP(H)$ and whose edges are all $T_i \rightarrow T_j$ ($i \neq j$) such that one of T_i's operations precedes and conflicts with one of T_j's operations in H.

Each edge $T_i \rightarrow T_j$ in $SG(H)$ suggests that T_i should precede T_j in any serial history that is equivalent to H. If we can find a serial history, H_s, consistent with all edges in $SG(H)$, the H_s is conflict equivalent to H and so H is *SR*. Clearly, we can do this as long as $SG(H)$ is *acyclic*. In other words, a history H is serializable iff $SG(H)$ is acyclic [8].

4.4 Recoverability

Recoverability means that the database management system behaves as if the database contains all the effects of committed transactions and none of the effects of uncommitted ones. Uncommitted transactions result from transaction programmatic aborts, aborts from the transaction manager upon the discovery of a non-serializable history, or unexpected interruption of transactions due to software or hardware failures. It can be said that recoverability is responsible for the atomicity and the durability of ACID transactions. Here again, there are certain restrictions imposed on the submitted transactions that ease the recovery process. The first condition, of course, is that the history should be recoverable in the first place. Like serializability, these properties can be conveniently formulated in the language of histories.

Definition 4.9. Recoverable history

> A history is *recoverable* (*RC*) if, whenever T_i reads a data object x from T_j ($i \neq j$) in H and $c_i \in H$, $c_j < c_i$. This means, a history is recoverable if each transaction commits after the commitment of all transactions from which it read.

Another desired property is that the abort of one transaction does not affect other executing transactions. This is achieved if the transactions are allowed to read only those values that are written by committed transactions or themselves. More formally,

Definition 4.10. ACA history

> A history H *avoids cascading aborts* (*ACA*) if, whenever T_i reads data object x from T_j ($i \neq j$), $c_j < r_i[x]$.

The set of ACA histories is a subset of RC histories. This is the minimum requirement for flat ACID transaction in centralized databases regarding recoverability. However, due to implementation reasons, database management systems restrict themselves further to a subset of the ACA histories. This subset is that of strict histories (ST).

Definition 4.11. Strict history

> A history H is *strict* (*ST*) if whenever $w_j[x] < o_i[x]$ ($i \neq j$), either $a_j < o_i[x]$ or $c_j < o_i[x]$ where $o_i[x]$ is either $r_i[x]$ or $w_i[x]$.

That is, no data object may be read or overwritten until the transaction that previously wrote into it terminates, either by aborting or committing.

In summary, all database management systems allow the processing of histories that are both *conflict serializable* and *strict*, illustrated by the shadowed are of Fig. 4.1.

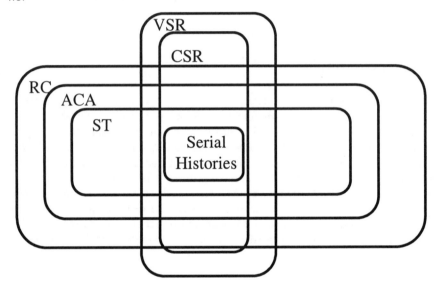

Fig. 4.1. Relationship between histories

4.4.1 Centralized Recovery

Fig. 4.2 illustrates a model of a centralized database management system. The *Recovery Manager* (RM) is responsible for guaranteeing the recoverability of the executed transactions. It receives database operations from the *Transaction Manager* (TM), whose role is to generate serializable schedules and makes the effects of only committed transactions permanent in the stable database. However, the Recovery Manager has no direct control over the *Cache Manager* (CM) and cannot usually enforce an instant flush of its write requests to the stable storage. That's why it makes use of *Logging*.

Conceptually, a log is a representation of the history of execution. A log entry is a tuple $[T_i, x, v]$ identifying the value v that transaction T_i wrote into data object x. Usually, v contains both the *before-image* value of the object, i.e., the value before the write operation, and the *after-image* value, i.e., the value after the write operation.

The recovery manager ensures the recoverability by means of two operations: *undo* and *redo*. An undo operation mainly restores the before-image value of each data object written by a transaction and a redo operation rewrites the after-image value. Depending on the degree of autonomy of the underlying Cache Manager, the recovery algorithm can be optimized to perform only one type of operations, either undo or redo. An optimization in space is also possible by storing either the before-images or the after-images.

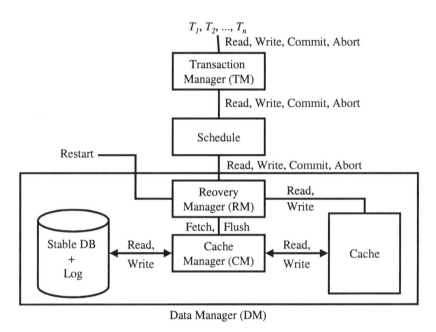

Fig. 4.2. Model of a centralized database management system

4.4.2 Distributed Recovery

In *Distributed Database Management Systems* (DDBMS), a single transaction might span several databases. In this case, the transaction is instantiated by a database node called the *coordinator* for this transaction and the other nodes are called the *participants*. In order to guarantee the commitment of a transaction at all sites, an *Atomic Commitment Protocol* (ACP) is needed. Several ACP are found in literature, e.g., [112]; but the most famous protocol is by far the *two-phase commit* (2PC) protocol. Assuming no failures, it goes roughly as follows [8]:

- The coordinator sends a vote request message to all participants.
- When a participant receives the vote request message, it responds by sending to the coordinator a message containing that participant's vote: *yes* or *no*. If the participant votes no, it decides to abort and stops.

- The coordinator collects the vote messages from all participants. If all of them were yes and the coordinator's vote is also yes, then the coordinator decides to commit and sends commit messages to all participants. Otherwise, the coordinator decides to abort and sends abort messages to all participants that voted yes. In either cases, the coordinator then stops.
- Each participant that voted yes waits for a commit or abort message from the coordinator. When it receives the message, it decides accordingly and stops.

Two-phase commit protocol is currently part of the X/Open standard [128] and is supported by many commercial DBMS. Several variations of the basic protocol for handling some failures and for a better optimization can be found in [7]. However, this protocol suffers from several disadvantages. In some cases, despite their rarity, the protocol can reach a blocking state for the participants or the coordinator. The most serious problem of this protocol is that all participants must provide a *prepare-to-commit* state and are blocked till the receipt of the coordinator's decision. In an autonomous multi-database environment, no database is willing to offer this state to the other participants alone due to administrative and organizational reasons and hence will not agree to participate in the protocol.

4.4.3 Semantic-Based Recovery

Due to the above-mentioned problem in the case of multi-databases or due to the application of advanced transaction models beyond the flat transaction model, some parts of a larger (and also distributed) transaction might be committed without any coordination with the rest of the transaction. If an abort decision of the whole transaction is made, the committed parts cannot be undone, because this would contradict the durability principle of committed transactions.

In this case only a *semantic recovery* is possible. Suggesting that semantic history and semantically consistent history [42] would suffice in place of traditional atomicity and syntactic serializability paved the way for this type of recovery. The approach is essentially based on *compensation*. A *compensating transaction* is a corrective action taken after the original transaction has been locally committed. It is used to revert the effect of the transaction. Compensation is used in various forms in advanced transaction models, as will be seen later in this chapter. The main challenge is to design such compensation transactions. Despite some research efforts to automatically generate them, e.g., [83], it is hardly possible for them to be designed without the help of the developer, since the semantic is largely dependent on the domain and the world model. *In fact, the task of specifying such compensating transactions might be more complicated than the original transactions themselves!* In some cases, compensation might not be even possible. For example, there is no possible compensating action for drilling holes in the flange of the robot gripper of Example 2.2, p. 13, after the drilling has taken place.

In the work of Mehrotra et al. [68], the authors divide actions in a distributed transaction into three categories: those that can always be compensated for (*compensatable*), those that will always eventually succeed if retried enough times (*retriable*), and at most one action that falls in neither category (*pivot*). In semantic-based recovery, care must be taken while executing a series of related transactions. They must be executed in the following order. Commitment proceeds by first committing all of the compensatable transactions. Then, the irrecoverable decision is made by committing the pivot. If it commits, then all of the retriable transactions must be executed till their commitment.

4.5 Multi-databases

Multi-Databases are information systems that provide interoperation and varying degrees of integration among multiple database management systems. In the literature, they are often referred to as federated databases [103] or more generally heterogeneous distributed databases systems [31].

Fig. 4.3 illustrates a typical architecture of a multi-database system. A multi-database system is a collection of independent local database management systems (LDBMS). An overlying layer, containing the Global Transaction Manager (GTM) module receives the operations from global transactions and directs them to the Local Transaction Managers (LTMs) of the appropriate LDBMS. Each LDBMS manages its own database and also processes its local transactions through its LTM without any interference from the GTM.

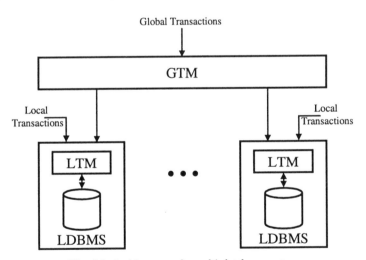

Fig. 4.3. Architecture of a multi-database system

One thing all multi-database systems have in common is that the participating systems have a high degree of autonomy. This autonomy manifests itself in four aspects [103]:

- *Design autonomy*: Local databases choose their own data model, query language, semantic, interpretation of data, constraints, functions and operations support, etc.

- *Communication autonomy*: Local databases decide when and how to respond to requests from other databases.
- *Execution autonomy*: The execution order of transactions or external/local operations is not controlled by foreign DBMSs. Local databases do not need to inform any other DBMS of the execution order of local or external operations. A local database does not distinguish among local and global operations.
- *Association autonomy*: Local databases can decide how much of their functions/operations and data to share with certain classes of users. The release of statistical information, such as costs efficiency, and execution speeds of processing information, is also determined by individual databases; thus, global query processing and optimization may be difficult. Local databases have the ability to associate or dissociate themselves from the network of databases.

In the following two subsections, we cast light on the effects of execution autonomy on transaction processing in multi-databases in view of the two robustness dimensions, namely, *serializability* and *recoverability*.

4.5.1 Serializability in Multi-databases

For this reason, the basic definitions introduced in Sect. 4.3 must be extended.

Definition 4.12. Global schedule

A global schedule H for n LDBMS is a schedule which:

1. includes the transactions $\bigcup_{i=1}^{n} T_i \bigcup T$, where T_i is the set of local transactions running at LDBMS$_i$ and T is the set of global transactions; and
2. $\forall i,\ 1 \leq i \leq n\ \Pi_i(H) = H_i$, where H_i is the local history of LDBMS$_i$.

Also the notion of conflicts must be divided into *direct* and *indirect* conflicts.

Definition 4.13. Direct conflict

Two transactions T and T' are in *direct* conflict in a local schedule H_i if $\exists p \in T$ and $\exists q \in T'$ where $p \not\!\!V q$.

Clearly, direct conflicts are no problem for the correctness of global schedules, since they can be solved within the LTM as usual using the local concurrency control algorithm.

Definition 4.14. Indirect conflict

Two transactions T and T' are in *indirect* conflict in a local schedule H_i if there exists a sequence of transactions $T_1, T_2, \ldots, T_r$ in H_i, so that T is in direct conflict with T_1, T_j is in direct conflict with T_{j+1} $(1 \leq j \leq r-1)$ and T_r is in direct conflict with T'.

As mentioned in Sect. 4.3, conflict serializability is the most applicable correctness criterion in view of the polynomial time needed for the verification of conflict serializable histories. Hence, the definition of conflict serializability is here extended to multi-databases.

Definition 4.15. Globally conflict serializable

A global schedule H is globally conflict serializable (GCSR), if a total order $<_H$ on $CP(H)$ exists, in which all local serial orders of the global transactions are the same, i.e., $\forall T_I$, $T_2 \in CP(H)$ $(T_I \neq T_2)$, and $T_I <_H T_2 \Rightarrow \forall H_i$, $1 \leq i \leq n$, T_1, T_2 are committed and $\exists H_i$, which H'_i is serial and $H_i \equiv_c H'_i$: $T_I <_{H'i} T_2$.

To ensure global serializability in multi-database systems, the possible indirect conflicts must be resolved. A problem with ensuring global conflict serializability results from the possible participation of local and global transactions in indirect conflicts and the restriction that no control information can be exchanged between the GTM and the LTMs of the participating LDBMS.

One of the simplest attempts to solve this problem is the *ticket method* [45, 46]. Here, conflicts are forced among global transactions using a data item called the *ticket*, maintained at each local database. Global transactions must read the ticket value, increment it and write the incremented value into the database. By doing so, any remote indirect conflicts between two local transactions at a site are converted into local direct conflicts that can be detected by the LDBMS. Hence, LDBMS can ensure serializability of their local transactions in the presence of global subtransactions. At the same time, the GTM does not have to be concerned with indirect conflicts between global subtransactions involving local transactions, since all global subtransactions at a site conflict directly [31]. Although this solution satisfies the global conflict serializability requirements, it is very inefficient since the tickets objects turn into real bottlenecks.

With an extra knowledge about the local concurrency control schemes employed at the LDBMS and in particular their ordering properties, more efficient solutions can be implemented. A good classification of these solutions can be found in [82]. Here, we mention one of these solutions. If all LDBMS produce rigorous schedules[5], the GTM does not have to perform any operation coordination; besides avoiding to commit any subtransaction of a global transaction at a site before all the operations of the global transaction have been completed [11].

Although global conflict serializability serves as a solid basis for formal correctness of transaction execution in multi-databases, it suffers from being hard to implement besides being *too* restrictive. In several advanced applications, a relaxed notion of global serializability will suffice. In [67], the notion of *two-level serializability* was first introduced. Under this relaxation, it suffices that every local schedule is serializable and the projection of the global schedule to a set of

---

[5] A schedule H is *rigorous* if it is strict and it satisfies the following condition:
$\forall T_I$ and $T_2 \in$ transaction set of H and $r_2[x] <_H w_I[x] \Rightarrow a_2 <_H w_I[x] \vee c_2 <_H w_I[x]$.

global transactions is serializable. *Quasi-serializability* [27] assumes that at most one subtransaction of a global transaction is allowed to execute on a particular LDBMS. The correctness of execution of a set of global and local transactions is based on the notion of a quasi-serial history, which specifies that only global transactions are executed serially, a history is quasi-serial if all local histories are conflict serializable and there exists a total order of all global transactions in which for each pair of global transactions, all the operations of the one transaction precede all the operations of the other in all local histories. Further forms of relaxed serializability can be found in [31].

4.5.2 Recoverability in Multi-databases

In general, there are two main approaches to maintaining atomicity in the presence of failures [31]:

- *Forward recovery*: the global transaction is completed successfully despite the failure. This means, a committed global transaction has, at every site where it has an original local subtransaction, exactly one committed local subtransaction.
- *Backward recovery*: The completion is achieved by continuing the transaction into an unsuccessful (aborted) completion. This means, that the global transaction is aborted and all the local subtransactions are locally aborted (or compensated). The approach is called *failure-exposing* in the sense that the application is notified about the failure.

After [12], the following is a categorization of the remedies that have been proposed in the literature:

- *Redo* (forward): A redo local subtransaction is executed. It consists of the all the commands changing the database state. For example, in the r/w database model, the write operations are re-executed and the read operation are ignored. The problem with this approach is that commercial DBMS do not allow their internal logging mechanisms to be used by an external entity such as the GTM.
- *Resubmit* (forward): A local subtransaction consisting of all the operations of the original subtransaction is executed [124].
- *Retry* (forward): Execute a transaction program corresponding to the failed subtransaction. This approach requires that global transaction programs be decomposed into global procedures [1] executing at participating sites.
- *Compensate* (backward): Compensating transaction, as mentioned in Sect. 4.4.3, are executed at the sites that had not failed.

4.6 Advanced Transaction Models

The limitations of classical ACID transactions have been discussed extensively in the literature [49]. In the context of traditional database applications, they perform very well so long as they are short-lived and access few data objects. However, this is not the case for distributed systems and data-intensive advanced applications, such as CAD systems, manufacturing control, workflows, etc. Here, transactions tend to be very long-lived compared to traditional ACID transactions. They access a huge amount of data objects and have a much more complex control flow. Another missing aspect in ACID transactions is the ability for cooperation between the various applications running these transactions.

In order to meet these requirements the flat ACID transaction model has been extended in several ways. All research efforts were dedicated to relax one or more of the ACID properties to encapsulate more semantic structure within the transaction declaration. Over the past ten years, many of the so-called advanced transaction models emerged. In the remaining sections of this chapter, we present only those models that are most relevant to our work.

4.7 ACTA

ACTA[6] [18, 20] itself is not a transaction model; but rather it is a formal first-order logic-based framework for characterizing the structure and behavior of existing advanced transaction models, and serves as a tool for relative comparison between them with respect to concurrency control and recovery. ACTA allows the specification of the effects of transactions on other transactions and also their effect on database objects.

In ACTA, database operations are represented as events. There are object events such as *reads* and *writes*. Other significant events are transaction management primitives, such as *begin* transaction, *commit*, and *abort*. Further primitives include *spawn* for nested transaction models. Also fundamental to ACTA is the use of histories to describe concurrent execution of transactions. ACTA captures the effects of transactions on other transactions and also their effects on objects through constraints and histories. This leads to definitions of transaction models in terms of a set of axioms, which are either invariant assertions about the histories generated by the transactions adhering to the particular model or explicit preconditions or post-conditions on operations of transaction management primitives.

The effects of transactions on each other in an advanced transaction model are characterized by the notion of *dependencies*. ACTA defines a long list of transaction dependencies like commit dependency, abort dependency, termination dependency, exclusion dependency, begin dependency, etc.

ACTA is used to characterize many of the different transaction models. For example, Sagas are characterized in the ACTA framework in [19]. In our work, we make use of ACTA to formalize the transaction dependencies in the proposed transaction model.

---

[6] ACTA means *actions* in Latin.

4.8 Sagas

Garcia Molina and Salem propose Sagas [41] as a transaction model for long-lived activities. A saga is a set of independent atomic short transactions $T_1, T_2, ..., T_n$ which are to be executed in a predefined order, usually sequential. Sagas are basically a *two*-level restriction of multi-level transactions (please refer to Sect. 4.11.2). On the lower level (component transaction), atomicity is the correctness criterion for transactions. The normal serializability theory governs the interleaving of execution in this layer. This requires no change in existing concurrency control modules built in commercial database management systems. At the upper (saga) level, concurrent sagas can interleave their transactions arbitrarily. This means, an upper layer module without a concurrency control is needed to manage sagas. This eases the integration of the saga transaction model in existing database management systems.

A saga commits, i.e., successfully terminates, if all its component transactions commit in the prescribed order. Under sequential execution, the correct execution of a committed saga is:

$$T_1 \, T_2 ... T_n$$

A saga is not failure atomic but neither can it execute partially, this means when a saga aborts, it has to compensate for the committed components by executing their corresponding compensating transactions. Compensating transactions are executed in the reverse order of commitment of the component transactions. Thus, in the sequential case, the correct execution of an aborted saga after the commitment of the ith component transaction, $T_i \, (1 \le i < n)$, is:

$$T_1 \, T_2 ... T_i \, C_i \, C_{i-1} ... C_2 \, C_1$$

where C_i is the compensation transaction associated with T_i. Note that the commitment of T_n implies the commitment of the whole saga and hence is not associated with a compensating transaction C_n.

In [43, 44], sagas are extended to a nested transaction model that provides more flexible transaction definitions, including adding provisions for alternative ways of accomplishing some operation and allowing for non-vital operations. In this extension, compensating transactions are instantiated recursively.

4.9 Flex

Flex transactions [30, 65] are designed to allow more flexibility in transaction processing. The model is developed with the premise that often parts of a transaction could be accomplished in one of several functionally equivalent ways. The model allows *functional replication* to provide a more failure-resilient transaction model. In our scenario of Chap. 2, getting a time slot for the drilling a hole in the flange can be done on drilling machine *A*. However, if this machine is not free, then a time slot can be acquired on a slower machine *B*.

Here also, the Flex transaction is defined as a set of subtransactions, some of which may be functionally equivalent, and a set of dependencies among these transactions. The dependencies occur among both the normal subtransactions and the compensating subtransactions. These dependencies define which subtransactions are actually executed in a Flex transaction, and in what order.

The Flex transaction model was implemented in the Vienna Parallel Logic (VPL) language [62]. The VPL programming language has explicit parallelism. The design of the VPL language is influenced mainly by the idea of compensated actions of the Flex transaction model [62]. The VPL language is a suitable environment for Flex transactions for the following reasons [29]: (1) VPL is a superset of Prolog; (2) committed computations can be automatically compensated with the convenient option of compensated actions; and (3) the programmer can easily specify Or/And parallelism, which facilitates the execution of the transactions and subtransactions sequentially or in parallel.

4.10 ConTracts

The ConTract model was first proposed in [95] and is well described in [117]. It provides a formal basis for defining and controlling long-lived, complex computations. It is inspired by the concept of spheres of control [24], and by the mechanisms for managing flow that are provided by some TP-monitors.

The ConTract model introduces a unit of work and control that consists of the whole application instead of individual database state transitions. ConTracts define a control mechanism above ACID transactions. It is rather a programming model that includes persistence, consistency, recovery, synchronization and cooperation. More formally,

Definition 4.16. The ConTract model

> A ConTract is a consistent and fault tolerant execution of an arbitrary sequence of predefined actions, called *steps*, according to an explicitly specified control flow description, called *script*.

The control flow is modeled by the usual elements, such as branching, looping, etc. while the steps are the elementary units of work and must be manually mapped into transactions on a database.

The system has a ConTract Manager, which is similar to modern Workflow engines. It implements an event-oriented flow management by using a transition net to specify activation and termination conditions for a step. The execution of a step is started if the event predicate for its activation becomes true and the required execution resources are available. The model uses exit invariants associated with steps in the ConTract. These invariants are used to maintain certain conditions in the database for the success of later steps in the ConTract. Thus, a step revalidates the invariance of a piece of information according to a previous step's exit invariant. Although the script model of ConTract seems to be powerful and relatively simple to use, the problem is that the model requires several special primitives in the underlying database and operating system to support its execution.

4.11 Nested Transaction Models

"All important concepts in computer science are recursive – why not transactions?" [6]. The nested transaction model was first introduced by Moss in [69]. Since then, the nested transaction model was further developed in several directions and appears in many variations. Sagas and Flex transactions can be viewed as special sort of nested transactions. Under this class of transactions, a transaction may contain any number of subtransactions, and each subtransaction, in turn, may contain any number of subtransactions; thus forming a *transaction tree*. In [50], the original definition of nested transactions by Moss is summarized as follows.

1. A nested transaction tree is a tree of transactions, the subtrees of which are either nested or flat transactions.
2. Transactions at the leaf level are flat transactions. The distance from the root to the leaves can be different for different parts of the tree.
3. The transaction at the root of the tree is called the root or top-level transaction; the others are called subtransactions. A transaction's predecessor in the tree is called a parent; a subtransaction at the next lower level is also called a child.
4. A subtransaction can commit or abort independently. If a child fails, its parent is not required to abort. Instead, the parent is allowed to perform its own recovery [29]. It may choose to:

   - ignore the condition (a non-vital subtransaction [43]);
   - retry the subtransaction;
   - initiate another subtransaction (a contingency subtransaction); or
   - abort.

5. The abort of a transaction anywhere in the tree causes all its subtransactions to rollback. This is the reason why subtransactions have only A, C, and I, but not D properties.

4.11.1 Closed-Nested Transaction Model

The most restrictive variation of nested transactions is the closed-nested transaction model. In some cases, it degenerates to the original ACID flat-transactions. Under this model, subtransactions are allowed to execute in parallel within their parent transaction. Transaction logic is encapsulated in the leaf nodes. All internal nodes are control nodes. Fig. 4.4 illustrates a closed-nested transaction tree for manufacturing the robot gripper of Example 2.2 (p. 10), independent from the product agents. However, subtransactions are allowed to see the results of their own subtransactions only. This leads to isolation over the whole transaction tree. Several protocols exist to synchronize the execution of subtransactions. For example, Moss [69] proposes an extension of the two-phase locking protocol, in which, after the end a subtransaction, its parent inherits all its acquired locks. The lock compatibility remains the same for the different subtransactions; but the parent is allowed to share the locks with its children.

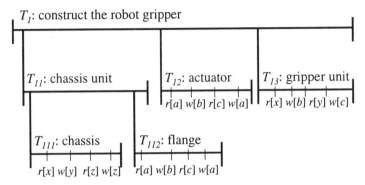

Fig. 4.4. Construction of a robot gripper as a closed-nested transaction tree

The internal nodes serve as save points for the execution of the transaction trees. In case of a subtransaction failure, the whole transaction tree does not need be undone. The first attempt is to backtrack to the previous save point and to retry the subtree once again. In case of resilient failures, the backtrack and retry could propagate till the first save point, which is the root transaction. The means to implement these save points is to inherit the before-images of updated objects together with the inheritance of the locks. This leads to the existence of more than one before-image of an updated data object at each save point.

This inheritance procedure imposes several limitations. First, lock inheritance reduces concurrency even between subtransactions of a same tree. If two subtransactions execute conflicting operations on the same data object, they cannot execute in parallel, though the structure of the transaction tree might allow it. Another problem is the need to change the internals of existing database management system. The transaction manager must be changed to implement lock inheritance and the recovery manager must be extended to handle multiple before-images for the same data object. Despite these problems, some TP-monitors, such as the Transarc Encina [114], support this model [50]. Some research has been done to supplement it with additional features such as automating the checking of integrity constraints under this model [26].

4.11.2 Multi-level Transaction Model

Multi-level transactions, also known as layered transactions, are a variant of nested transactions where the nodes in a transaction tree correspond to executions of operations at particular level of abstraction in a layered system [119]. The model is based on the seminal work on sphere of control [24]. Unlike the closed-nested transaction model, all transaction trees have the *same height* and the transaction logic is present in all levels with increasing degree of abstractions as we move towards the root.

The edges in a transaction tree represent the *implementation* of an operation that is invoked at level L_{i+1} by a sequence of operation executions at the next lower level L_i. The implementation of an operation is state-dependent; i.e., an L_i operation that is executed in two different transactions may invoke different L_{i-1} operation in these two transactions.

Concurrency control is achieved on a multi-level basis. It is meant to exploit the semantic of cooperation in level-specific *conflict relations* that reflect the compatibility of operations [42]. On the lowest level, the conflict relation is the normal read/write conflict in the r/w database model. On a higher level, two increment operations on the same data objects are compatible and can commute their execution order. More generally, serializability of the schedule at level L_i is provided by considering the L_{i+1} subtransactions as normal transactions with the conflict relation defined for the operations of the level L_i.

Again here, multi-level transactions cannot be directly applied to commercial database management systems, since a concurrency control mechanism is needed for each level. Also the non-trivial task of defining the conflict relations at the various levels is completely the responsibility of the developer. The main advantage of multi-level transactions is their extension of the formal definition of the conflict relation and hence the ability to define the concurrency control generically. This serves as a basis for other advanced transaction models, such as the Interaction transaction model (Sect. 4.12). Note that also Sagas (refer to Sect. 4.8) are special case of multi-level transactions with only *two* levels and an *empty* conflict relation at the higher level.

4.11.3 Open-Nested Transaction Model

The open-nested transaction model is the most general case of transaction nesting. In this model, subtrees in the transaction tree are allowed to have different nesting depths, just as the original nested model. In contrast to the closed-nested model, the open-nested transaction model attempts to relax all ACID properties.

Considering the aspect of *isolation*, each subtransaction makes its results available immediately after its commitment for all other subtransactions, whether within the same transaction tree or across the other coexisting trees. Hence, the need for lock inheritance is eliminated as opposed to the closed-nested transaction model. However, the limited isolation leads to the use of the most relaxed notion of *atomicity*. Under this transaction model, atomicity means masking the existence of aborted subtransactions to all subtransactions that will be subsequently executed [119]. Due to this relaxed atomicity, dependencies between the subtransactions of an unfinished transaction tree are created. In case of failure, backtracking to previous save points cannot be performed by simply restoring before-images, even if multiple of them are stored within each save point as in the closed-nested model.

The alternative in this transaction model is the extensive use of semantic-based recovery mentioned in Sect. 4.4.3. Each subtransaction is associated with a compensating transaction, which is to be executed to recover from failures. In our robot gripper example (Example 2.2, p. 13), a compensating transaction for the time slot allocation subtransaction for the drilling machine that drill holes in the flange is simply another simple transaction that frees the allocated time slot and transfers the sum paid to the corresponding production unit back to the product agent. Compensation offers a greater flexibility in recovery at the price of extra effort from the side of the system designer to define the appropriate action.

Durability of subtransactions is affected by the relaxed definition of the atomicity. A persistent subtransaction may have non-persistent as well as persistent descendants. The difference is that the non-persistent descendants are made persistent when the lowest persistent ancestor completes successfully, whereas persistent descendants are made persistent upon their own successful completion [119]. Under this large flexibility of the model, *consistency* is completely the responsibility of the application programs. The transaction manager guarantees the consistency across the subtransaction borders (*outer* consistency) but can do nothing against the weak conflicts resulting from the interactions between them.

Due to its large expressive power, the open-nested transaction model serves as basis for many advanced data-intensive applications such as CAD-systems as well as within advanced database management systems. For example, the model is used by the rule-based ULTRA language [120] to specify logical update queries in a modular form [32]. In view of its great potential, an extension to the Object Management Group (OMG) Transaction Service (OTS) [87] is suggested to add the open-nested transaction model to its standard [98].

4.12 Interactions

The Interaction transaction model [82] is based on the open-nesting paradigm. It is used to define flexible transactions that represent long-lived tasks accessing multi-databases. It is designed for supporting AI-like planning applications, such as travel planning assistants. In such domains, a certain degree of reaction is required to deal with unpredicted changes in the environment.

Similar to ConTract, Interactions are composed of primitive procedures called *steps* that operate on the local databases. Different steps of an Interaction operating on the same local database can be grouped together into a single local transaction. The definition of control logic is done using a declarative language called TaSL[7]. [84] contains a definition of the language. Using TaSL, the planning application is able to define the interaction tree. The model allows forking and joining of subtasks. Task flexibility is represented as alternative subsets of short atomic

---

[7] TaSL stands for Task Specification Language.

transactions, each of which accomplishes the same subtask. The model also allows for prioritization of alternative subtasks. A detailed description of the tree model can be found in [81].

Because of the long-lived nature of planning applications, other transactions running on the local databases change the information in those databases, potentially overriding information set by the Interaction and necessary for its correct completion. For this reason, the notion of *weak conflicts* is introduced in the model. Weak conflicts define a set of conditions set by the Interaction, which should be preserved for a specific span of the Interaction's execution. Conditions are violated as a result of an update of a specific data object in the database. Here, also compensation is the means for recovering from such weak conflicts.

A prototype architectural design for a multi-database called *Mongrel* is designed for the execution management of Interactions as well as the monitoring of events and evaluation of weak conflict conditions. Mongrel contains a global transaction manager that is responsible for scheduling steps in the Interactions against the local databases. The interaction Manager itself has a private local database for storing the internal states of the Interactions. Fig. 4.5 illustrates the system modules in Mongrel [84].

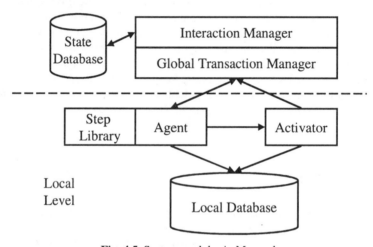

Fig. 4.5. System modules in Mongrel

At first sight, the Interactions model seems appealing for the application in MAS due to the large similarity between AI-planning applications and MAS. However, the model lacks several aspects central to MAS. For example, the model does not directly support the explicit coordination between the execution of various agent plans. Furthermore, the internals of the transaction specification together with its contingency behavior do not put up with the high rate and variety of disturbances inherently present in MAS. On the task definition level, a declarative language such as TaSL is not adequate due to the high degree of interaction between planning and execution. Certainly, an interactive conversation-oriented protocol is more suitable for the continuous refinement and adaptation of the transaction trees. On the architectural level, a multi-databases approach is not applicable in the highly autonomous multiple database environments that are expected in MAS domains. For this reason, all functionality embedded in Mongrel must be distributed across several light-weight agents. Finally, although the Interactions model enjoys very good theoretical foundations, the performance of the model has never been tested for scalability.

4.13 Conclusion

Over the past 25 years, transaction processing proved itself to be a solid means for providing formal guarantees on the robust execution of database operations. The original theory is easily extended to handle the case of multiple heterogeneous databases, which form the landscape of today's information systems.

The model of flat ACID transactions was extended in many ways to accommodate advanced data-intensive applications. Over the past ten years, many research efforts were proposed in the literature. Models based on nesting transactions appear to be the most appealing to be used in a transaction model for MAS due to their flexibility and their expressive power. Unfortunately, none of these models found its way to large-scale commercial applications. The reasons lie in that the majority of the already-developed models are tailored to specific applications and are not general enough to be used in a generic MAS architecture. Many models require internal changes in underlying database management systems and come with their own proprietary language, architecture, and infrastructure, which makes them again unsuitable for MAS.

In the next chapter, we exactly state the requirements for a transaction model to be used for increasing the robustness of MAS and show how we extend these advanced transaction models and integrate such a model in a MAS architecture.

5 Proposed Approach: Transactional Agents

The focus of the thesis is the increase of *robustness* of MAS by providing the necessary middleware to guarantee the robust execution of agent actions. After presenting an application scenario in Chap. 2 to illustrate an example for the application of MAS in large-scale applications, we gave an overview of MAS and transaction processing in databases in Chaps. 3 and 4, respectively. Now, we move forward to present our approach for increasing robustness in MAS applications. In this chapter, we begin with a statement of the problem under consideration. Then, our approach, namely that of *transactional agents*, is presented. We justify the choice of the open-nested transaction model as a basis for the proposed transaction model. Embedding the transaction model into a general MAS architecture is then discussed. Here, we introduce a new component, called the *Execution Agent* to the architecture. Then, all architectural components are exposed with a special emphasis on the Execution Agent. Finally, a concluding section summarizes the chapter and motivates the following chapters.

5.1 Problem Statement and Objectives

The use of redundancy and specially tailored organizational structures in MAS have been the traditional way for increasing robustness of MAS over the last decade. This had a great implication on the design process. Designing robust MAS is a highly complicated process since robustness aspects are to be designed and implemented step by step by the system designers. This significantly increases the complexity of the system and the solution is often tailored to a specific domain. Porting the specially-designed solution to other domains or adapting it to changes in the application requirements is hardly feasible.

The aim of this work is to increase the robustness of MAS *through an underlying middleware*. This relieves the MAS designers from designing and implementing the robustness ensuring aspects and let them concentrate on their real assignment, namely, designing the MAS that solves the original problem. Providing robustness through a *middleware component* in the infrastructure and separating this aspect from the development of the MAS itself ease the portability of a MAS from one domain to the other by always relying on the middleware for achieving robustness. Moreover, the middleware will be able to provide formal guarantees on the robustness of the system by itself and independently from the original structure of the MAS architecture.

K. Nagi: Transactional Agents, LNCS 2249, pp. 63–78, 2001.
© Springer-Verlag Berlin Heidelberg 2001

However, a middleware cannot encapsulate the whole semantic of the application. Some parts of the logic of the system will always remain invisible to the middleware. Thus, we define the *robustness* provided by the middleware in terms of guarantees given on a *technical basis*. Thus, we consider the robustness problem from its technical side, which is guaranteeing the *correctness* and *recoverability* of the system.

- By *correctness*, it is meant that, in normal operation modes, the agent plans are executed in a way that guarantees the absence of any *undesired* side effects that might result from the concurrent execution of agent actions in the multi-agent environment. This definition of correctness is a generalization of the serializability theory [8] used in database technology.
- By *recoverability*, it is meant that, in case of disturbances, the system reaches a well-defined consistent state. Due to the reactivity of MAS, this state is not necessarily its state before the occurrence of the disturbance as compared to the traditional recoverability theory [8] employed in databases. It can be any state as long as it is consistent, desirable, and expectable by the MAS designer.

From the above definition of robustness provided by the middleware, it is clear that we restrict ourselves to the robustness of the execution of agent actions, and not to the mental states of the agents or to the planning process itself. The necessity of the need for robustness was already argued above. Now, it is our turn to argue that restricting robustness to the execution is even *sufficient* to be guaranteed by the middleware.

- Considering the correctness aspect, the simple agent actions, such as allocating a time slot for a production step in our application scenario, are the ones that enter into contest on acquiring shared resources, i.e., data objects stored in the underlying databases [33]. The planning process itself runs within the agents and is, by nature, isolated within the borders of the agents. It is, hence, protected from any undesirable side effects resulting from concurrent execution.
- The recoverability of the whole agent including its mental internal status and the planning process is not feasible, since it requires logging the whole agent trace in persistent storage. Moreover, it is also not desirable, since changes in the real world during the down time of the agent outdate much of its internal knowledge. Therefore, it is wise to identify the parts of the agent mental states that must be recovered. It is reasonable to assume that the plan development process itself is *idempotent* and can be restarted any time. However, it is vital to know which actions were already performed by the agent against the database and which messages were interchanged with the other agents before the crash. It is also desirable to automatically undo the effects of all incomplete actions.
- Even if the robustness of parts of the planning process are needed to be guaranteed by the middleware, these parts can be easily translated to special sorts of internal actions, which can be temporarily stored in an underlying database. In that case, the middleware can handle these parts as any normal agent action and is able to provide them with the required robustness guarantees.

From these requirements, it is obvious that the desired robustness goes far beyond a mere syntactical aspect as in traditional transaction processing in database management systems. We obviously need a *structure* that captures the semantic of the plan of each agent [76]. This structure must fully represent the plan of the agent. The middleware is then responsible for executing this structure. This way, we enable:

- The middleware to provide formal guarantees on the robustness of execution of agent actions, and
- The planning process to concentrate on its original task, which is solving the logical problem and achieving the agents' goals.

The choice of this structure is a huge challenge. Clearly, the structure must be based on a transaction model because of *two* strategic reasons:

1. Transactions are the means for achieving robustness in databases environments over the past 25 years. It is unwise simply to ignore research efforts done in this area.
2. The traditional flat ACID transactions are the understandable form of submitting actions to the underlying environment, namely, the underlying heterogeneous databases representing the real world.

The structure must be *powerful* enough to represent the agent plans. This is not an easy task since there is no canonical form for representing agent plans. This is primarily caused by the variety of domains in which MAS are applied and the variety of approaches and methodologies employed in developing them.

Besides being powerful, the structure must also be *flexible* to allow the evolution of the agent plans. The middleware must be able to accept and execute incomplete parts of the plan and allow its further refinement and reconfiguration during the execution. This requires the support for an intensive conversation between the planning entity and the structure executing entity to capture the dynamics of the plan generation process.

Since the social aspect is the milestone in the MAS paradigm, the structure must support *cooperation* between agents trying to achieve a common goal by executing a common plan. It is reasonable to assume that each plan is represented by one structure to preserve the autonomy of the agent and to allow a nearly one-to-one correspondence between the plan and the structure representing it. The support for cooperation must be done through the implementation of various coordination primitives between the components of these independent structures.

A key to the success of any introduced structure is the capability of capturing both *the plan* and *the contingency behavior* of the plan in the face of disturbances. This is very important for the following reasons.

- It allows the middleware to provide the required robustness guarantees, since the contingency behavior is defined within the structure and can be automatically executed by the middleware when required.
- It increases the reactivity of the middleware and hence of the whole system in face of rapid changes or disturbances in the system as well as in the real world.

- It provides the necessary coupling between planning and execution, which is vital to the success of any MAS architecture [28]. By defining the cases for the contingency and capturing the desired behavior within the structure, the execution is no longer isolated from the changes in the real world.
- It relieves the planning process from the tedious monitoring for minor disturbances in the real world that do not affect the course of plan development, but yet require a rapid reaction.

As with the plan itself, the structure must be *powerful* enough to capture the contingency behavior and yet *flexible* enough to allow its refinement, adjustment, and redefinition during execution. This flexibility is even a more important aspect in the contingency behavior as compared to the normal behavior, since the planner, in general, tends to elaborate on the plan development itself and leave much of the definition of the contingency behavior incomplete or even open. This is due to the low frequency of occurrence of the disturbances for which the contingency is defined and the variety of contingencies that must be considered and designed to face the various forms of disturbances. In many systems, it is more economical to adopt an optimistic approach and to leave the definition of contingency behavior to the point when it is actually needed.

To support the execution of such contingencies, the proposed middleware must automate several *patterns of behavior* for error handling that are usually executed in cases of disturbances. Some of the most famous patterns include the following.

- The automatic *retrial* of actions in case of simple failures caused by the temporary unavailability of required resources, conflicts over common resources, or system crashes, either software or hardware.
- Automatic *restoring* of parts of the agents after a software failure leading to their crash.
- Automatic *backtracking* facilities in case of persisting failures or drastic changes in the real world invalidating parts of the already executed plans.
- Automatic *reactivity* to changes in the real world leading to inconsistency in parts of the plans, which can be reconverted to a consistent state by reactively readjusting parts of the plan.

On the *implementation* level, any proposed solution must fit in the existing IT-landscape. Commercial DBMS, either relational or object-oriented, have established themselves as the standard middleware for data storage, access, and manipulation. With their traditional flat ACID transactions as work units, they constitute the design constraint from the lower layer for any proposed solution. Any change in the internals of these DBMS is deemed to failure. Also, posing one centralized layer above them, as in multi-databases, is not applicable in the MAS paradigm that is inherently against any centralization. Moreover, we are dealing with loosely coupled heterogeneous databases sources that join in and out the system. This, in turn, is not in favor of a centralized middleware. From the overlying layer, the MAS poses also several constraints. Unlike the DBMS layer that enjoys a well-established standard, MAS are very different in nature, organization and function. Any solution should meet a generic MAS architecture. However, it must be flexible enough to be tailored to fit the MAS it is employed for. The key to solve this paradox is to use an open architecture that only defines the interfaces between the components and their main functionality, but not their internal functioning.

Robustness is a deciding factor if the MAS is to be applied outside the research labs in industrial large-scale applications, such as the domain of PPC applications. These, in turn, have other requirements than research prototypes. The most important one is *performance*. Of course, guaranteeing robustness has its price but, under no circumstance should performance drastically decrease because of the proposed solution to the robustness problem. That's why any new middleware components introduced to the MAS as part of the IT-infrastructure should be of a light-weight nature, both in processing costs and storage capacity. These components should also be transparent and of a plug-in nature so that one or more robustness guarantees, such as recoverability, could be deactivated on some occasions, where they are not needed.

By no means, the system should have a centralized instance. For one reason, this disagrees with the MAS paradigm with its tendency to extreme decentralization. The other reason is to enable the *scalability* of the system. Scalability is vital to any serious application of MAS in industrial domains. Through simulation, the performance of the introduced solution must be analyzed and proven to be scalable. Through an extensive simulation model, the *predictability* of the MAS can be dramatically improved since one of the main problems of MAS is their unpredictable nature through simple analytical tools, such as mathematical models. Extensive simulation tools are the means for solving this problem.

5.2 Proposed Approach: Transactional Agents

The proposed approach relies on choosing the structure for representing the agent plan within the domain of database technology. This way, MAS will gain in robustness by being based on the well-established robustness techniques of database systems, namely *transactions* [76]. More precisely, the structure is based on an extension to one of the *advanced transaction* models presented in Chap. 4. The IT-infrastructure is, hence, supplied with components, namely, the *transaction agents* that execute the structure and ensure the required robustness guarantees.

The nested transaction models seem to be the best candidate in the choice of the structure. Since their introduction in the early 80s, the nested transaction models have been suggested for representing long-lived activities due to their relaxation of the ACID properties and their great flexibility. Specially, the family of open-nested transactions is suitable for AI planning-like applications and were used in several transaction models applied in these domains. Examples are found in the Interactions transaction model [82] and nested-Sagas [43, 44].

Due to the following properties, the open-nested transaction model also forms the basis for our proposed transaction model.

- *Recursive Structure*: The vast majority of agent planning strategies is based on hierarchical decomposition of problems [28]. The recursive structure of the transaction trees allows the decomposition of subplans in subtransactions and preserves their hierarchy within the tree structure.

- *Localization*: The nested transaction model allows the separation of subplans into relatively independent subtrees. This increases the controllability of the planner over the execution. This high controllability is crucial for MAS that require both reactivity and flexibility in face of disturbances. The nested transaction model generally supports this by allowing the dynamic configuration of subtrees in the transaction tree even during the execution.

- *Capturing the normal behavior as well as the contingency behavior*: The nested transaction model defines both the normal course of action and the contingencies within the same structure. The definitions of save points and compensations act as exception handlers in case of failures. By using them, it is possible to semantically undo some already executed actions and to retry them or their alternatives at a later point in time.

- *Multilevel handling of contingencies*: Defining multiple save points across a tree path together with hierarchical compensation allows nesting of exception handling by performing multi-layered recovery. This is essential for MAS applications, which always attempt to localize the damage caused by a failure and try to recover only the affected part.

- *Support for extended recovery mechanisms*: Beside the ability of nested transactions to define different recovery levels, the open-nested transaction paradigm offers extra recovery mechanisms by allowing both *forward* and *backward* recovery. This is a substantial feature for MAS. An agent controls and executes long sequences of complex actions. In case of disturbances, the agent must recover with the lowest possible overhead. In light of the accomplished tasks, the agent must be given the chance to choose between the direction in which to carry its recovery and the open-nested transaction model provides it with both directions.

- *Support for long-living activities*: In the open-nested transaction model, a subtransaction makes its results directly available to all other transactions. This avoids locking the data objects for long periods. This is very useful for MAS. Executing agent plans is a very long process and it is not acceptable to block shared resources for the whole duration of the plan execution.

- *Support for cooperation*: Another huge advantage of the early release of resources is enabling the cooperation between the transaction trees. The social behavior is central to MAS. In other words, cooperation between the agents achieving a common goal must be mapped onto the transaction layer. If each agent is to execute a transaction tree, the first step is to be able to share the intermediate results of each other during their execution and not after their termination.

- *Applicability in heterogeneous Information Systems*: MAS are add-on software components that must coexist with existing information system components. Any introduced transaction model cannot change the internals of the underlying DBMS. Implementing the open-nested transaction model does not require drastic changes in existing DBMS as compared to the closed-nested transaction model that needs lock inheritance and the storage of multiple before-images per updated data object (refer to Sect. 4.11.1). Additionally, the open-nested model has shown to be particularly suitable in structuring applications that need to access data stored in data repositories managed by systems that do not support any global atomic commit protocol such as the two-phase commit protocol [21]. Due to large autonomy of the DBMS on which MAS operate, such repositories are expected to be the common case.

Having chosen the open-nested transaction model as a basis for the proposed transaction model, the structure must be introduced into the general MAS architecture. Conceptually, the transactional agents can be embedded within any existing agent architecture. For example, a BDI-agent could be made transactional by introducing a *transaction-processing unit* to each agent in the system as shown in Fig. 5.1.

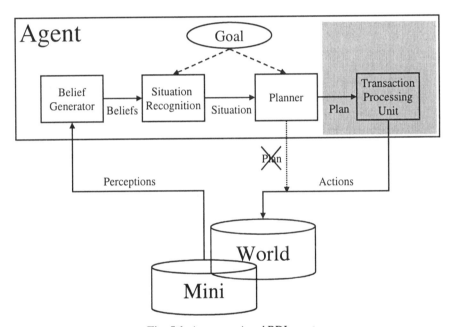

Fig. 5.1. A *transactional* BDI agent

Although on the conceptual level, this is exactly the desired solution, this is not applicable on the architectural level for the following reasons.

- This mixes two completely different architectural aspects, namely the internal architecture of the agent including its foundational theory with the robustness aspects with their focus on coping with real life interactions and disturbances together with their side effects.
- This requires drastic changes in the internals of already existing MAS and their architectures.

- Building the robustness components within the agent has the consequence of forcing multi-agent designers to go into the details of the new component within their own systems as compared to the ideal case where only the functionality and the interface to the component must be known.
- In case the robustness component is not needed for a period of time, it would be very difficult to unplug the integrated component.

In summary, building the transaction processing unit into the agent itself leads to the loss of the generality of the MAS architecture. In the next section, we discuss how to bring in the execution structure into a generic MAS architecture.

5.3 System Architecture

5.3.1 A Generic MAS Architecture

A generic MAS architecture that can be, for example, employed in a decentralized PPC application is illustrated in Fig.5.2. The MAS is situated in an environment that is modeled in a mini world of federated heterogeneous and loosely coupled databases. Agents can perceive the environment by reading the databases and can modify it by writing to the databases. Agents wrap their database actions in flat ACID transactions, since most commercial DBMS support this transaction model. The agents are cooperating with each other to achieve a common goal, e.g., the

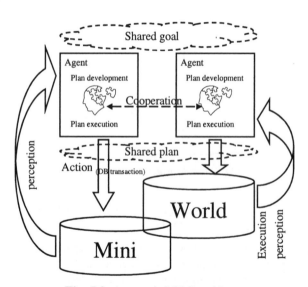

Fig. 5.2. A generic MAS architecture

production of the robot gripper unit of the application scenario. For this purpose, they develop a shared plan based on their perceptions, whose various parts are executed by the single agents. During execution, the agents make execution perceptions to observe the effect concerning the success or failure of their actions on the mini world.

5.3.2 A Robust MAS Architecture

The MAS remains above the layer of federated databases representing the mini world as illustrated in Fig.5.2. Agent actions are still wrapped in flat ACID transactions to remain open to almost all existing commercial DBMS. All possible agent actions are represented as independent work units with their definitions stored in the *Action Repository*. Central to our approach is that each agent is actually divided into two physical entities: a *Planning Agent* and an *Execution Agent*. The Planning Agents still have their common goal and cooperate with each other by forming agent groups to develop the common shared plan. Due to the autonomous nature of agents, each Planning Agent develops its agent-specific part of the

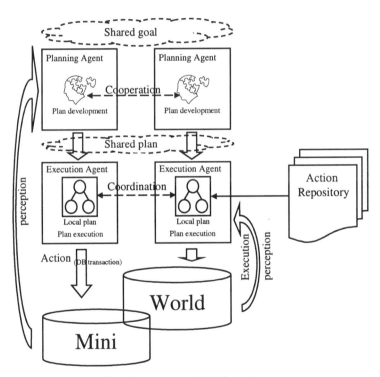

Fig. 5.3. Proposed MAS architecture

overall plan shared by the members of an agent group. Then, each Planning Agent delegates its part of the shared plan to a peer Execution Agent. The execution of these *local* plans must be then coordinated by means of *coordination protocols*. As mentioned in Sect. 5.2, we extend the model of open-nested transaction trees to represent the plan. The Execution Agents receive these trees and are responsible for the robust execution of agent actions. In these trees, agent actions are defined together with the corresponding control flow and control parameters governing them. When the Execution Agent is about to execute a work unit, i.e., a flat ACID transaction, within the agent plan, it fetches its definition in the action repository and submits the transaction to the appropriate DBMS. The cooperation between the individual agent plans is reflected in a series of *Event*, *Condition*, *Action* (ECA) rules connecting the transaction trees at the Execution Agents and building the coordination primitives. The details of the transaction tree are described in Chap. 6.

The life cycle of the Execution Agent is completely controlled by its peer Planning Agent. The Planning Agent instantiates it, hands it over the execution of the plan, and kills it upon the completion of the plan execution. If required, the Planning Agent delegates the plan execution to more than one Execution Agent. The autonomy of the Execution Agent manifests itself in the fact that it is completely free in scheduling the agent actions as long as they obey the general execution dependencies implied by the transaction tree. It is entitled to autonomously execute any of the predefined contingency behavior in case of disturbances. Nevertheless, the Planning Agent is allowed to monitor the status of execution of its plans. If necessary, it interacts with its peer Execution Agent during the execution phase to change the course of actions and readjust its original plan.

To keep the MAS architecture open for arbitrary agent frameworks joining the system, all the interactions between the Planning Agent and its peer Execution Agent as well as the interactions between the Execution Agents belonging to the same agent group obey a certain standard. As seen in Chap. 3, the FIPA standard [37] is emerging as the standardization body for software agents. Thus, we design the interactions between the various architecture components on the basis of the FIPA standard.

In the following, we describe each of the components of the architecture with a special focus on the Execution Agent, since it is the central and novel component in the architecture.

5.4 The Planning Agent

The Planning Agents are the planning instances in the MAS architecture. They are responsible for developing the solution of the given problem. For this purpose, they may employ any of the AI-planning methodologies to achieve this goal. They are also responsible for developing the contingency behavior in order to be able to react to emerging disturbances inherently present in the system either on the operational or the technical levels. Planning Agents perceive the real world by reading the databases in the mini world and, according to their competence and the nature of the problem, divide themselves into agent groups to solve their problem and achieve their common goal. This common goal is divided within the group to local goals for which local plans are to be developed. Plan development occurs through cooperation between the Planning Agents of the same group. The sum of all local plans in an agent group thus forms the common shared plan for this group.

The Planning Agent delegates the execution of its local plan to a peer Execution Agent. The plan is formulated in a transaction tree to be executed by the Execution Agent. Before the begin of execution, the Planning Agent must instantiate the Execution Agent. If necessary, it can instantiate more than one agent for the execution of different parts of the tree. If requested, the Planning Agent can be informed on the execution status of the transaction tree. At any time, it can interfere in the course of execution, refine, and readjust parts of the transaction tree. This interaction between the Planning Agent and the Execution Agent is based on the exchange of XML structures encapsulated in FIPA *Agent Communication Language* (ACL) messages. These messages contain communication performatives to define the desired effect of the interactions. These interactions are described in details in Chap. 8.

This way, the Planning Agent is able to concentrate on the original task of the MAS, namely, solving the conceptual problem by defining the normal and the contingency behavior. It is hence relieved from the executive perception and directly dealing with every slight disturbance by delegating the execution to its peer Execution Agent.

Another advantage of restricting the robustness guarantees to the execution is that the Planning Agent need not be modified to embody the robustness guaranteeing components. In fact, the internals of the Planning Agent are completely irrelevant to the architecture as long as it is able to express its generated plan in terms of transaction tree and engage itself in the conversation protocols with its peer Execution Agent. Regarding the Planning Agents as black boxes makes the architecture open to any agent framework with its proprietary implementation.

Example 5.1. The Planning Agent for the production of the robot gripper unit

> In the application scenario of Chap. 2, a group of Planning Agents has the shared goal of manufacturing the robot gripper unit. This includes both the production scheduling phase and the follow-up process. This common task is divided into several subtasks such as the manufacturing of the chassis unit, the manufacturing of the actuator, and the manufacturing of the gripper unit, etc. Each Planning Agent develops its own plan for the subtask for which it is in charge of. The plan identifies the construction dependencies between the production steps and reflects these dependencies into execution dependencies between the time slot allocation actions. A certain degree of cooperation between the Planning Agents is required while developing the local plans, especially while allocating time slots for the assembly phase. Then, the Planning Agents instantiate their peer Execution Agents in order to execute the plan. In this scenario, it is very reasonable to create two Execution Agents for each Planning

Agent: one for the time slot allocation phase and the one for the follow-up process during the manufacturing phase.

5.5 The Execution Agent

The Execution Agent is the main contribution of this work to the MAS architecture. Its presence is central to our approach since it is actually the *transactional agent* in the architecture. After being instantiated by a Planning Agent, the Execution Agent receives the plan in the form of a transaction tree. The transaction tree can be completely specified or incrementally transmitted from the Planning Agent to the Execution Agent using the conservation-based interaction protocols. Using the same communication protocol, the transaction trees can be anytime redefined, refined, and readjusted by the Planning Agent as long as these plan fragments did not yet execute. The Execution Agent has complete autonomy on the execution of the transaction tree and the execution of contingency behavior, defined within the plan, in case of disturbances to guarantee the robust execution of the transaction tree.

The main modules of the Execution agent are illustrated in Fig. 5.4. The *Agent Transaction Manager* (ATM) module resides at the heart of the Execution Agent. It receives the definition of the transaction tree and is responsible for the robustness of execution. For the correctness of execution, the ATM has a scheduler component that is responsible for submitting the agent actions to the underlying DBMS according to the execution dependencies specified in the transaction tree. Moreover, the ATM checks on the feasibility of the aggregation of the transaction trees to be executed by the Execution Agents of the agent group. Of course, the Execution Agent cannot know much about the internal consistency and semantic of the transaction trees but it can guarantee that the execution of the transaction trees does not end up in endless loops if the coordination primitives between the subtrees are not set properly.

Before executing a predefined agent action, the ATM loads its definition from the action repository upon demand. If any of the parameters is missing, the ATM requests it from its master Planning Agent. To ensure the recoverability of the Execution Agent, the ATM logs the activities of the Execution Agent. Depending on the services provided by the system hosting the Execution Agent, logs can be stored in physical files or in database relations. Since the various components, such as the DBMS and the message queues, of the architecture have their own mechanisms for guaranteeing recoverability, these mechanisms must be coupled to the logging mechanisms of the ATM. Details of the operation of the ATM are explained in Chap. 7.

The *Database Interface* module lies between the ATM and the underlying DBMS. Through this module, the database transactions defined in the agent actions are submitted to the underlying databases. The module is responsible for establishing the connection to the database by loading the appropriate database connection driver using the connection information supplied as part of the agent action parameters. Using the connectivity driver, such as a JDBC driver, the SQL commands are submitted and the execution results of the transaction are returned in the action parameters. The result of the execution itself, which is either the *success* or *fail* of the ACID transaction, is transmitted through the module to the ATM. Furthermore, the Database Interface module provides the ATM with the necessary information about the logs of the underlying DBMS in order to couple robustness mechanisms of the DBMS with those of the Execution Agent.

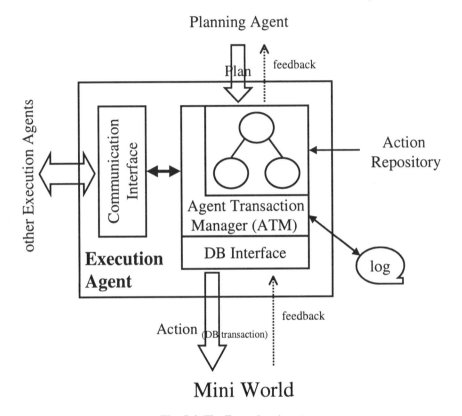

Fig. 5.4. The Execution Agent

On the other hand, the *Communication Interface* module is responsible for the communication with other Execution Agents of the same agent group. The module is in direct contact with the communication channel shared by the Execution Agents. This channel can be as simple as an Internet port or as complex as a transactional message queues service, such as IBM MQ-series [57]. The module receives the incoming messages and is responsible for parsing and interpreting them. Then, it reports the status of the relevant parts of the various transaction trees to the ATM. The Communication Interface module also sends all outgoing messages used in the coordination process between the actions of the various Execution Agents. Here, it is responsible for the encapsulation of the message in the FIPA compliant communication primitives. Similar to the Database Interface module, the Communication Interface module provides the ATM with the necessary information for coupling the robustness mechanisms of the communication channel with those of the Execution Agent.

In summary, the Execution Agent is the transactional agent in the architecture that is responsible for the following tasks.

- The execution of agent plans.
- Formally guaranteeing the robustness of the execution of agent actions.
- The interaction with the Planning Agent.
- The interaction with the underlying databases representing the mini world.
- The interaction with other Execution Agents to coordinate the execution of their shared plans.

5.6 The Action Repository

All possible agent actions are defined in the action repository, illustrated in **Fig. 5.5**. Agent actions define the work units executed by the Execution Agents. The Planning Agents use these actions as building blocks to develop their plans. In other words, the plan developed by a Planning Agent defines a set of agent actions to be executed on the underlying DBMS together with the necessary control flow between these actions and the control parameters governing their execution. Each agent action wraps a flat ACID database transaction.

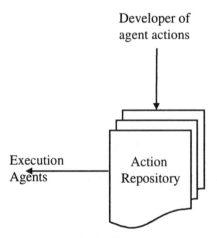

Fig. 5.5. Action repository

In the prototype implementation of this architecture, agent actions are expressed in the form of Java classes with embedded SQL statements. Data is exchanged between the Java code and the SQL statements using the JDBC standard. Through a graphical user interface, the developers of agent actions define the classes in the repository. These classes extend a generic class for agent actions. Through this inheritance and the use of reflection, the repository stores the definition of the action together with several meta data about the actions themselves. These meta data include textual descriptions of the action, the number of the parameters and their types, etc.

Example 5.2. Meta data for an agent action

An agent action that reserves a time slot for a certain manufacturing step might have the following meta data in the action repository.

- *Java class name*: DE.uka.ira.ipd.Action.Schedule.
- *Class description*: this agent action reserves a time slot for a production step x on a production unit of type y within the time period $t1$ and $t2$ with a maximum budget of a DM.
- *Class Path*: ~KRASH/Repository/Schedule.class
- *Source Path*: ~KRASH/Repository/Schedule.java
- *Executable Method*: Boolean execute();
- *Number of Parameters*: 5
- *Parameters*:

Type	Name	Description	Calling
Integer	ProductionStep	The identifier to the production step	By value
...	...	...	...

5.7 Integration with the FIPA Platform

To ensure that the proposed MAS architecture remains open for the joining and leaving of agents belonging to arbitrary agent architectures, the proposed architecture complies with a standard agent platform, namely, FIPA [37]. As seen in Sect. 3.4, FIPA has established itself as the standardization body in the software agent community. FIPA provides the framework for defining agent communication languages, ontologies, and standard negotiation protocols. In our prototype implementation, we use the FIPA implementation FIPA-OS developed at the labs of Nortel Networks [92]. This open-source software is Java-based and is one of the most widely spread implementations of FIPA.

The first step is to incorporate the Execution Agent in the FIPA standard platform. Fig. 5.6 is a schematic illustration of such integration. After the instantiation of the Execution Agent, it registers itself at the white pages service and the yellow pages facility of the FIPA platform. Here, it is necessary to map the Execution Agent names to unique FIPA agent addresses. A FIPA agent address contains the IP address of the hosting system, the port number listened to by the agent, and the agent name. We do not enforce a naming scheme for the Execution Agent, but suggest that the name of the Execution Agent contains the identifier of its peer Planning Agent and a unique sequence number within the Planning Agent to guarantee the uniqueness of the name. Furthermore, the lifecycle of the Execution Agent can be monitored by the *Agent Management Service* (AMS) of the FIPA platform.

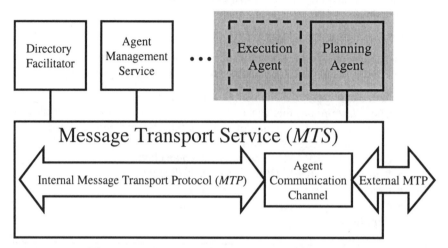

Fig. 5.6. The Execution Agent as part of the FIPA platform

On the communication level, we define the messages exchanged between the Execution Agents and their master Planning Agents as well as the coordination messages between the execution Agents of the same agent group using the FIPA ACL. An ambitious step would be defining the transactional ontology we use as well as the interaction protocols as standard negotiation protocols within FIPA. This would certainly contribute to a wider spread of our approach of transactional agents. The first steps in this direction have already begun within the KRASH project ([79, 80]).

5.8 Conclusion

In this chapter, we first presented our approach of having *transactional agents* to increase the robustness of execution of agent actions. After listing the requirements that our solution must fulfill, we justified the choice of open-nested transaction model as basis for our transaction trees. Then, we described the general MAS architecture and exposed each of its components with a special focus on the Execution Agents that are responsible for the robust execution of the transaction model.

In the next chapter, we describe the transaction model executed by the Execution Agent in details. Then, in the following two chapters, we go into the details of operation of the Execution Agent and describe its interactions with the other components of the architecture.

6 The Agent Transaction Model

From the previous chapter, it is clear that the agent transaction model forms the heart of our proposed solution for increasing the robustness of MAS. The scope of this chapter, as illustrated in Fig. 6.1, is the definition of the proposed transaction model. Here, we describe the transaction model itself from a formal and a theoretical perspective.

First, we begin with explaining the need for extending the open-transaction model to fulfill MAS requirements. Then, we describe the transaction tree itself and describe the various modes for recovery that provide the necessary control flow for defining the contingency behavior. Having described the operation of the transaction tree, we go into each node type in detail. Finally, we give a formal proof of correctness for the transaction model in view of serializability and recoverability. A concluding section ends the chapter. In subsequent chapters, we concentrate on the issues of embedding the transaction model in the MAS architecture.

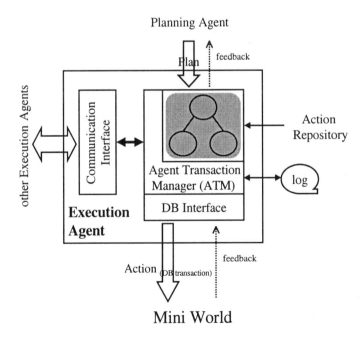

Fig. 6.1. Scope of Chap. 6

K. Nagi: Transactional Agents, LNCS 2249, pp. 79–115, 2001.
© Springer-Verlag Berlin Heidelberg 2001

6.1 The Need for Extending the Open-Nested Transaction Model

In Sect. 5.2, we argued for the use of the open-nested transaction model as basis for the proposed agent transaction model. Unfortunately, there is no standard variation of the open-nested transaction model directly applicable for the MAS environments. Therefore, we need to devise an extension to the existing family of that model, which additionally supports the following requirements.

- *Additional support for non-recursive structures*: The transaction model must also support non-recursive structures such as a general partial orders between the agent actions. However, this support must preserve the presentation of the plan in some structure. The support should not result in the creation of a new intermediate programming or scripting language, such as in the Flex transaction model [30] (presented in Sect. 4.9) or the ConTract model [95] (presented in Sect. 4.10).
- *Conversation-oriented interaction between the transaction tree and the applications*: In all nested transaction models, the application program usually defines transaction trees in a purely declarative manner, such as TaSL in the Interaction transaction model [84]. In MAS, all interactions between the agents are based on message-based negotiation protocols. For more flexibility and a better reactivity of the model, it is wiser to control the interaction between the planner and the transaction tree by means of interactive negotiation protocols instead of using purely declarative languages.
- *Bounding the execution of contingencies within a framework*: A well-defined framework must be defined for exception handling during contingency situations. The framework must be rigid enough to be able to provide some formal guarantees for correctness of execution and yet flexible enough to deal with the high reactivity requirements of MAS. Providing such a powerful framework is crucial for suitably bundling contingencies with normal behavior.
- *Support for cooperation*: Although the open-nested transaction provides the first steps for cooperation by revealing intermediate results, the transaction trees running by the various agents must be coupled by some sort of coupling mechanism that provide coordination, notification, and synchronization between subtrees of different agents.
- *Complete decentralization of the underlying middleware*: All nested models require the presence of an extra transaction manager layer above all the DDBMS that implement the model and correctly schedules the actions to the corresponding LTMs, e.g., Mongrel in the Interaction model [82]. In a MAS, there is no place for such centralized components, hence all their functionality must be incorporated within the agents themselves, while remaining as lightweight software components.

In light of these extra requirements, we define the transaction model in details starting from the following section.

6.2 The Transaction Tree

6.2.1 The Tree Structure

In line with the standard definition of the nested transaction model summarized in Sect. 4.11, p. 56, [50], a transaction in our model can launch any number of subtransactions, thus forming a transaction tree. The root node represents the whole plan to be executed. The distance from the root to the leaves is different for different parts of the tree. Executing the transaction tree starting from the root is the execution of the agent plan. Fig. 6.2 illustrates the mapping of the manufacturing of the robot gripper of Example 2.2 (p. 10) into a single transaction tree, assuming that the scheduling of the whole manufacturing process is done by one product agent.

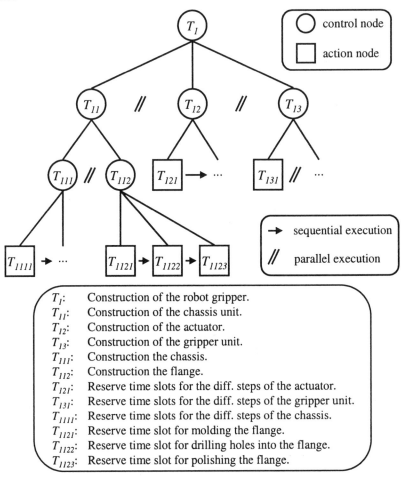

T_1:	Construction of the robot gripper.
T_{11}:	Construction of the chassis unit.
T_{12}:	Construction of the actuator.
T_{13}:	Construction of the gripper unit.
T_{111}:	Construction the chassis.
T_{112}:	Construction the flange.
T_{121}:	Reserve time slots for the diff. steps of the actuator.
T_{131}:	Reserve time slots for the diff. steps of the gripper unit.
T_{1111}:	Reserve time slots for the diff. steps of the chassis.
T_{1121}:	Reserve time slot for molding the flange.
T_{1122}:	Reserve time slot for drilling holes into the flange.
T_{1123}:	Reserve time slot for polishing the flange.

Fig. 6.2. Manufacturing of the robot gripper in one transaction tree

Action nodes can only be at the leaf level. These outer nodes encapsulate flat ACID transactions and contain the programming logic of the agent actions. They include the data manipulation commands, expressed as SQL statements embedded in Java. *Control nodes* are inner nodes. They express the control flow and represent the execution dependencies between the action nodes. They are executed by the ATM of the Execution Agent according to the control parameters supplied to it by its peer Planning Agent [72]. Typical control parameters include the *number of retries* in case of failure, the *time interval* between successive retries, and *must undo* flag in the case of aborts. A variety of control parameters are described in Sect. 6.4. During normal execution, the children of a control node can execute either in *parallel* or *sequentially*. Finding the correct sequence for scheduling the subtransactions of a transaction tree is easily determined from the so-called the *Precedence Graph* for the transaction tree, which expresses the execution dependencies identified by the ACTA framework [18], such as the begin and commit dependencies.

Definition 6.1. The Precedence Graph for a transaction tree

> The Precedence Graph represents the partial order relation over the execution of the transaction tree. The *Precedence Graph* (PG) for transaction tree T is a directed graph (N, E), where N is the set of nodes and E the set of edges connecting these nodes.
>
> More formally, this is the mapping from the transaction tree T to its *PG*. The elements of N are those:
>
> $N = \{\, b_i \mid \forall$ transaction node T_i in T; where b_i represents the begin of transaction node $T_i\,\} \cup \{\, e_i \mid \forall$ transaction node T_i in T; where e_i represents the end of subtransaction node $T_i\,\}$
>
> The tuple $(n_i, n_j) \in E$ iff:
>
> 1. $n_i = b_i$, $n_j = b_j$ and T_i is the parent node of $T_j \wedge (T_i$ executes its children in parallel $\vee T_j$ is the first node to be executed in a sequential execution of the children of $T_i)$,
> 2. $n_i = e_i$, $n_j = e_j$ and T_j is the parent node of $T_i \wedge (T_j$ executes its children in parallel $\vee T_i$ is the last node to be executed in a sequential execution of the children of $T_j)$,
> 3. $n_i = b_i$, $n_j = e_i$ and T_i is a leaf node, or
> 4. $n_i = e_i$, $n_j = b_j$ and T_i and T_j share the same parent $\wedge$ the execution of T_i directly precedes the execution of T_j in a sequential execution.

Following the execution dependencies identified by ACTA, rule 1 corresponds to *begin* dependency. Rule 2 corresponds to the *commit* dependency in the case of parallel execution, and the *strong-commit* dependency in the case of sequential execution. Rule 3 is the internal dependency within the transaction; while rule 4 corresponds to the *begin-on-commit* dependency.

Lemma 6.1.

> The Precedence Graph is always acyclic due to the hierarchical structure of the transaction trees.

Fig. 6.3 illustrates the precedence graph for the transaction tree of Fig. 6.2.

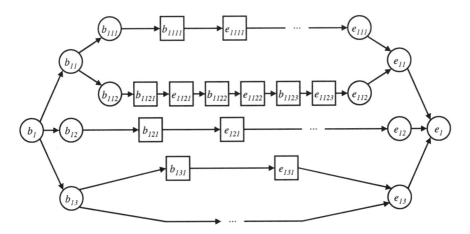

Fig. 6.3. Precedence Graph for the transaction tree of Fig. 6.2

Action nodes can commit or abort independently. In case of commitment of an action node, it directly releases its locks and makes its results persistent in the database and hence visible to other subtransactions directly after reaching its commit point. That's why the underlying DBMS can process action nodes as any other normal ACID transaction running in the system. In case one of the children fails, its parent does not have to abort. It has the choice between:

- ignoring the failure,
- retrying the subtransaction,
- initiating another alternative transaction, or
- aborting.

Typical to the open-nested transaction model, the commit dependency for an inner node is defined as such: *the commitment of all the children leads to the commitment of the parent node* [21]. While this remains the prevailing criterion for committing control nodes in our model, we allow for a much more flexible commitment dependency.

Definition 6.2. Commitment of a control node

> A control node is allowed to commit after satisfying a predefined condition over the state of any transaction nodes either in the same transaction tree or in any other transaction tree executed by any other Execution Agent in the system.

This is the key difference to existing open-nested transaction models. By allowing this arbitrary commit dependency, we move away from the strict hierarchical structure of the transaction trees and can hence support non purely-recursive execution structures such as general partial orders. By these means, we also support the coupling mechanism to provide coordination, notification, and synchronization primitives for cooperating agents.

A problem arises from this generalization, namely, how can a control node observe status changes of nodes outside its subtree or even in other agents? Here, the *synchronization nodes* come in play. These nodes operate according to the *Event*, *Condition*, and *Action* (ECA) rules principle. ECA rules simply mean that a predefined action is executed whenever a condition is satisfied. The evaluation of the condition is triggered by the occurrence of an event. There are *two* types of synchronization nodes:

- *Sender* nodes, and
- *Receiver* nodes.

These nodes can be situated in different transaction trees. They communicate by exchanging messages through the Communication Interface modules of the corresponding Execution Agents.

Synchronization nodes are superimposed on existing transaction nodes in the transaction tree. They can be control nodes or action nodes. A sender node sends a message to a receiver node if an event occurs. *Events* are restricted to changes in the state of the sender node. The message contains the condition and action parts of the ECA rule. The *condition* is evaluated by the receiver node and can be defined over the states and modus of the receiver or the sender nodes. A pre-evaluation of the condition can take place at the sender node if the predicates in the condition can be solely evaluated there. This optimizes the exchanged messages. An example of the condition part of an ECA rule is:

Example 6.1. A condition of an ECA rule

Condition: (state_sender = commit) ∧ (state_receiver = wait)

Actions are commands to change the state of the receiver node or to stop/resume the execution of the other transaction tree. The receiver node can be an empty leaf node or a full-functioning action or control node. Examples of possible actions are: *commit the receiver leaf-node* or *abort the receiver control node*. The states of a transaction node and the possible state transitions are described in the following subsection. The ECA rules play the major role in implementing the general commitment policy of control nodes stated in Definition 6.2.

Technically, a control node only watches the change in state of its direct children. However, it also can execute a status changing command encapsulated in an incoming message from the Communication Interface module. By adding empty receiver leaf nodes to its children, which replicate the same change of state of their sender nodes, the control node can *practically* watch the change in state of *any* other transaction in an *any* transaction tree executed by *any* other Execution Agent. Note that by means of this mechanism further execution dependencies, such as the begin dependencies, can be expressed across different transaction trees as well. The following simplified example clarifies the function of ECA rules in defining dependencies.

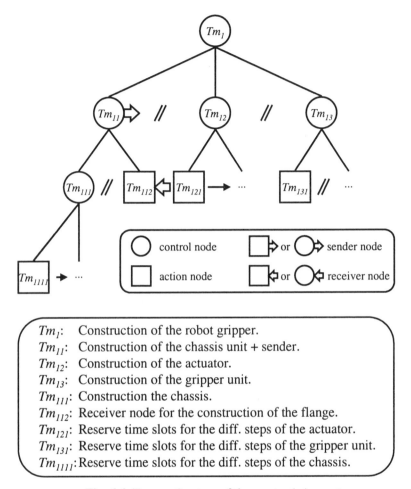

Fig. 6.4. Transaction tree of the master (m) agent

Example 6.2. Defining ECA rules for begin and commit dependencies

Similar to the task delegation example of Chap. 2 (Example 2.3, p. 13), it is desired to delegate the production of the flange to a separate product agent. This means that the subtree with root T_{112} of Fig. 6.2 will be executed by the slave Execution Agent. For clarity, we identify the nodes of the master transaction tree with the extra symbol m and those of the slave transaction tree with the symbol s. The subtree at T_{112} at the master Execution Agent is replaced by a receiver leaf node Tm_{112}, as illustrated in Fig. 6.4, and the original subtree of T_{112} is transferred to the slave Execution Agent beginning with the control node Ts_{12}. At the slave Execution Agent, two new nodes are added, Ts_1 and Ts_{11} as illustrated in Fig. 6.5. The coordination is then configured as follows. First, a mechanism is needed to trigger the slave Execution Agent and to notify the completion of the execution of its transaction tree to its master agent. Tm_{11} is reconfigured to include a sender node. The receiver node is Ts_{11} at the slave Execution Agent. The exchanged message contains:

- Condition: (state_sender = execute) ∧ (state_receiver = execute)
- Action: change state of receiver node Ts_{11} to commit.

Before the arrival of this message, the slave Execution Agent is blocked at the receiver node Ts_{11}. The receipt of the message dispatches the tree at the slave Execution Agent. Its ATM then proceeds with the execution of its transaction tree. Upon its completion, the sender node (i.e., the root node Ts_1) sends a message to Tm_{112} of the master Execution Agent containing:

- Condition: (state_sender = commit) ∧ (state_receiver = execute)

- Action: change state of receiver node Tm_{112} to commit.

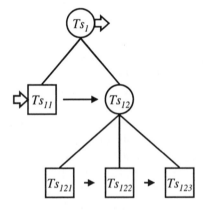

Ts_1:   Sender on slave termination.
Ts_{11}:   Receiver node for starting execution.
Ts_{12}:   Construction steps for the flange.
Ts_{121}: Reserve time slot for molding the flange.
Ts_{122}: Reserve time slot for drilling holes into the flange.
Ts_{123}: Reserve time slot for surface finishing the flange.

Fig. 6.5. Transaction tree of the slave (s) agent

Upon the receipt of this message, the master Execution Agent is informed about the accomplishment of the scheduling part for the construction of the flange.

6.2.2 Node States

For a better understanding of the operation of ECA rules and the agent transaction model in general, we describe the operation modes and the execution states of the transaction nodes in this section as well as the possible state transitions. In Sect. 6.4, we revisit these modes and state transitions for each node type.

A transaction subtree, represented by its root node, can be in one of *three* operation modes:

- The *Normal* mode: in the absence of disturbances,
- The *Compensation* mode: for backward recovery, and
- The *Reassessment* mode: for forward recovery.

The transition between these modes is illustrated in Fig. 6.6. In the absence of disturbances, a transaction subtree operates in the *Normal* mode. In case of disturbances leading to a backward recovery, the subtree operates in the *Compensation* mode. After the successful completion of the compensation, it returns again to the Normal mode. In case of disturbances leading to a forward recovery, the transaction subtree moves to the *Reassessment* mode. It stays in this mode till the completion of the execution of the whole tree. Meanwhile, further disturbances can lead to starting another round of reassessment. If the forward recovery fails for any reason, a backward recovery takes place and the transaction subtree moves to the compensation mode. Within each of these operation modes a transaction node can be in one of *six* states.

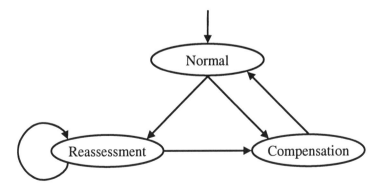

Fig. 6.6. Transition diagram for operation modes for a subtree

Fig. 6.7 illustrates a simplified state transition diagram between these states. This diagram generally applies to all node types. At the beginning, the transaction node is in the *Wait* state of the normal operation mode until the ATM starts it. It then moves to the *Execute* state. According to the result of the execution (e.g., success or fail of an action node), the node moves either to the *Commit* state or to the *Abort* state. If aborted, the node waits for a time interval before moving again to the Execute state as long as the number of retries is not yet exhausted. A committed node in the normal operation mode moves to the *Wait* state in the *Compensation* mode if the *must undo* flag is set in its control parameters and its parent node fails. This state transition is accompanied by a mode transition from Normal to Compensation of the involved transaction subtree. The node follows the same state transition, previously described, in the new operation mode. After the completion of the compensation, the subtree restores its normal mode of operation. Similarly, if a forward recovery takes place and a committed transaction is affected, it moves to the *Wait* state in the *Reassessment* mode till its dispatching by the ATM. Note that after the completion of reassessment, the subtree remains in the Commit state till reaching the *Terminate* state. Meanwhile, a disturbance can lead to another forward recovery and hence a new reassessment. If forward recovery persistently fails, a backward recovery takes place and the transaction subtree moves to the Compensation mode. However, if the root node fails and exhausts all its retries, all of its descendents recursively enter the *Abandon* state. Conversely, the commitment of the root node leads to the recursive termination of all its descendents. In some way, the Terminate and Abandon states are analogous to commit and abort in flat ACID transactions. The two states define the durability guarantees. A terminated subtransaction will never be undone and an abandoned subtransaction will never be retried.

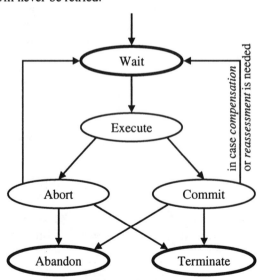

Fig. 6.7. General state transition diagram for a transaction node (applicable for all operation modes)

6.2.3 Global Precedence Graph

By defining the generalized ECA rules for execution dependencies between transactions, we can no longer consider the precedence graph of each transaction tree individually. We need to combine all graphs of all trees running at the Execution Agents on the system in one *Global Precedence Graph* (GPG) and include the extra edges resulting from the ECA rules.

Definition 6.3. The effect of an ECA rule on the precedence graph

> An ECA rule is mapped to the precedence graph by a means of a directed edge from the sender node to the receiver node. In the precedence graph, the edge starts from the end node (*e*) corresponding to the sender transaction node if the condition part of the ECA rule contains a positive assertion that the state of the sender is in one of the following states: *abort*, *commit*, *abandon*, or *terminate*. Otherwise, the edge starts at the begin node (*b*) of the sender. Similarly, the edge ends at the end node (*e*) corresponding to the receiver transaction node if the action part of the ECA rule causes the change of the state of the receiver node to *abort*, *commit*, *abandon*, or *terminate*. Otherwise, the edge ends at the begin node (*b*) of the receiver to trigger its execution. No edges are added for ECA rules with commands stopping/resuming the execution for the receiver nodes.

Note that *not* all edges resulting from these ECA rules are *applicable* at one time. Which subsets of the edge remain applicable at a certain point depends on the condition part of the rule. Applicable rules are those whose condition might evaluate to true under the current operation mode of the transaction node. For example, in normal operation mode, no edge resulting from a rule involving conditions over compensation or reassessment modes can be applicable. Also the applicability of some edges can be mutually exclusive. For example, two ECA rules, one with condition over the abort state of a certain node and the other over the commit state of the same node, cannot simultaneously be applicable.

Definition 6.4. Global Precedence Graph

> The *Global Precedence Graph* (GPG) of a set of transactions T is the union of all Precedence Graphs PG_i for T_i where $T_i \in T$ with extra directed edges resulting from *applicable* ECA rules.

Fig. 6.8 illustrates the GPG for the task delegation example (Example 6.2, p. 85).

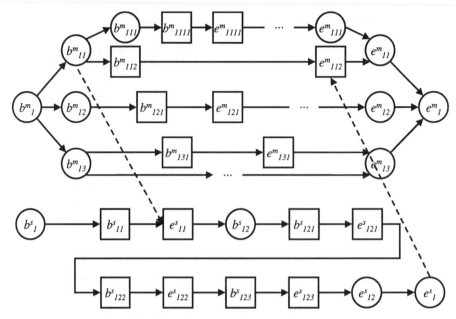

Fig. 6.8. Global Precedence Graph for Example 6.2

In some cases, the Execution Agents can test for such cycles and, if present, refuse to execute the transaction trees before the begin of execution. This provides one way of checking for the validity of the agent common plans only by examining the syntax of the trees. This check is a by-product offered by the Execution Agents to their peer Planning Agents. However, due to the evolving nature of the transaction tree, the Execution Agent might not be able to detect cycles in the Global Precedence Graph before the actual begin of execution. But, they are always able to discover a cycle before entering one. Therefore, the cycle detection is continuously performed during runtime. Another problem is that cycles spread across several Execution Agents due to the fact that the global precedence graph is inherently distributed and there is no central instance that can detect the cycles. It is, hence, required to discover them in a purely distributive way by the Execution Agents. To perform this check in distributed manner, all Execution Agents run a cycle detection algorithm based on path-pushing protocol, whose details are explained in Chap. 7.

6.3 Recovery

6.3.1 Recovery Strategy

Whether the transaction trees are coupled or not, the general correctness criterion maintained by the transaction model remains either:

- The complete execution of the transaction tree, or
- Through compensation, it semantically appears to not have executed at all.

More formally, at the end of execution of a transaction tree, the ATM of the Execution Agent should be either after e_{root} or before b_{root} of the precedence graph of the transaction tree. In case of failures, the transaction tree should be able to recover itself to maintain the general correctness criterion. One advantage of the transaction model is that it can recover in either direction as the model allows for both *forward* and *backward* recovery. The decision in which direction to recover is not an easy one.

In early work of Mehrotra et al. [68], backward recovery is allowed as long as the execution has not yet reached its pivot transaction and forward recovery can only take place after the commitment of the pivot transaction. This is necessary for the correct execution transaction models with rigid structures. An overhead is always present, since determining the type of the transaction, whether compensatable, retriable, or pivot, must be done by the user prior to the execution. In our transaction model, the definition of the transaction tree together with its contingency (i.e., compensation and reassessment) actions evolve during the execution of the transaction tree. Given the information about the transaction nodes, being either retriable, compensatable, or pivot, the transaction model can perform the same checks as in the work of Mehrotra et al. and report a possible violation in the form of a *warning* to the Planning Agent, but not as an error, since the pivot can change its place in our model as the execution proceeds. Another clear problem with the approach of Mehrotra et al. arises with the presence of more than one pivot. Here, the model refuses the execution; whereas we adopt a more optimistic approach and only provide a warning. This is more appropriate in the dynamic environment of MAS, which cause the change in the type of the node (e.g., being compensatable instead of pivot) by defining a new compensation action that can be applied in the new environment.

In general, we allow both modes for recovery in all phases of execution. The direction of the recovery is decided according to the lowest possible overhead endured by undoing committed work. In resilient transaction aborts of isolated subtrees, the usual decision is to perform a backward recovery and then restart execution from the save point. In case of coupled subtrees and an ECA message invalidating already committed transactions, the first attempt is to recover in the forward direction. In that case, forward recovery is the best way since the abort message invalidates not only the committed transaction but also all succeeding transactions in the GPG that were committed before the arrival of this message. In this case, backward recovery should only be attempted if the forward recovery fails. A comprehensive example of choosing the right direction for recovery is presented in the recovery example of Sect. 6.3.4 coming after the full definition of backward and forward recovery given in the next two subsections.

6.3.2 Backward Recovery

In case of transaction abort, a backward recovery to the first save point of the next parent node - whose number of available retries has not yet reached zero - must take place. To satisfy the general correctness criterion, the effects of all committed subtransactions of the aborted subtree must be undone by executing compensating transactions. Compensating transactions are defined for the action nodes as well as for the control nodes. Compensating transactions for the action nodes mitigate their permanent effects. Often, it suffices to reverse the actions of the original transactions. The compensation of the control nodes serves as an extra clean-up process that is executed after the compensation actions of the child subtransactions. In either case, the compensating transactions can be left empty if there is no need for them in reconstructing the consistent state of the database. Clearly, these compensating transactions need not be executed in the same order of execution of the original transactions.

Finding the correct sequence for scheduling the subtransactions of a transaction tree in the backward recovery is easily determined from the Global Precedence Graph. In order to compensate a subtree it suffices to do the following.

Algorithm 6.1. Backward recovery

1. Replace *end* with *begin compensation* and *begin* with *end compensation* for leaf nodes.
2. Remove *end transaction* for control nodes.
3. Replace *begin* for control nodes with *begin compensation*, *end compensation*, and the *connecting edges* connecting them.
4. Reverse the directions of all edges in the subgraph.
5. Activate all edges resulting from ECA rules with conditions over the compensation mode for all nodes in the subgraph.
6. Deactivate all edges resulting from ECA rules with conditions over the normal execution mode, or the reassessment mode for all nodes in the subgraph.
7. Run the cycle detection check starting from the former sink node of the subgraph. Note that under any arbitrary case of compensation the graph must remain acyclic.
8. Begin the execution of the compensation from the former sink node of the subgraph to the new sink. Of course, non-committed subtransactions are directly skipped and need not be compensated.

In the following, we illustrate the precedence graph in case the subtree with root T_{11} of the transaction tree of Fig. 6.2 is under compensation due to the persistent failure of a child node, e.g., T_{1122}. Originally, the PG of this transaction tree looks as in Fig. 6.9.

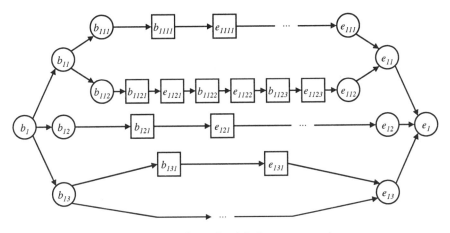

Fig. 6.9. Precedence Graph before compensation

In order to compensate the subtree with root T_{11}, the following must be done. All the leaf nodes, e.g., T_{1111}, must exchange their begin and end nodes in the PG (step 1). The end transaction nodes e_{111}, e_{112}, and e_{11} of the control nodes are removed (step 2). Then, each begin for a control node, e.g., b_{11}, is replaced by begin compensation, end compensation (e.g., b^c_{11} and e^c_{11}, respectively), and the connecting edge $e^c_{11} \rightarrow b^c_{11}$ (step 3). Then, the directions of all edges in the subgraph are reversed (step 4). Since, there is no ECA rules, steps 6 and 7 are skipped. The PG looks as in Fig. 6.10. Finally, the cycle detection check is started and the execution of the compensation is started from the original place of e_{11}. At the end of the compensation, the precedence graph is restored to its original configuration of Fig. 6.9 and the execution of the compensated subtree is resumed starting from b_{11}.

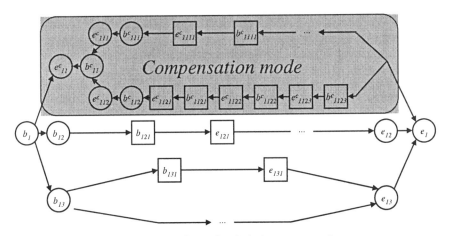

Fig. 6.10. Precedence Graph during compensation

6.3.3 Forward Recovery

In case of coupling transaction subtrees by means of ECA rules, transaction aborts result in sending invalidation messages to already committed transactions in other subtrees, possibly in other Execution Agents. The problem is that the execution of several transaction nodes might have followed since the commitment of this transaction node till the receipt of the message. A backward recovery of all these affected transactions is too costly as it might instantiate a chained reaction of cascaded invalidation messages. That's why a forward recovery is attempted to reassess all affected transaction nodes.

With some luck, a reassessment action might be found whose effects are so similar to the original transaction such that it does not necessitate the invalidation of succeeding committed transaction nodes. That's why each action node can be supplied with a *boundary condition* defining its validity. If this condition still holds after the reassessment of a preceding transaction node, it does not have to be reassessed.

Example 6.3. Boundary condition

A condition for T_{1122} of Fig. 6.2, p. 81, that reserves the time slot for drilling holes into the flange might be:

Time slot acquired by T_{1122} - time slot acquired by $T_{1121} \geq 7$ days.

The following are the steps for carrying out forward recovery.

Algorithm 6.2. Forward recovery

1. All execution threads succeeding the invalidated transaction node are suspended. Determining the succession relation is straightforward using the Global Precedence Graph.
2. Activate all edges resulting from ECA rules with conditions over the reassessment mode of all nodes in the subgraph starting from the begin node of invalidated transaction node to the suspended threads.
3. Deactivate all edges resulting from ECA rules with conditions over the normal or compensation modes of all nodes in the subgraph starting from the begin node of invalidated transaction node to the suspended threads.
4. An execution thread is started from the invalidated transaction node and advances till reaching all succeeding execution threads previously suspended in step 1.
5. Subtransactions whose validity checks still hold are simply skipped over.
6. (a) Forward recovery is successfully completed, if execution reaches all the suspended threads. The edges resulting from ECA rules are reactivated according to the normal mode of operation. Finally execution of suspended threads is resumed.

(b) If execution during reassessment fails and the failure persists and exhausts all predefined retries, backward recovery takes place as described in the previous section. The save point to which the transaction tree recovers is determined as being the lowest possible node containing all nodes with the suspended execution threads in its subtree.

6.3.4 Example for Recovery

The scenario of Chap. 2 provides the best illustrative example for recovery in the transaction model. The main tasks of the product agents are:

- Contracting the production units for reserving the time slots needed for the manufacturing (step 5), Fig. 2.6, and
- The follow-up process (step 6) in order to readjust the production schedule data (step 8) in case of a reported disturbance (step 7).

In order to implement the follow-up process, the transaction tree of Fig. 6.2 must be supplemented with another transaction tree that supervises the actual manufacturing process. For simplicity, we assume that the time slot reservation phase is not divided between several Execution Agents. By coupling the transaction trees of the time slot allocation and the follow-up using the ECA rules, the follow-up and readjustment procedures are made perfect.

The second transaction tree does not necessarily have the same depth as the reservation tree. It suffices to hang each follow-up transaction node directly to the root transaction. The transaction trees are illustrated in Fig. 6.11 and Fig. 6.12.

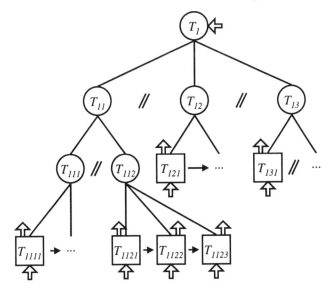

Fig. 6.11. Transaction tree of the Execution Agent responsible for the time slot reservation

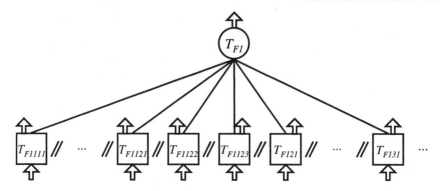

Fig. 6.12. Transaction tree of the Execution Agent responsible for the follow-up process

For each action node in the reservation transaction tree, there is exactly one follow-up transaction node in the follow-up tree. An ECA rule instantiates the follow-up transaction directly after the commitment of the reservation transaction. For example, the subtransaction T_{1121} is configured as sender node and has:

- Condition: (state_sender = commit) $\wedge$ (mode_sender = normal $\vee$ reassessment)
- Action: change state of receiver node T_{F1121} to execute.

To notify the reservation transaction node about the failure of the allocated production unit, an ECA rule is associated with each leaf-node of the follow-up transaction tree. So, the follow-up transaction T_{F1121}, responsible for monitoring the production control data of the molding production unit has:

- Condition: (state_sender = abort) $\wedge$ (state_receiver = commit) $\wedge$ (mode_receiver = normal $\vee$ reassessment)
- Action: change mode of receiver node T_{1121} to reassessment.

Finally, the root node of the follow-up transaction tree is a sender node to notify the completion of the manufacturing of the robot gripper. Fig. 6.13 illustrates the GPG at the moment of begin of execution (without only a subset of the applicable edges actually drawn for readability). Assuming that the subtransaction T_{1123} fails during execution and exhausts its number of retries, *backward recovery* takes place. Assuming that also T_{112} has exhausted its number of retries, the next save point would be T_{11} and the GPG would look as in Fig. 6.14. Note the deactivation of the previously existing coupling edges. After the accomplishment of the backward recovery process, execution is resumed in the normal direction and hence the follow-up edges are reactivated one by one through the coupling edges, thus, reverting back to Fig. 6.13.

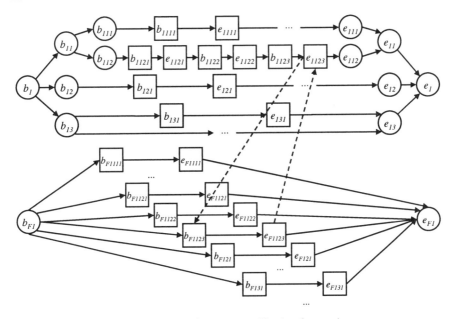

Fig. 6.13. GPG at the moment of begin of execution

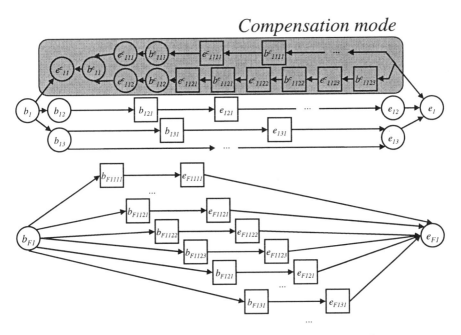

Fig. 6.14. GPG at the moment of begin of compensation mode

Now assume that before the execution of T_{1123}, the follow-up subtransaction T_{F1121} is notified about a disturbance in the molding production leading to the unavailability of the time slot already allocated for T_{1121}. T_{F1121} sends a message to the Execution Agent of the product agent responsible for the time slot reservation. First, the execution thread is suspended at subtransaction T_{1123} and the whole path from T_{1121} to T_{1123} enters the reassessment mode. This is illustrated in Fig. 6.15. Other execution threads are not affected and continue to execute in their current modes. T_{1121} is reassessed by freeing its allocated time slot and trying to find another time slot on another molding production unit. Assuming it finds one free slot at exactly the previously allocated time slot on the former unit, the reassessment of T_{1122} is skipped, since the guarding condition still holds, and the execution of T_{1123} is resumed. After the completion of the reassessment, the corresponding follow-up transactions are automatically activated since the condition part of the corresponding ECA rule contains an assertion on the reassessment of the reservation transaction that makes the condition evaluate to true.

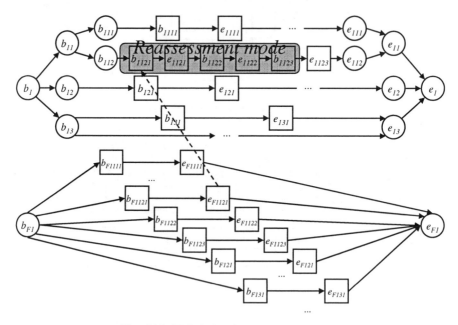

Fig. 6.15. GPG during the reassessment phase

6.4 Node Types

As seen in the previous section, there are basic types of nodes in the transaction model: *action* nodes and *control* nodes, which can be augmented by *synchronization* nodes. Synchronization nodes are, in turn, divided into *sender* and *receiver* nodes. Each of these nodes can be superimposed on either control nodes or action nodes. Common to all node types is that they must be uniquely identifiable. Each node has a node identifier that includes the agent identifier, the tree identifier, and a unique node identifier within the tree. In the following subsection, we describe these node types in more details.

6.4.1 Action Nodes

Action nodes carry the program logic of agent actions. This means they also include the data manipulation language that reads from and writes to the underlying database. Each action encapsulates exactly one flat ACID transaction. This transaction usually operates only on one database of any DBMS that supports ACID transactions, but may access more than one database provided that the underlying DBMS support the Two-Phase Commit protocol, described in Sect. 4.4.2. The action node returns either success or fail according to the commitment or abort of the submitted transaction. The action node also provides means to communicate the execution parameters from the Planning Agents to the executed action and vice versa.

In our implementation, we use Java as hosting language for embedding SQL commands using the JDBC standards. Other techniques, such as SQLJ [96], can be also employed. For this reason, all agent actions must inherit a predefined Java class that implements basic interface methods for parameter exchange between the Execution Agent and the underlying DBMS. By defining analogous classes in other languages, such as C++, we can support other hosting languages. The following is a summary of the most important control parameters that must be supplied to the action nodes.

- *Parent node*: is a pointer to the parent node of this action node.
- *Position*: marks the order of the node among the children of the parent node.
- *JAVA class name*: contains the full name of the class from which the action node instantiates an object and executes a predefined method. The definition of this class must be found in the action repository.
- *Database connection information*: contains all information necessary to connect to the database. In case of access to multiple databases in one transaction, this becomes a list of connection information to each database. This information includes:
- JDBC driver information: contains the address of the JDBC driver,
  - URL of the database,
  - Username, and
  - Password.
- *Action Parameters*: is a list of parameters that are passed to and from the executed method of the class. Each element of the list includes the parameter name, type (whether string, integer, object, etc.), value and the type of calling (e.g., whether by value or by reference).
- *Need Confirmation*: indicates whether the commitment of the node needs to be confirmed by the Planning Agent.
- *Number of Retries*: indicates, in case of failure, the number of retries that must be carried out before the node returns a *Fail* result to its parent node.
- *Time Interval*: defines the time interval between two consecutive retries.

- *Must Undo* flag: if this flag is set, the committed action node must be compensated if its parent node fails.

The same information is repeated for defining the compensation and reassessment actions associated with this action node.

These control parameters can be altered at any time as long as the action node is not yet executing. A missing parameter is requested by the Execution Agent from the Planning Agent before execution through the interaction protocol used to pass the definition of the transaction tree to the Execution Agent. At the latest, all the parameters will be supplied before the begin of Execution of the action node. This conversation protocol is based on the exchange of XML documents encapsulated in FIPA messages. Fig. 6.16 sketches such an XML document that supplies these control parameters in one shot to the action node T_{1121} of Fig. 6.2.

```
[...]
<ActionNode name="T1121" parent="T112" ...>
   <noTrials
       normal="2"
       compensation="4"
       reassessment="4"/>
   <timeInt
       normal="2000"
       compensation="4000"
       reassessment="4000"/>
   <db  url="jdbc:oracle:thin:@florenz
.ipd.uka.de:1521:dbipd"
           userid="krash"
           passwd="******" />
   <normal action="DE.uka.ipd.Schedule">
      <p>2001-02-01 10:00</p> <!--EarliestTimeSlot-->
      <p>2001-02-05 10:00</p> <!--LatestTimeSlot-->
      <p>Molding</p>          <!--MachineType-->
      <p>100</p>              <!--MaxBudget-->
   </normal>
   <compensation action="DE.uka.ipd.Deschedule">
      <p>MoldingUnit_12</p>   <!--MachineID-->
   </compensation>
   <reassessment action="DE.uka.ipd.Schedule">
      <p>2001-02-01 10:00</p> <!--EarliestTimeSlot-->
      <p>2001-02-05 10:00</p> <!--LatestTimeSlot-->
      <p>Molding</p>          <!--MachineType-->
      <p>100</p>              <!--MaxBudget-->
   </reassessment>
</ActionNode>
[...]
```

Fig. 6.16. Sketch of an XML document for defining subtransaction T_{1121} of Fig. 6.2

State Transition Diagram for Action Nodes

Action nodes can operate in all three different modes: the Normal (N) mode, the Compensation (C) mode, and the Reassessment (R) mode. Fig. 6.17 illustrates the state transition diagram for action nodes, which coincides with the general state transition diagram presented in Sect. 6.2.2.

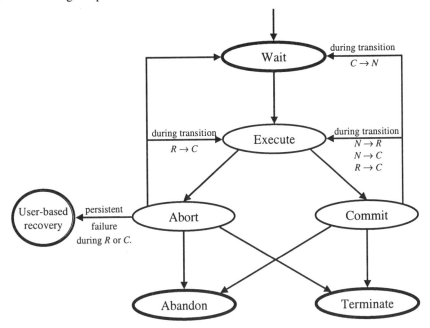

Fig. 6.17. State transition diagram for action nodes applicable for all operation modes

In the Normal operation mode, the node first starts in the wait state. It then moves to the execute state after submitting the begin transaction command to the DBMS. If the transaction succeeds, the action node moves to the commit state. If the transaction fails, the action node moves to the abort state and decrements the number of available retries. As long as this number is above zero, a new retry is started and the node moves to the wait state again for the time period specified by the time interval control parameter. If the number of available retries reaches zero, it reports its final failure to its parent.

In case of commitment, the action node remains in this state till the root node finishes execution. Accordingly, the action node moves to the terminate or the abandon state. Meanwhile, if a parent node of the action node fails, the committed action node changes its mode to the Compensation mode if its *must undo* flag is set and changes its state to the execute state. After the successful termination of the compensation of the subtree, the committed action nodes change their mode of operation to the normal one and move to the wait state for another round of processing. However, if compensation fails and exhausts its number of retries in compensation, control is returned to the user (in this case the Planning Agent) for a user-based recovery. In that case, the user can change the semantic of the compensation transaction or simply orders the Execution Agent to ignore this failure relying on the fact that the parent node has its own clean-up compensation.

Similar transitions occur in case of forward recovery. A committed action node changes to the execute state as its mode of operation changes from Normal to Reassessment. Also user-based recovery is instantiated if the reassessment persistently aborts and exhausts the number of retries specified in the control parameters. State transitions in the reassessment mode are the same as in the normal mode. The transitions from the commit or abort states to the execute state can occur in case of failure of the forward recovery. The action node changes then its mode to compensation mode when the forward recovery fails and is replaced by a backward recovery.

6.4.2 Control Nodes

Control nodes are the inner nodes in a transaction tree. They are completely executed by the ATM in the Java virtual machine hosting the Execution Agent. This is in contrast to action nodes, which execute their program logic on the host Java virtual machine and the SQL statement on the machine hosting the DBMS. Control nodes do not carry any program code. Through the various control parameters, they control the flow of execution between the action nodes and manage the execution dependencies between them. Control nodes and action nodes have some control parameters in common. For example, control parameters supplied to control nodes also include:

- *Parent node*: is a pointer to the parent node of this action node.
- *Position*: marks the order of the node among the children of the parent node.
- *Need Confirmation*: indicates whether the commitment of the node needs to be confirmed by the Planning Agent.
- *Number of Retries*: indicates, in case of failure, the number of retries that must be carried out before the node returns a *Fail* result to its parent node.
- *Time Interval*: defines the time interval between two consecutive retries.
- *Must Undo* flag: if this flag is set, the control node must start its compensation transaction if its parent node fails.
- *Compensation information*: similar to the information supplied by action nodes for their compensation. This information includes the Java class name of the class containing the compensation action, database connection information, compensation action parameters, number of retries and time interval between retries in compensation.

The compensation associated with the control node serves as a clean-up process that is carried out after the completion of the compensation actions of its children. However, if this process is not needed the compensation information is simply left empty.

Special to the control nodes, the following is another set of parameters that actually control the flow of execution of their children.

- *The list of children*: is a list of pointers to the children nodes of the control node. The list may include pointers to action nodes or other control nodes.
- *Execution order of children*: determines the execution sequence of the children. Children can be executed in:

  - *Parallel*: in which all children are simultaneously started when the control node enters the execute state.
  - *Sequence*: in which only one child is executed at a time. Only the first child is directly started when the control node enters the execute state. The succeeding child remains in the wait state and is not allowed to enter the execute state before the commitment of its predecessor.
  - *Alternative*: in which only one child is chosen for execution. The choice is first made when the Execution Agent begins executing this control node. It contacts the Planning Agent that decides which of the children to execute based on its observation of the underlying database and its mental state. The Planning Agent takes its decision by executing a condition evaluation method and sends this decision back to the Execution Agent.

- *Alternative-choosing function*: is a pointer to a method in the Planning Agent that chooses the child to be executed in the case of alternative children execution.
- *Commit condition*: is a condition over the state of the children of this control node. *AND*, *OR*, and *NOT* logical operators, nested parentheses as well as predicates in the form of $state\_child_i$ = state form the condition. By means of synchronization nodes, this condition can be virtually extended to all subtransactions in arbitrary transaction trees. This, together with the various ways for defining execution sequences, the control nodes provide powerful means to flexibly determine their commitment strategy and define a wide range of execution combinations.

Here again, the control parameters can be altered at any time as long as the node is not yet executed. A very useful feature is to leave the list of children empty to be defined just before the execution of the control node. This can be recursively done to represent open-ended plans that evolve during their executions. Fig 6.16 sketches an XML document that defines the control node T_{112} of Fig. 6.2.

```
[...]
<ControlNode name="T112"
             parent="T11"
             mode="parallel">
    <noTrials
        normal="2"
        compensation="4"/>
    <timeInt
        normal="2000"
        compensation="4000"/>
    <compensation action="DE.uka.ipd.CleanUpT1121">
        [...]
```

```
    </compensation>

    <!--Children-->
    <ControlNode>
       [...]
    </ControlNode>
    <ActionNode>
       [...]
    </ActionNode>
       [...]
</ControlNode>
[...]
```

Fig. 6.18. Sketch of an XML document for defining subtransaction T_{112} of Fig. 6.2

State Transition Diagram for Control Nodes

Control nodes operate only in two different modes: the normal (N) mode, the compensation (C) mode. During the reassessment of action nodes, the control nodes behave as in the normal mode. Fig. 6.19 illustrates the state transition diagram for action nodes, which coincides with the general state transition diagram presented in Sect. 6.2.2.

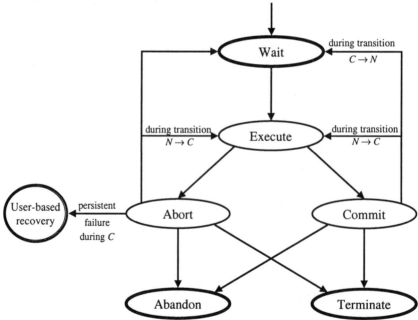

Fig. 6.19. State transition diagram for control nodes applicable for the Normal and Compensation modes

The control node first starts in the wait state. It then moves to the execute state after starting one or more of its children. The choice of the children to start executing depends on the execution order parameters, the decision of the Planning Agent in case of alternative execution, and the commit condition parameter. With each change in the state of the children nodes, the commit condition is evaluated; and the control node either continues execution, moves to the commit or abort states. If the decision is to abort, the children are forced to change their modes to compensation. After the completion of their compensation, the control node switches to the compensation mode itself to start its clean-up compensation action. In case of persistent failure of the compensation, the user, the Planning Agent in that case, is asked to manually execute its own compensation action. Otherwise, the control node moves to the abort state, decrements the number of available retries. As long as this number is above zero, a new retry is started and the node moves to the wait state again for the time period specified by the time interval control parameter. If this number reaches zero, it reports its final failure to its parent. This can propagate to the level of the root node whose abort causes the whole transaction tree to move to the abandon state. This is highly undesirable as it indicates the failure of the Execution Agent to execute its entrusted plan.

In case of commitment, the action node remains in this state till the root node finishes execution. Accordingly, the action node moves to the terminate or the abandon state. As with action nodes, if a parent node of the control node fails, the committed node changes its mode to the Compensation mode if its *must undo* flag is set and changes its state to the execute state. After the successful termination of the compensation of the subtree, all the transaction nodes in the subtree change their mode to Normal and move to the wait state for another round of processing.

6.4.3 Synchronization Nodes

Synchronization nodes are the building blocks for implementing the ECA rules that couple the execution of transaction trees. They are not an independent node type. They are superimposed on existing control nodes or action nodes. Synchronization nodes come in pairs: *sender node* and *receiver node*.

A node is configured as a sender by setting the sender flag in its control parameters and by defining the following parameters.

- *Receiver node*: contains the full node identifier (including Execution Agent and transaction tree identifiers) of the receiver node.
- *Condition*: defines the condition part of the ECA rule to be evaluated.
- *Action*: defines the action part of the ECA rule to be sent to the receiver node for execution.

Note that the event part of the ECA rule is implicitly defined as the change in the state of the sender node. Fig. 6.20 sketches the configuration of a sender node in an XML document.

```
[...]
<ControlNode name=...
              parent=...
              mode=...>
    [...]
   <Sender>
         receiver_node=PA1EA2XT1NT112
         <condition>
                <expression predicate=state_sender
                       operator="="
                       value=Commit />
         </condition>
         <action      action_type=Change_state
                       new_state=Commit>
         </action>
   </Sender>
      [...]
</ControlNode>
[...]
```

Fig. 6.20. Sketch of an XML document for configuring of a sender node

A node is configured as a receiver by setting the receiver flag in its control parameters and by defining the following parameters.

- *Condition*: defines the condition part of the ECA rule to be evaluated.
- *Sender node*: contains the full node identifier (including Execution Agent and transaction tree identifiers) of the sender node needed for the authentication of the receipt messages.

Fig. 6.21 sketches the configuration of a sender node in an XML document.

```
[...]
<ControlNode   name=...
               parent=...
               mode=...>
    [...]
   <Receiver>
      sender_node=PA2EA1XT1NT11
     <condition>
        <expression predicate=state_receiver
                     operator="="
                     value=Commit/>
     </condition>
   </Receiver>
      [...]
</ControlNode>
[...]
```

Fig. 6.21. Sketch of an XML document for configuring of a receiver node

Synchronization nodes do not have their own propriety state transitions. Configuring a transaction node as a sender does not affect its state transitions. It is the other way round; an event is triggered with each state transition of the sender node. Yet, receiver nodes change their states and sometimes mode of operation according to the incoming command encoded in the action part of the ECA rule[8]. Nevertheless, they always follow the rules for state transitions of the nodes in which they reside, stated in Sect. 6.4.1 for receiver leaf nodes and in Sect. 6.4.2 for receiver control nodes.

6.5 Relaxation of the ACID Properties

The transaction model is based on the open-nested transaction paradigm. As seen in Chap. 4, all advanced transaction models relax their notion of ACID properties and, hence, define relaxed correctness criteria using their extra knowledge of the semantic of the transaction structure.

In this section, we summarize the relaxation made in the model compared to the rigid ACID flat transactions. These relaxations are central to the proof of correctness for the *serializability* and the *recoverability* of the model presented in the following two sections.

- *Atomicity* is defined on the level of the leaf nodes since they are only flat ACID transactions operating on one DBMS or a multi-database transaction running under the *2PC* atomic commit protocol. On the level of transaction trees themselves, atomicity is simulated by forcing the Execution Agent either to execute the transaction to its completion (even by using forward recovery in case of failure) or it appears as if it did not execute at all by means of compensation and notification of other transaction trees in case of backward recovery.
- *Consistency* is a problem in open-nested transaction models. The limited isolation in these models leads to execution dependencies between subtransactions in different transaction trees. Original open-nested transactions do not model this type of weak conflicts leading to consistency problems between depending subtransactions. The Interaction model [82] is the first to model these conflicts and allows them to invalidate the dependent subtransactions. In our transaction model, we model these conflicts in a stronger and a more explicit form by means of the ECA rules of the synchronization nodes. With them, the source of the weak conflict is explicitly modeled at the sender node whose explicit task is to notify the dependent subtransaction and also to define the behavior to be exhibited at the receiver node. By restricting the behavior only to allowable state and mode transitions, we guarantee the general correctness criteria.
- *Isolation* is limited to the level of leaf nodes on purpose. This is to support cooperation within and between transaction trees. For one thing, the results of committed subtransactions are needed by other cooperating subtransactions for

---

[8] For an example, please refer to Sect. 6.3.4.

further processing and the synchronization nodes need this limited isolation to coordinate agent actions.

- *Durability* is strongly affected by the relaxed notion of atomicity. Again, durability is simulated by forcing the Execution Agent either to execute the transaction to its completion or it appears as if it did not execute at all. In the transaction model, the *Terminate* and *Abandon* states define the durability guarantees. A terminated subtransaction will never be undone and an abandoned subtransaction will never be retried.

6.6 Serializability

Clearly, the traditional serializability theory, introduced in Chap. 4, cannot be applied to our transaction model on the level of the whole transaction tree due to above-mentioned relaxation of the ACID properties. For the same reason, this strong notion of serializability is not desirable as it hinders the interaction and hence the cooperation between the subtrees of the various transaction trees. Thus, we first need to formalize our correctness criterion concerning serializability.

Definition 6.5. Serializability in the transaction model

> The commit projection of the resulting history of subtransactions on the leaf-node level of the transaction trees must be serializable and this history must be conflict equivalent to a serial history that is consistent with the execution dependencies defined by the transaction trees and the associated ECA rules coupling their subtrees.

First of all, we use conflict equivalence for determining the serializability. This is in harmony with almost all standard work in serializability theory, since determining this equivalence can be done in polynomial time.

Here, we define the serializability on the level of leaf-nodes, i.e., the level of subtransactions actually submitted to the LTMs of the underlying DBMS. For one thing, this is the desirable level of serializability as it supports the interaction between the subtransactions. The other thing is that the LTMs need not consider any higher levels in the transaction trees. For them, these action nodes submit their subtransactions as any other application submits its flat ACID transactions. In other words, the transaction trees remain transparent to the LTMs and, hence, the LTMs do not need to be re-implemented to support the transaction model.

Due to this transparency, the LTM does not identify the nature of the submitted transaction, whether it is a normal, compensation, or reassessment transaction. Therefore, the commit projection includes all committed subtransaction in all modes of operations.

Action nodes submit flat ACID transactions either to one LDBMS or to more than one LDBMS using the *2PC* protocol. In the first case, the LTM of the LDBMS can guarantee the serializability of the resulting history. In the latter case, global serialization must be guaranteed by one of the techniques employed in the multi-database environments presented in Sect. 4.5.1. One of these is the ticketing method. This method can be easily supported by the transaction model, as the implementation supports the presence of the ticket object as will be seen later in Chap. 7. In all cases, the LTMs can guarantee that the global serializability of the history or, in other words, that the global serialization graph remains acyclic.

The following still remains: the resulting history must be equivalent to a serial history that is consistent with the execution dependencies of the transaction trees and the associated ECA rules coupling their subtrees. By consistent, the following is meant.

Definition 6.6. Consistency between the serial history and the execution dependency of the transaction model

> The equivalent serial history is consistent with the execution dependencies of the transaction model, if the serial history does not order any two subtransactions in such a way to contradict an execution dependency specified by the transaction trees or the associated ECA rules coupling their subtrees.

Although this appears intuitive to the reader according to the definition of the transaction model, we try to prove this formally in the remainder of this section. Definition 6.6 can also be formalized by means of graph theory. If we merge the global serialization graph and the global precedence graph, the merged graph must remain acyclic. However, in order to merge the two graphs, we need to change their format to a common one.

The global serialization graph builds a partial order between action transactions, which represents all possible serial histories that are conflict equivalent to the actual history. Each node in the graph represents an action transaction. These nodes must be split into two nodes: *one marks the begin of the transaction* and *the other marks the end of the transaction.* An edge starting at the begin of transaction node and ending at the end transaction node is also added to the graph. This does not change the overall topology of the graph regarding its cycles. This change cannot introduce any new cycles that did not previously exist and cannot eliminate possibly existing cycles either. The new graph is called the *Modified Global Serialization Graph* (MGSG).

As for the global precedence graph of the transaction trees, the inner nodes are no longer interesting and can thus be removed together with their out- and ingoing edges. However, during the removal of the edges, any precedence relations between action nodes must be preserved, including the ones resulting from the transitive closure of the precedence relations involving inner nodes. This applies for normal edges as well as edges resulting from ECA rules. This necessitates the introduction of edges between action nodes so that *the transitive closure of the edges represents the same execution dependency relations expressed by the transitive closure of the original edges in the presence of inner nodes.* The following example illustrates a GPG before, Fig. 6.22, and after, Fig. 6.23, the removal of the edges. The new graph is then called the *Modified Global Precedence Graph* (MGPG). Again, this does not change the overall topology of the graph regarding its cycles. This change cannot introduce any new cycles that did not previously exist and cannot eliminate possibly existing cycles either.

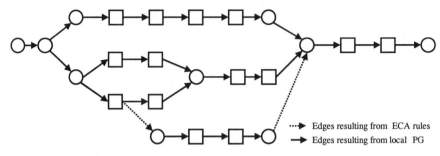

Fig. 6.22. A *GPG* before the removal of the inner nodes

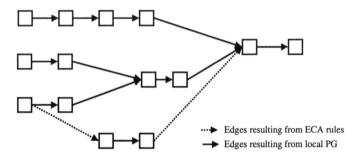

Fig. 6.23. A *GPG* after the removal of the inner nodes

Now, the *Merged Execution Graph* (MEG) can be formed by merging the *MGSG* and the *MGPG* as follows. The *Merged Execution Graph* is a graph (N, E), where:

- $N = $ nodes($MGSG$) = nodes($MGPG$), and
- $E = $ edges($MGSG$) $\cup$ edges($MGPG$).

Now, for the serializability correctness criterion, the *MEG* must be proven to be cycle-free.

Proof. There are *three* possibilities for forming cycles in the *MEG*:

1. Some edges in the *MGSG* form a cycle:

   As seen in Chap. 4, the LTMs do not allow for cycles in their local graphs. Also, the application of a global serializability mechanism, such as ticketing guarantees that the global serialization graph and hence the *MGSG* is cycle-free. This possibility for forming cycles is not applicable, since we assume the global serializability of the history.

2. Some edges in the *MGPG* form a cycle:

The presence of a cycle in the *MGPG* at any point of time is logically incorrect. This would simple ruin the notion of precedence in the precedence graph. In other words, the Execution Agents would not be able to consistently and correctly schedule their subtransactions. We mentioned that the ATMs of the Execution Agents can detect these cycles before or during the beginning of execution (the details of the algorithm will be presented in Sect. 7.1.2), and hence refuse to execute them. Again, this possibility for forming cycles is not applicable.

3. A combination of *MGSG* and *MGPG* edges form a cycle:

Without loss in generality, consider the *MEG* illustrated in Fig. 6.24 and the precedence relation <.

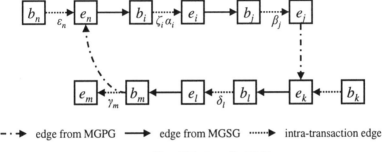

- ·▶ edge from MGPG   ⟶ edge from MGSG   ······▶ intra-transaction edge

Fig. 6.24. A cyclic *MEG*

- Since the edge $(e_i, b_j) \in MGSG$, then $\exists\ \alpha_i \mathbb{W} \beta_j$ such that $\alpha_i < \beta_j$. Due to the use of locking protocols (such as the *two*-phase locking protocol) that produce *strict* histories, we can deduce that $e_i < e_j$.
- Since the edge $(e_j, e_k)^9 \in MGPG$, this means that $e_j < e_k$.
- Similarly, the edge $(e_k, b_l) \in MGSG$ leads to $e_k < e_l$.
- From the edge $(e_l, b_m) \in MGSG$, we can deduce that $e_l < \gamma_m$, where $\delta_l \mathbb{W}$ γ_m. Due to the conflict equivalence to the serial history in which $T_l < T_m$, $e_l < \gamma_m$ can be changed to $e_l < b_m$.
- From the edge $(b_m, e_n) \in MGPG$, we deduce that $b_m < e_n$.
- Using the transitivity property of the precedence relation <, we conclude that $e_i < e_n$.

However, the existence of edge $(e_n, b_i) \in MGSG$ means that $\exists\ \varepsilon_n \mathbb{W} \zeta_i$ and again to the strict protocols used, $e_n < \zeta_i < e_i$. This contradiction eliminates the presence of such cycles in an *MEG*. (*Q.E.D.*)

---

[9] A directed edge between two end nodes in the *MGPG* is the result of an ECA rule.

6.7 Recoverability

Recoverability has *two* main aspects:

- In case of a crash of an Execution Agent, the exact state of execution of the transaction tree before the crash is restored.
- Guaranteeing the general correctness criterion of the transaction model, mentioned in Sect. 6.3, which is either the complete execution of the transaction tree or it *semantically* appears to not have executed at all.

We leave the proof of the first aspect till presenting the internal operation of the Execution Agent, its logging, and recovery algorithms in Chap. 7. Now, we concentrate on the second aspect under the consideration of the *backward* and *forward* recovery algorithms, presented in Sects. 6.3.1 and 6.3.3, respectively.

Obviously, we cannot provide a proof of correctness following the scheme of centralized recovery, presented in Sect. 4.4.1, solely based on the syntax of the transaction tree. Since we are dealing with *semantic*-based recovery, we must follow a proof with a higher abstraction level as done with Sagas [41].

Proof framework. The framework of the proof is as follows. *Under certain assumptions over the semantic of the compensation actions and the reassessment actions, we can have a history, in which a submitted transaction tree is either executed to completion or the history is semantically equivalent, denoted $\equiv_S$, to a history, in which the transaction tree has not executed at all.*

Assumption. We take the assumption made about compensation in Sagas as basis for our assumption. In the Sagas transaction model, let T_i be a subtransaction of a Saga S, whose semantic compensation subtransaction is T_i^C.

Given a history $H = T_i < H' < T_i^C$,

$$H \equiv_S H' \text{ iff } \neg(\exists\, T_j \in H' \wedge T_i <_S T_j);$$

where $<_S$ is the total order of subtransactions of the Saga S.

This simply means that executing the compensating subtransactions in the reverse order *semantically* undoes the effect of the original subtransactions, regardless of the execution of other subtransactions belonging to other Sagas in the time period between the original and the compensation subtransactions. This is called the *isolation assumption* of Sagas.

In our transaction model, we can generalize that assumption to consider the MGPG[10].

Given the history $H = T_i < H' < T_i^C$,

$$H \equiv_S H' \text{ iff } \neg(\exists\, T_j \in H' \wedge T_i <_{\text{MGPG}} T_j);$$

where $<_{MGPG}$ is the partial order of action nodes in the MGPG.

---

[10] From the proof of the serializability, the predecessor relation in the MGPG is compatible to the predecessor relation in the MGSG, and hence we could use the MGPG in this proof.

The meaning is here extended to the fact that executing the compensation actions in the reverse order of the partial order *semantically* undoes the effect of the original action nodes. This goes in agreement with the correctness proof [82] of the recoverability of the Interaction model (Sect. 4.12).

Correctness of backward recovery without ECA rules and under the isolation assumption. Considering a MGPG without edges resulting from ECA rules and applying the backward recovery Algorithm 6.1 of Sect. 6.3.1, the proof of the semantic equivalence of the history with the compensated subtree, H, to a history, in which the subtree did not execute at all, H', becomes trivial. Considering the subtree to be a whole transaction tree at an Execution Agent, we achieve the correctness criterion of having a history, in which the failed transaction tree *semantically* appears to not have executed at all.

Dropping the isolation assumption. Note that the compensation actions of the control nodes have no direct function in the proof *under the isolation assumption*. However, their informal cleanup purpose serves in reality to overcome the isolation assumption, which does not always hold in real life situations. Being hierarchically nested in the same nesting structure of the control nodes makes them always able to catch any inconsistency at all nesting levels.

Correctness of backward recovery with ECA rules. The real problem in the proof arises due to the presence of edges in the MGPG resulting from ECA rules. Such an edge outgoing from the subgraph in the normal mode might not necessarily have a corresponding edge in the compensation mode. Here, the ATM can only *warn* the Planning Agent about the absence of such ECA rule before the begin of execution. However, due to the flexibility of the model, the Planning Agent has *three* choices:

- It can preserve the original correctness criterion and defines an ECA rule in the compensation mode to induce a backward recovery for the subgraph to which the end of the ECA edge points. An example of such behavior will be given within the pragmatic presentation of the coordination patterns between the Execution Agents in Sect. 8.3.1.
- Ignore the case if we are dealing with non-vital actions, whose semantic allows them to remain persistent even if their triggering action is undone. Example of such actions is read-only transactions whose read values can simply be dropped without affecting the further computations.
- The compensation of the subgraph at the destination of the ECA edge is either not possible or is too expensive. Then, the transaction tree at the destination of the edge is to be recovered in the forward direction to its completion although its triggering action is undone. Purely syntactical, forward recovery is incorrect in this case since it violates the causality principle (the source node that triggered the ECA rule is undone and hence all its semantic effect must appear as not to have happened). However, semantically, it might be the desirable decision as seen in the recovery example of Sect. 6.3.4 and will be also seen in the coordination pattern of Sect. 8.3.2.

Correctness of forward recovery. The still open problem about the forward recovery is the assumption made about the semantic of the reassessment actions, whose purpose is to *semantically* fix the invalidated action nodes. Say we have a history $H = H' < T_i < T_j < H''$, where $<$ is the partial order in the MGPG.

Let $I(T_i)$ be the invalidated representation of action node T_i, and T_i^R be the reassessment action of T_i. Obviously, T_i^R must *semantically* eliminate the effects of the invalidated T_i and *re-execute* T_i under the current state of the world. More formally, $I(T_i) < T_i^R \equiv_S T_i$.

However, actions dependent on $I(T_i)$ have been executed before T_i^R. In the transaction model, these are subsequently invalidated by the execution of the T_i^R, which eases the requirements on the reassessment actions. This can be expressed as

$$I(T_i) < H < T_i^R \equiv_S I(H) < T_i; \text{ where } I(H) \text{ is the invalidated form of } H.$$

Note that the invalidation function, I, is by definition idempotent in the sense that $I(I(H)) = I(H)$.

Here, we also work under the generalized notion of the isolation assumption. According to Algorithm 6.2 of the forward recovery, presented in Sect. 6.3.3, executing actions in the reassessment mode for an invalidated action, say $I(T_i)$, in history H has the same original partial order topology as in the normal mode; especially if the active ECA rules in the normal mode are the same as in the reassessment mode.

Given the history $H = H' < T_i < T_j < H''$, and the invalidation of T_i, the resulting reassessment history H^R of H, according to Algorithm 6.2, becomes:

$$
\begin{aligned}
H^R \quad &= H' < I(T_i) < T_j < H'' < T_i^R < T_j^R < H''^R \\
&\equiv_S H' < I(T_j) < I(H'') < T_i < T_j^R < H''^R \quad &&(\text{using } I(T_i) < H < T_i^R \equiv_S I(H) < T_i) \\
&\equiv_S H' < I(I(H'')) < T_i < T_j < H''^R \quad &&(\text{using } I(T_j) < H < T_j^R \equiv_S I(H) < T_j) \\
&\equiv_S H' < I(H'') < T_i < T_j < H''^R \quad &&(\text{using } I(I(H)) = I(H)) \\
&\equiv_S H' < T_i < T_j < H'' \quad &&(\text{using recursion}) \\
&\equiv_S H \; (Q.E.D.)
\end{aligned}
$$

Note that the boundary conditions, mentioned in Sect. 6.3.3, do not affect this proof as they can be viewed as a shortcut to performing the reassessment action for a given action node.

6.8 Conclusion

Realizing the shortcomings of existing open-nested transaction models, we presented an extension to these models that is suitable for MAS in this chapter. Particularly, the support for non-recursive structures and the extensive support of cooperation through ECA rules coupling the transaction trees are completely new to the open-nested paradigm.

Considering the application-oriented requirement analysis presented in Chap. 2 and the technical requirements analysis of Chap. 5, we strongly feel that the proposed transaction model can face all its challenges specially through the powerful and yet flexible definition of the transaction trees and its bundling of normal and contingency behaviors in one structure. The transaction model allows for a full decentralization of the underlying middleware by introducing the Execution Agents. They are responsible for the robust execution of the transaction model. Although, we have formally proven the correctness of execution of the transaction model concerning its serializability and recoverability, the implementation of the model within the Execution Agent remains open. This is addressed in the following chapter.

7 Robustness Guaranteeing Mechanisms

Transactional agents are our means for increasing the robustness of execution in MAS. In the previous chapter, the proposed transaction model is described in details. The chapter ends with a formal proof of correctness of the transaction model concerning its guarantees on serializability and recoverability.

In this chapter, we show how the Execution Agent internally implements this transaction, marked by the shaded area in Fig. 7.1. First, the aspects guaranteeing the correctness of execution are exposed. We describe how the ATM, the heart of the Execution Agent, schedules the agent actions according to the local Precedence Graph, checks the validity of the coordinated trees using the Global Precedence Graph, and ensures the global serializability of the concurrently submitted transactions.

In the second part of the chapter, we concentrate on the implementation of the recoverability guaranteeing aspects. We describe the mechanisms employed by the Execution Agent to guarantee it own recoverability and the techniques to couple these mechanisms with those of the other components in the system, such as the DBMS of the mini world.

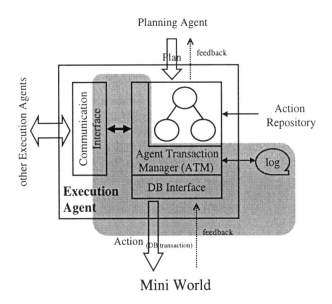

Fig. 7.1. Scope of Chap. 7

K. Nagi: Transactional Agents, LNCS 2249, pp. 117–133, 2001.
© Springer-Verlag Berlin Heidelberg 2001

7.1 Guaranteeing Correctness

As seen in Sect. 5.1, the first element in guaranteeing the robustness of execution of agent actions is to guarantee the correctness of execution in normal operation. Since it is the responsibility of the transaction managers of the underlying DBMS to guarantee the serializability of transactions submitted to their local databases, the responsibility of the ATM of the Execution agent lies mainly in scheduling the agent actions according to their execution dependencies predefined in the transaction tree.

The ATM is also responsible for validating the logical correctness of the coordination mechanisms employed between subtrees of different transaction trees based on the definition of ECA rules controlling the synchronization nodes. Since the Execution Agent has no exact knowledge over the semantic of the cooperation between the Planning Agents, it can only verify that the execution dependencies always remain cycle free. In case multi-database transactions are employed within single agent action nodes, the Execution Agent can provide automatic implementation mechanisms for guaranteeing global serializability. In the following subsections, we describe how the Execution Agent handles each of these issues.

7.1.1 Scheduling Actions

In order to find the correct scheduling order of execution of agent actions, the ATM constructs its local part of the *Global Precedence Graph* for the transaction tree, as described in Sect. 6.2. This Precedence Graph can change by adding further nodes and edges as the Planning Agent refines its plan or due to failures leading to the compensation of subtrees. The ATM begins its execution with the begin node of the root node and follows the directed edges along the Precedence Graph, hence, starting further nodes in the transaction tree. Reaching the end node of the root transaction node indicates the successful termination of the whole transaction tree. The ATM keeps track of the active nodes in a list called *Active Path List* with each entry in the list pointing to the a currently executing node. The contents of this list are illustrated for the example Precedence Graph of Fig. 7.2 in Table 7.1.

To execute an action node, the ATM starts a separate thread in which the program logic of the action node is executed including the interaction with the database through the Database Interface module. The death of the thread is the indication that the action node has executed. According to the success or fail of the transaction, the action path list is adjusted.

7.1.2 Decentralized Cycle Detection

One of the main tasks of the ATM is to check on the feasibility of execution of the aggregation of transaction trees in the Execution Agents of an agent group. The correctness criterion that the execution agent provides to the overall correctness of execution of a group of coordinated transactions is given in Definition 6.6. According to the proof of Sect. 6.6, the consistency between the equivalent serial history and the execution dependency of the transaction model is guaranteed as long as each Execution Agent schedules its agent actions correctly and the *Modified Global Precedence Graph* (MGPG) remains cycle-free.

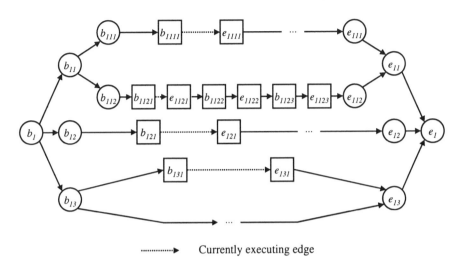

............▶   Currently executing edge

Fig. 7.2. A Precedence Graph under execution

Table 7.1. Active Path List for Fig. 7.2

| Edge | | Final destination | Node type | Actual number of retries | ... |
Starting from	Ending at				
b_{131}	e_{131}	e_1	Action Node	1	...
b_{121}	e_{121}	e_1	Action Node	1	...
b_{1121}	e_{1121}	e_1	Action Node	1	...
b_{1111}	e_{1111}	e_1	Action Node	1	...
...	...	...	...	...	...

The problem is that there is no central component that keeps track of the MGPG to assure that it remains acyclic. Each Execution Agent holds only a part of the MGPG locally. Hence, the cycle detection algorithm must be executed in a fully decentralized manner between the ATMs of the Execution Agents through their Communication Interface modules. For this purpose, we use a variation of an algorithm called *path pushing* [8] that was originally used for discovering dead-locks in distributed transactions.

All Executing Agents have their own local cycle detection for their part of the MGPG. Then, each Execution Agent searches for paths ending with an ECA edge in its local MGPG. If it finds one, it sends the whole path (starting from the begin node of the root transaction node to the node with the ECA edge) to the Execution Agent having the receiver node of the ECA edge. This Execution Agent, in turn, inserts this path into its local graph and investigates the presence of a cycle in this modified graph. This procedure propagates for all Execution Agents. In this way, a possibly existing distributed cycle can be discovered without the presence of a centralized cycle detector instance. The algorithm can be summarized as follows.

Algorithm 7.1. Decentralized cycle detection at an Execution Agent

1. Upon the receipt of a plan fragment from the Planning Agent or a path from an Execution Agent, the new consolidated local precedence graph is constructed.
2. The Execution Agent runs the cycle detection on its local part of the precedence graph. If a cycle is detected, all Execution Agents involved in this cycle are notified.
3. In the absence of any new cycle, the Execution Agent searches for paths starting from its the begin node of the root transaction node and ending with an ECA edge in its local MGPG.
4. If such a path is found, it is sent to the Execution Agent having the receiver node of the ECA edge. This triggers the same algorithm on the side of this Execution Agent.

Of course, the detailed algorithm is more complex. For example, the Execution Agent must keep track of the paths they have already sent in order to ask for their retraction in case the execution of the transaction tree is terminated or if a subtree involved in the path is being compensated, which makes the path sent no longer valid. Also, phantom cycles can be incorrectly identified due to an out-of-date path that is not removed on time due to the asynchronous nature of message exchange between the Execution Agents. Fortunately, these problems are similar in the original algorithm, which makes porting these solutions to our algorithm trivial.

7.1.3 Guaranteeing Global Serializability

An action node can define a transaction that accesses more than one database using the atomic 2PC protocol. In this case, the LTMs of these databases are not able to guarantee the global serializability of the history. Therefore, one of the techniques for achieving global serializability in multi-databases must be employed. Some of these techniques are described in Sect. 4.5.1. The simplest technique is the *ticket method*. A description of this method is also available in Sect. 4.5.1. If required in a multi-database transaction, the Database Interface module can automatically implement it by reading, incrementing, and then writing the ticket data object after establishing the connection to the databases. This makes guaranteeing the global serializability of the history completely transparent to the Planning Agent and the whole planning process.

7.2 Guaranteeing Recoverability

Recoverability is the second element in guaranteeing the robust execution of agent actions. The original components of the architecture, such as the underlying DBMS of the mini world and the communication channel, already have their own mechanisms for ensuring the recoverability of the actions executed under their control. For a complete recoverability guarantee by the MAS middleware, the Execution Agent must also have its own mechanisms. Intuitively, all these mechanisms must be coupled to each other. In the following subsections, we present these mechanisms. The need for coupling the mechanisms is discussed, and three approaches for the coupling are presented with their pros and cons.

7.2.1 Recoverability Mechanisms in Each Architectural Component

The Database Layer

As seen in Sect. 6.4.1, the leaf-nodes of the transaction tree are action nodes that contain flat ACID transactions. Each of these transactions is executed at one database of the underlying DBMS of the mini world. In case of the use of the 2PC protocol, these transactions spread across several databases.

In either case, the DBMS is responsible of guaranteeing the recoverability of those transactions according to the ACID paradigm. For this purpose, they log the submitted database operations (e.g., database read and write operations) in physical log files containing before and after images according to the principles discussed in Chap. 4. This means that the Execution Agent does not have to worry about the recoverability of the actions themselves. Unfortunately, the commercial DBMS do not allow the access to these logs not even for reading their contents, which is the main problem in coupling the robustness mechanisms as will be shown later.

The Communication Channel

As seen in Sect. 6.4.3, the synchronization nodes exchange FIPA messages for coordinating the execution between subtrees in different Execution Agents. With the increasing tendency for distribution over the last decade, several commercial products appeared in the market for guaranteeing the robustness of the communication channel against the potential loss of messages.

A commercial product, IBM's MQSeries [57], guarantees for example the delivery of exactly one copy of a sent message through the so-called persistent transactional message queues. This means that the Execution Agent does not have to worry about the recoverability of the messages themselves. As in the DBMS, these message queuing systems deny the access to their internal logging systems.

The Execution Agent

In contrast to action nodes, the inner nodes of the transaction tree are completely executed within the Execution Agent. Hence, it is the responsibility of its ATM to ensure their recoverability. According to the definition of recoverability, the status of the execution of agent actions before the failure must be restored, this means any incomplete actions must be undone and all complete actions must be identified so that they are not resubmitted after restart. The atomic property of the leaf nodes guarantees the first part automatically through the DBMS. However, for the second part, the execution of the transaction tree must be *logged*.

7.2.2 Logging at the Execution Agent

In order to reconstruct the transaction tree that has been running at the Execution Agent at the time of the crash, the log must contain both *static* and *dynamic* information of the transaction tree. The format and content of the log are dependent on the facilities offered by the system hosting the Execution Agent. Typically, the hosting system will allow the storage of these two logs in sequential files in the persistent storage. In this case, the Execution Agent creates two files: one for the static information and the other for the dynamic information.

By *static* information, we mean information about the definition of the transaction tree itself. This information is needed to reconstruct the tree after the crash of the Execution Agent. This information includes the node identifier, the identifier of its parent nodes, its order within its brother nodes, the node type and the control parameters such as the number of retries, the time interval between retries, etc. Source of this information is the conversational communication between the Planning Agent and the Execution Agent.

Algorithm 7.2. Logging the static information of the transaction tree

1. At the receipt of a message from the Planning Agent altering the definition of the transaction tree, write this message in the static log file.
2. First after the completion of the write operation in the log, update the definition of the transaction tree according to the incoming message.

Table 7.2 sketches such a static log file.

Table 7.2. Example of a static log file

Performative	Node Id	Parameters
add node	T_1	ControlNode, sequential, 2 retries, ...
add node	T_{11}	ActionNode, order 1, 5 retries, ...
add node	T_{12}	ControlNode, order 2, sequential, 2 retries, ...
redefine node	T_{12}	ControlNode, order 2, sequential, 3 retries, ...
...	...	...

The *dynamic* information is about the execution status of each of the transaction nodes. Dynamic information for a node is illustrated in Table 7.3. This information must be logged in order to reconstruct the execution status of the transaction tree after a crash. Using this information, it is possible to identify the already completed actions, the actions under execution before the crash, and the actions that have not yet executed.

Table 7.3. Dynamic information for a transaction node

Element	Description
Node id	The identifier of the transaction node.
Number of retries	The actual number of retries for this node.
State	The state of the node; either: wait, execute, commit, abort, abandon, or terminate.
Mode	The mode of operation of the node; either: normal (N), compensation (C), or reassessment (R).

Algorithm 7.3. Logging the dynamic information of the transaction tree

1. When the ATM reaches the point of changing the state or mode of execution of a transaction node, either inner or outer node, it first writes the new state or mode in the dynamic log file.
2. Afterwards, the ATM applies the change to the transaction node.

Table 7.4 sketches a dynamic log file.

Table 7.4. Example of a dynamic log file

Node id	Number of retries	State	Mode
T_1	0	Execute	Normal
T_{11}	0	Execute	Normal
T_{11}	0	Abort	Normal
T_{11}	1	Execute	Normal
T_{11}	1	Commit	Normal
T_{12}	0	Execute	Normal
...	...	...	...

In case of the reconstruction of the Execution Agent after a crash, the ATM must read both log files in the recovery process and perform the following recovery algorithm.

Algorithm 7.4. Recovery algorithm after a crash of an Execution Agent

1. Construct the definition of the transaction tree by parsing the static log file sequentially from the beginning to the end and re-executing the actions in the stored messages defining the transaction tree.
2. Initialize the state of all transaction nodes of the tree to *Wait* and their operation mode to *Normal*.
3. Construct the state of the transaction nodes, by parsing the dynamic log file sequentially from the beginning to the end. The last entry of each node identifies its status before the crash.

From this algorithm, it is clear that the log entries cannot be removed until all the nodes of the transaction tree reach either the *abandon* or the *terminate* states.

If the hosting system has a DBMS and allows the Execution Agent layer to install its own tables, the logs become much more compact by storing them in database relations. In this case, the execution does not log each entry in the database; but only stores the effects of the actions (e.g., the newest state of the transaction node) in the database tables. During its instantiation, the execution Agent can sense which type of service it can obtain from the hosting system. Hence, the ATM can load the appropriate logging module.

The definition of the transaction trees can only be reconstructed from the static log of the Execution Agent under the assumption that the receipt of the message defining the transaction tree from the Planning Agent and the registration of this message in the log file is done using an *atomic* operation. This is technically not possible but can be easily emulated. The Planning Agent always waits for an acknowledgement of its messages. The Execution Agent, in turn, does not send this acknowledgement before successfully registering it in the static log file. If this acknowledgement message is lost due a failure in the communication channel, the Planning Agent can always resend the original message. Since the actions defining the transaction tree are all idempotent, there is no fear of duplicated messages coming to the Execution Agent.

The states of each of the inner nodes can be easily reconstructed from the dynamic log file. Since the inner nodes are executed within the Execution Agent whose ATM registers each state transition before it is accomplished, no state transition can be lost.

The problem arises with the outer nodes, since they execute partially at the system hosting the Execution Agent, whereas the database manipulation part executes at the system hosting the DBMS. Clearly, we need some sort of coordination between the two systems. In the following section, we investigate the recovery of outer nodes in more details to complete the proof.

7.2.3 The Need for Coupling Recoverability Mechanisms

From the above section, it is clear that the recoverability of the leaf nodes is the responsibility of the underlying DBMS and the recoverability of the inner nodes is the responsibility of the execution agent and its ATM. Moreover, the communication channel guarantees that the messages will be delivered and without any duplication. However, a complete separation of these mechanisms results in a critical window, in which it is not possible to correctly recover the status of the Execution Agent if the crash occurs during this time window. This time window is illustrated in the protocol diagram of Fig. 7.3 between the Execution agent and the underlying DBMS [52]. The same applies to the protocol between the execution agent and the communication channel.

Normal Operation in the Absence of Disturbances

During the normal execution of a transaction tree, the Execution Agent starts the execution of an action node, say T_{11}. Directly before starting the execution, it inserts a BOT-entry (Begin of Transaction) in the dynamic log file. This BOT-entry is illustrated in Table 7.5.

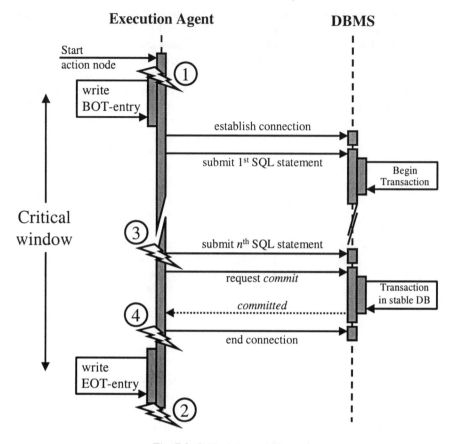

Fig. 7.3. Critical time window

Table 7.5. BOT-entry in the dynamic log file

Node id	Number of retries	State	Mode
T_{11}	i	Execute	Normal

Then, the Database Interface module establishes the connection with the appropriate database and the transaction is started on the side of the database with the first SQL statement. At the end of the transaction, the Database Interface module receives either success or fail. Accordingly the ATM inserts the EOT-entry (End of Transaction) to the dynamic log file. This EOT-entry looks as in Table 7.6 in case of commit or Table 7.7 incase of abort.

Table 7.6. A commit EOT-entry in the dynamic log file

Node id	Number of retries	State	Mode
T_{11}	1	Commit	Normal

Table 7.7. An abort EOT-entry in the dynamic log file

Node id	Number of retries	State	Mode
T_{11}	i	Abort	Normal

Operation in the Presence of Disturbances

In case of disturbances leading to the crash of the Execution Agent, it might be impossible to correctly restore the whole status of the Execution Agent before the crash. To illustrate this case, we must investigate all possible time intervals in which the crash can occur. These are illustrated by the lightning signs in Fig. 7.3.

1. There exists no BOT-entry in the dynamic log file. This means that the action node in question did not start before the crash.
2. Both BOT- and EOT-entries are found in the dynamic log file. This means that the action node in question was already executed and the result of execution is found in the EOT-entry.
3. Only the BOT entry is found in the dynamic log file. In this case, the Execution Agent cannot know whether the ACID transaction was aborted or committed. Suppose the Database Interface module did not yet sent the request commit signal and the DBMS aborted the transaction after the loss of connection. However, the ATM cannot know about this abort, because the EOT-entry is missing.
4. The same as in the previous case with the exception that the request commit signal was sent and the Execution Agent occasionally knew the outcome of the Transaction but it did not register it in its log before the crash took place. Here also, there is no way to reconstruct the status of the ACID transaction in question.

In summary, a critical time window exists between the time of writing the BOT-entry and the time of writing the EOT entry due to the separation of the recoverability guaranteeing mechanisms at the different components of the architecture. This critical time window can hinder the restoration of the status of execution of the transaction tree after the crash of the Execution Agent as in cases 3 and 4. After having passed this critical window, the log cleaning process can remove the BOT and the EOT-entries.

7.2.4 General Solution for Recoverability Coupling

By coupling the logging mechanisms of the various components of the architecture, it is possible to close this critical time window [52]. The key to this coupling is the use of a *transaction identifier* (TID) for uniquely identifying the flat ACID transactions of the leaf nodes. To guarantee the uniqueness of the TID, it must be constructed by concatenating the following identifiers.

$$TID = <Agent-id> + <Tree-id> + <Node-id> + <operational\ Mode>$$

The main idea for the coupling is to write the TID in the log files used by the various components. During the recovery process, if the Execution Agent finds that an action node was in its critical time window before the crash, it gets the TID of the transaction from its BOT-entry in the dynamic log files, which must be extended as in Table 7.8 to include the TID.

Table 7.8. Dynamic log file with TID

Node id	Number of retries	State	Mode	TID
T_{11}	i	Execute	Normal	$EA_1\text{-}TR_1\text{-}T_{11}\text{-}N$

By searching the log files of the other components, e.g., the corresponding DBMS in the mini world, the execution agent can determine the exact status of the node before the crash. However, hardly any commercial system allows external programs, such as the Execution Agent, to access their log files. As a workaround for this problem, we present three solutions in the following sections. Each solution has its pros and cons and is only applicable under certain circumstances.

7.2.5 Solution 1: Distributed Transaction

The basic idea behind this solution is to write the TID to the dynamic log in the database as part of the simple transaction and to execute this combined distributed transaction in a *single* atomic transaction under the 2PC protocol (refer to Sect. 4.4.2). To implement this strategy, the Database Interface module must introduce an SQL statement to the original transaction that writes the TID in the dynamic log table as illustrated in Fig. 7.4.

During the recovery process, we rely on the atomic property of distributed transactions to provide information about the state of the action nodes. During the critical window of the transaction, the existence of the TID in the log indicates the successful completion of the transaction. Due to the use of the atomic commit protocol, the TID will never be made persistent in the database if the transaction did not commit. On the contrary, the absence of the TID entry is the proof that the transaction was aborted, since the abort of the transaction will cause the automatic undo of the write operation for the TID within the transaction.

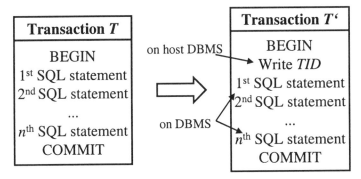

Fig. 7.4. Extending a transaction to include the TID

This method can only be implemented if two conditions are satisfied:

- The system hosting the Execution Agent has a DBMS that can store the dynamic log table and that is capable of taking part in the 2PC protocol of the distributed transaction.
- The underlying database of the mini world is capable and is also *willing* to take part in the 2PC protocol. This is not always the case in an autonomous environment, which is expected to build the mini world for the MAS application. It is not likely for highly autonomous databases to involve themselves in 2PC protocols with foreign entities such as the Execution Agent, since the protocol causes the blocking of resources until the global commit is reached.

If the underlying DBMS is cooperative enough to allow the implementation of the protocol, this solution sounds the simplest and the most elegant one. A further advantage is that the database used to write the TID can also be used to write the ticket object used to guarantee the global serializability of the distributed transactions submitted to the multi-database within the action nodes. Fig. 7.5 sketches this solution.

7.2.6 Solution 2: Database Relation with *TID*

This solution is similar to the former one and is meant to be used if the DBMS of the mini world does not engage itself in the 2PC protocol with the Execution Agent, but is willing to dedicate a table in its database to be used by the Execution Agent. In this case, the Execution Agent can still log its dynamic and static log files either in its physical file or in its local database and use the extra table offered by the underlying DBMS to store the TID. This certainly causes a slight change in the schema definition of the database to include the extra table but avoids the use of the 2PC protocol. The system configuration for this solution is illustrated in Fig. 7.6.

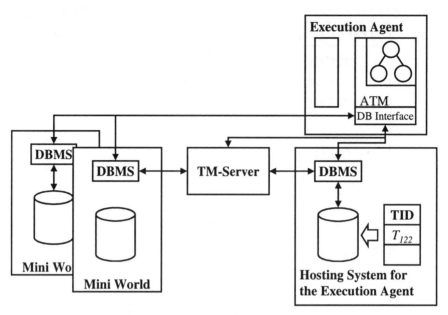

Fig. 7.5. System configuration for solution 1

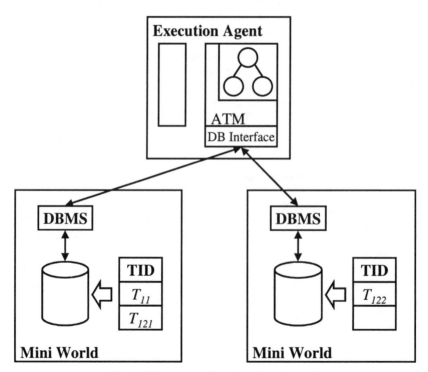

Fig. 7.6. System configuration for solution 2

7.2.7 Solution 3: DBMS-Specific Solutions

If the underlying databases do not allow either the involvement in a 2PC protocol or the extension of their schema to define an extra table for the TID, a workaround must be found to gain some sort of information about the logs of the DBMS. Since it is impossible in almost all commercial DBMS to gain access to the internal logging information itself, a solution with a similar effect must be found. For this solution, we rely on DBMS-specific features such as the system monitors provided by DBMS for the use to monitor database events. The original purpose of these services is to allow the user to tune the performance of the DBMS.

For example, Oracle 8*i* [86] provides a set of performance monitoring tables with extra fields that can be used to register the TID. IBM's DB/2 Universal Database [56] provides log data similar to internal log files for the external usage by the user for performance monitoring reasons. These meta data help in developing our solution. This solution, however, has the great disadvantage of being dependent on the DBMS and the version used. This means that for each database type and possibly each database version a driver for communication with the special monitoring facility is required. For the database access, the Database Interface module loads the corresponding driver. In the following, we present an outline of the solution based in the system monitoring logs of IBM DB/2 Universal Database [55].

IBM DB/2 Universal Database offers the so-called *system monitoring facility* that logs the database events as illustrated in Fig. 7.7. The system monitors have the following functions:

- *Activity monitoring*: by registering all events submitted to the database including the SQL statements.
- *Problem identification*: by logging problems occurring during normal operation such as deadlocks.
- *Performance analysis*: by logging the start and stop times of SQL commands.
- *Supporting system configuration*: by fine-tuning the system through the information it supplies to the database administrators.

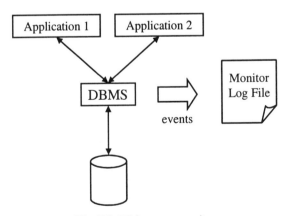

Fig. 7.7. DB2 system monitor

The system monitor logs the following events:

- Deadlock events,
- Connection events,
- Statement events, and
- Transaction events.

By translating the monitor file to ASCII, the statement event entry and the transaction event entry are illustrated in Fig. 7.8.

Statement Event...	**Transaction Event...**
`Appl Handle:5`	`Appl Handle:5`
`Appl Id:`	`Appl Id:`
`*LOCAL.DB2.000530144000`	`*LOCAL.DB2.000530144000`
`...`	`...`
`Text: SELECT * from`	`Completion status: Com-`
`Production Schedule;`	`mitted`
`Start Time: 05-30-2000`	`Start Time: 05-30-2000`
`16:40:01.689603`	`16:40:00.246034`
`End Time: 05-30-2000`	`End Time: 05-30-2000`
`16:40:01.753978`	`16:40:02.518362`

Fig. 7.8. Statement and Transaction event entries

By executing the dummy SQL statement containing the TID, illustrated in Fig. 7.9, the TID will be present in the log file. During the recovery process, the ATM parses the log file for the TID, gets the application handle number, which is internally generated by the DBMS, and parses the files in the forward direction till it finds its corresponding transaction event entry and can hence determine the status of the transaction in question before the crash.

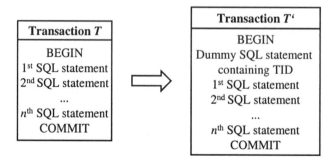

Fig. 7.9. Extending the transaction to include the TID for solution 3

7.3 Conclusion

This chapter describes the internal structure functioning of the execution agents and demonstrates their capabilities of executing the transaction trees and guaranteeing the robustness of execution of agent actions. But a robust transaction model alone does not guarantee the success of the approach of transactional agents. The main challenge is to formulate the agent plan in the transaction trees and to communicate the plan to the Execution Agents. In the following chapter, we concentrate on the interaction with the other agents in the system. Using the conversation-oriented protocols, we should be able to transfer the various planning constructs and coordination patterns to the layer of Execution Agents middleware.

8 Interacting with the Execution Agent

After presenting the transaction model in Chap. 6 and describing the internal structure of the Execution Agent and its robustness guaranteeing mechanisms in Chap. 7, we finalize the definition of the concept of *transactional agents* with a description of the interaction with the Execution Agent, as illustrated by the shaded area of Fig. 8.1. The aim of this chapter is to demonstrate the feasibility of transferring the distributed agents to the coordinated transaction trees through a set of predefined performatives. We first start with describing the main interaction primitives used in the conversation between the Planning Agents and their Execution Agents as well as between the Execution Agents of an agent group. With the aid of these primitives, we show how the proposed transaction model supports the various planning constructs. Then, we move to the social aspect of agents and show how cooperation between several Planning Agents developing a shared plan can be supported by implementing typical coordination patterns using the transaction trees and the synchronization nodes coupling them. Finally, a concluding section summarizes the chapter and ends the part of the thesis describing our approach of transactional agents.

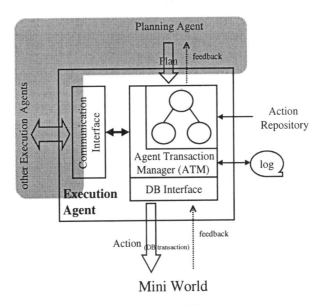

Fig. 8.1. Scope of Chap. 8

K. Nagi: Transactional Agents, LNCS 2249, pp. 135–150, 2001.
© Springer-Verlag Berlin Heidelberg 2001

8.1 Interaction with the Other Agents

The key to the success of the Execution Agents is the simple, and yet semantically rich, interaction of these agents with the rest of the components of the MAS. In Chap. 7, the interaction with the underlying databases is thoroughly described. However, the description of the interaction with the other agents still remains open. This interaction exists through the exchange of FIPA ACL messages taking part in a conversational protocol between either the Planning Agent and the its Execution Agent or the Execution Agents of an agent group.

In this section, we do not go into the definition details of the protocols and their automata. We restrict ourselves to the definition of the primitive actions and requests resulting through these conversations. These serve as building blocks for implementing the various planning constructs and coordination primitives.

8.1.1 Actions Started by the Planning Agent

The Execution Agent provides several actions to be invoked by the Planning Agent through an interaction protocol. These actions fall in four groups.

Actions Managing the Agent Life-Cycle

Through a *createAgent* action, an Execution Agent can be created. We do not enforce an agent factory model. The Planning Agent can create an Execution Agent on any arbitrary platform. The Execution Agent then registers itself at the yellow pages and white pages services of the FIPA platform. However, the Planning Agent is responsible of providing its peer Execution Agent with a unique name. Other agent life-cycle actions as well as the AMS of FIPA allow the monitoring of the life cycle of the Execution Agent. The life of the Execution Agent is ended with the invocation of a *killAgent* action by its peer Planning Agent.

Actions Defining the Transaction Tree

The action *insertTree* takes the identifier of the parent node, the order of the subtree in question and the various control parameters as input parameters. It inserts a subtree into the children list of a control node (or creates a new root node in case a transaction tree does not already exist). This is the way for the Planning Agent to transform its plan to a transaction tree and submit it to its peer Execution Agent for execution. The Planning Agent can retract parts of its plan by invoking *deleteTree*, which deletes a transaction node and all its children. This action takes mainly the name of the root node of the subtree to be deleted. Of course, insertion is only possible if the ATM of the Execution Agent did not start this part of the tree yet. Similarly, a deletion of a subtree is not possible if it is under processing or has finished execution.

The action *redefineNode* allows the Planning Agent to change the configuration of the transaction tree and hence parts of the agent plan at run-time. By requesting this action, the Planning Agent can either change the control parameters of a given node, change the action to be executed in case of action nodes, or pass it the input parameters. In Sect. 8.2, the major role that these actions play in the development of plans, based on incremental or interactive planning strategies, are illustrated.

Actions Controlling Execution

By invoking the action *startExecution* the Planning Agent signals the begin of execution of the transaction tree to the Execution Agent. If, through perceptions of the mini world, the Planning Agent discovers that the execution of its plan is going in the wrong direction, it has the option of interfering and stopping the execution of a subtree starting from its root node by invoking the *stopExecution* action with the root node as parameter. However, execution is only stopped in a consistent state. This means that the agent actions, wrapping the flat transactions in the executing state are carried out till reaching their committing or aborting states. In order to resume execution, the Planning Agent must request the execution of the *resumeExecution* action with the corresponding subtree as parameter.

Actions Monitoring Execution

If, for any reason, the Planning Agent wants to enquire about the node status of the transaction tree under execution, it can invoke a family of requests. In order to enquire about the static properties of a transaction node, the Planning Agent issues a *getNodeProperty* request and for the dynamic status and actual operation modes, it requests a *getNodeState*.

8.1.2 Actions Requested from the Planning Agent

From the side of the Execution Agent, requests can be sent to the Planning Agent for acquiring further information about the plan, in case they are needed for the execution. These requests must be honored by the Planning Agent to carry on with the execution. They fall into the following four categories.

Request for Plan Fragments

During the execution of the transaction tree, if the ATM of the Execution Agent encounters a control node without children, it calls *requestPlanFragment* with the node identifier of the control node from the Planning Agent and suspends execution of this subtree. The Planning Agent then provides the missing children nodes according to its developed plan by invoking a sequence of *insertTree* actions. Execution is resumed as soon as the missing children are supplied.

Request for Missing Parameters

If the ATM of the Execution Agent reaches the point of executing a node and a needed parameter is missing, it issues a *requestParameters* from the Planning Agent. The missing parameter can be either a control parameter of the node in question or an execution parameter in case of an action node.

Request for Function Evaluation

If the children nodes of a control node are configured as alternatives, the ATM must evaluate an associated branching condition to determine the child to be executed. Since this condition is usually based on an observation of the mini world, this is typically done by the Planning Agent. In this case, the ATM issues a *requestForEvaluation* from the Planning Agent and passes it the condition to be evaluated as parameter. The Planning Agent, in turn, evaluates the condition and identifies the node to be executed.

Request for Progress Confirmation

It is possible for the Planning Agent to deprive its peer Execution Agent from much of its autonomy by setting a special *consultPlanner* flag at the control nodes. If this option is set for a control node and its children reach a state where it can commit, the Execution Agent does not commit the node before calling a *requestProgressConfirmation*. The Planning Agent can make a final observation of the mini world and only if it returns *true*, the node is committed. If not, ATM of the Execution Agent changes the state of the node to aborting, and abort takes place instead of commit preceded by a compensation of the children.

8.1.3 Actions Invoked by the Execution Agent at Other Execution Agents

Transaction trees at different Execution Agents can be coupled through the synchronization nodes. As seen in Sect. 6.2, ECA rules control the operation of these nodes. The *event* takes place completely at the sender node and hence need not be transmitted to the receiving node. However, the *condition* evaluation part can take place at the sender node, the receiver node, or both depending on the predicates in the condition. This means that if a condition cannot be completely evaluated by the sender node, the remaining part of the condition must be sent to the receiver node. In all cases, the *action* part is always sent to the Execution Agent hosting the receiver node. Possible actions fall in two categories.

Actions Changing Node State

The action *changeNodeState* carries the identifier of the receiver node and its effect is to change the state of the node and, possibly, also its mode of operation.

The ATM of the Execution Agent updates the new status by executing the appropriate state transition action, such as an abort action or transforming the operation of the subtree in question to another operation mode by beginning a compensation or a reassessment process.

Actions Controlling Execution

Here, the Execution Agent can control the execution of subtrees at another Execution Agent with which it coordinates its actions. Through these actions, it can start the execution of a subtree, stop or resume its execution.

8.2 Supporting the Various Planning Constructs

From Sect. 3.2, we can conclude that, although the planning strategies are very different, plans have, in general, a control flow that is a mix between regular control flows of programs and a declarative description of the parallel execution of the various actions of a plan manifesting itself in the most general form of a partial order of executions between these actions [80].

In this section, we use the primitive actions of the conversation protocol between the Planning Agent and the Execution Agent presented in Sects. 8.1.1 and 8.1.2 to build primitive planning constructs. The following subsections contain by no means an exhaustive listing of all possible planning constructs. We believe these constructs to be the most important ones, and further, more complex constructs can be built by combining them.

8.2.1 Step-by-Step Planning

Plans are developed incrementally. In several planning agent frameworks, such as DESIRE [70], planning and execution is done in a continuous cycle of mini world perception, plan fragment development, execution, and new perception to assess the change in the world model and so on. On the programmatic level, this typical cycle is expressed in the form of non-unfoldable iterations in which the number of loops is not known in advance, or recursion with an unknown depth.

Example 8.1. Step-by-step planning

A single manufacturing step, such as polishing, is in reality an iteration of several simple polishing processes. The number of iterations can only be *estimated* for time planning purposes but the decision to polish the product for another round cannot be met before analyzing the roughness of the product after the polishing process. This loop of polishing followed by roughness checking must be repeated until the quality specifications are reached.

The transaction model must hence allow the representation of an incomplete transaction tree with the identification of the place of the missing plan fragment in the tree for further extension. A control node without children serves as a place-holder for the missing plan fragment as illustrated in Fig. 8.2. First, the Planning Agent submits the incomplete transaction tree using the *insertTree* actions followed by *startExecution*. The Execution Agent executes the transaction tree till it reaches the control node with the missing children (1). The Execution Agent then sends a message with a *requestPlanFragment* (2). The Planning Agent reacts by invoking *insertTree* actions to define the missing plan fragment (3). This fragment, in turn, can contain further control nodes with missing children for further plan extensions. Once the conversation protocol is over, the Execution Agent resumes the execution with the new nodes (4).

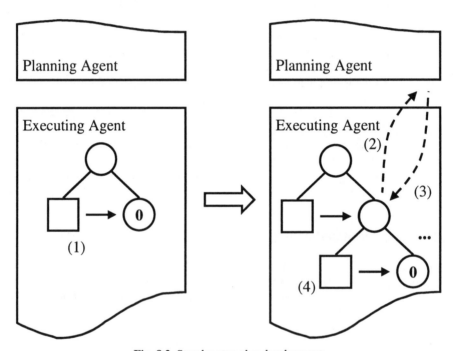

Fig. 8.2. Step-by-step plan development

8.2.2 Plans with Branching

With branching, the Planning Agent develops all the alternative steps during the plan development phase. For this purpose, it also defines the branching condition. The branching condition, which usually includes predicates from the observation of the mini world, is to be evaluated during the execution and the Execution Agent is to load the proper branch.

Example 8.2. Plans with branching

In the manufacturing of our robot gripper, holes must be drilled in the flange. According to the quality of the allocated drilling machine, the flange needs afterwards either one milling process on a normal rotation speed machine or two consecutive milling processes, the first with a high rotation speed and the second with a low rotation speed. Fig. 8.3 illustrates the plan as developed by the Planning Agent.

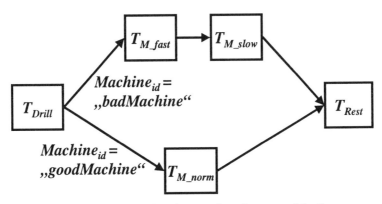

Fig. 8.3. Plan for scheduling the manufacturing steps of the flange

In order to map the branching of Example 8.2 to the transaction tree, the Planning Agent sets the mode of execution order of the children of the control node to *alternative*, as illustrated in Fig. 8.4. Children of this node are the two branches inserted as two subtrees using the *insertTree* action. As the ATM of the Execution Agent reaches the execution of the control node, it sends the *requestForEvaluation* message to the Planning Agent (1). As response to the request, the Planning Agent evaluates the condition and returns the identifier of the root node of the subtree containing the correct branch to the Execution Agent (2). This subtree, in turn, is loaded as the current subtree and is executed by the ATM of the Execution Agent (3).

8.2.3 Graph-Based Plans

The vast majority of planning algorithms are based on a hierarchical decomposition of the problem into several subproblems [28]. For each of these subproblems, a subplan is successively developed and further refined till reaching the detailed overall plan containing the simple actions. This decomposition appears very appealing for the mapping of agent plans to transaction trees. Nevertheless, the planning strategies often use problem solvers (theorem provers) [97] for developing plans for the lowest levels of the subproblems.

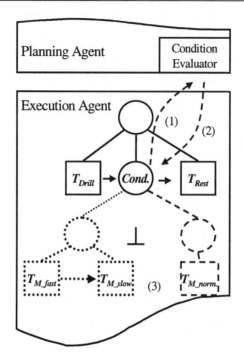

Fig. 8.4. Transaction tree with branching

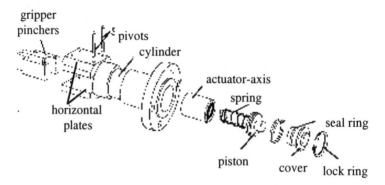

Fig. 8.5. The various parts of the robot gripper

Problem solvers identify the goal of their problem through their desired final state and consider the current state of the mini world to be their initial state [97]. Since each simple action has a predefined start condition and a known end condition in the absence of disturbances, problem solvers build their plan by combining the various simple actions using a search procedure in the solution space. This results in graph-based instead of tree-based plans, as seen in the following example.

Example 8.3. Graph-based planning

A clear example of graph-based planning appears in the application of problem solvers in scheduling the assembly of the robot gripper. Fig. 8.5 illustrates the various parts of the robot.

The following assembling actions can be identified to be the necessary steps for building the robot gripper.

- T_1: mounting the horizontal plates to the cylinder.
- T_2: mounting the gripper pinchers to cylinder.
- T_3: installing a jig.
- T_4: assembling the various parts of the actuator unit together and building it into the cylinder chassis.
- T_5: linking the gripper pinchers to the piston.
- T_6: removing the jig and sealing the pivots.
- T_7: mounting the pressure conducting tube to the actuator.

Building an execution dependency graph between these actions results in the graph illustrated in Fig. 8.6. At the first sight, this type of graph is similar to the Precedence Graph for the transactions trees described in Sect. 6.2. However, there is no hierarchical transaction tree representing this graph.

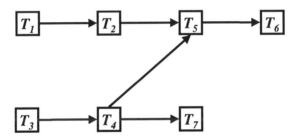

Fig. 8.6. Graph-based plan for scheduling the assembly of the robot gripper

In order to represent this execution dependency in the transaction model, we seek help in the synchronization nodes of the transaction model. Beside their normal role of coupling transaction trees at different Execution Agents, we use them here within the same transaction tree. Fig. 8.7 is a simple representation of the transaction tree expressing the execution dependencies of Fig. 8.6. *Placing both sender and receiver nodes in the same transaction tree practically changes the hierarchical tree to a graph.* The root node has two control nodes executing in parallel. The first node controls the actions T_1, T_2, T_5, T_6, while the second one represents the path T_3, T_4, T_7. Configuring T_4 as a sender node whose commitment leads to the commitment of a dummy node attached to a control node containing T_2 simulates the execution dependency $T_4 \rightarrow T_5$.

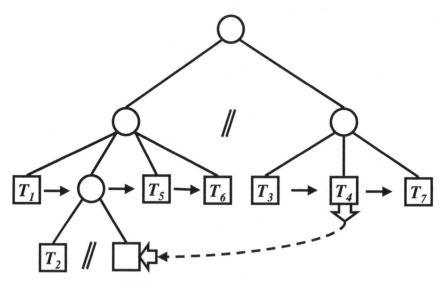

Fig. 8.7. Transaction tree for graph-based plans

8.2.4 Flexible Definition of Success

Supplementary to the traditional open-nested transaction model, we allow for a more flexible definition of success of agent actions. This flexibility manifests itself in the implementation of two strategies. A wise mix of these strategies establishes the right amount of autonomy for the Execution Agent at each control node individually.

One strategy is the use of the versatile commit condition of the control node. According to Definition 6.2, the definition of the commitment of a control node can be formed by combining any conditions on the states of the children and joining this condition with *AND*, *OR*, and *NOT* operators. This way non-vital actions as well as mutually exclusive actions can be defined within the same control node. Here, the Execution Agent has a high autonomy in choosing which of the possible outcomes to execute. For example, the Execution Agent is free to decide on the fate of the children executing in parallel and linked with the *OR* operator in the commit condition after the commitment of the first child.

The other strategy reduces the autonomy of the Execution Agent by setting the *consultPlanner* flag at a control node as in Fig. 8.8. After satisfying the commit condition for the control node (1) and (2), the Execution Agent sends a *request-ProgressConfirmation* message to its master Planning Agent (3). This, in turn, observes the mini world and either accepts or refuses the commit decision. In the latter case, the Execution Agent treats the refusal as if the commit condition has evaluated to false.

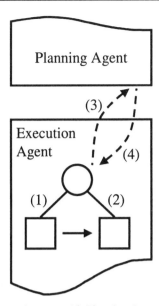

Fig. 8.8. Transaction tree with Planning Agent confirmation

8.3 Supporting the Various Coordination Patterns

The social aspect is central to the MAS paradigm. A lot of research effort is dedicated to building agent societies. Through the various cooperation protocols developed on the MAS macro level, we identify several coordination patterns. These patterns are used as building blocks in the implementation of these protocols [74].

In this section, we use the primitive communication actions invoked between the Execution Agents of an agent group, presented in Sect. 8.1.3, to build some basic agent coordination patterns. Further patterns can certainly be added using these communication primitives. A very appealing approach is to construct a library with coordination patterns.

8.3.1 Task Delegation

Often a Planning Agent delegates the development and the execution of part of its plan to another agent. Reasons for this task delegation include better use of domain specific knowledge of an agent or a better load distribution. Task delegation is introduced in Example 2.3, p. 13, as part of the application scenario of Chap. 2. Here, the transaction tree developed by the delegated Planning Agent must be coupled to the transaction tree of the delegating Planning Agent.

A first attempt for this coupling is presented in Fig. 6.4 and Fig. 6.5 of Sect. 6.2. In this coupling, there exist two pairs of synchronization nodes. One pair (1)

starts the execution of the slave transaction tree and the second pair (2) reports the end of execution of the slave transaction tree to its master. However, this simple coupling supports the task delegation coordination pattern only in the normal operation mode. For a full support also in the compensation mode, two further pairs of synchronization nodes are needed. Consider the case in which Tm_{12} fails and the master transaction tree must be compensated. Here, the slave transaction tree must also be compensated. Through the receiver node Ts_2 of the pair (3), the termination of the slave transaction tree is delayed till after the commitment of the root node of the master transaction tree. This way, the slave transaction tree has the chance to be notified for compensation. The pair synchronization nodes (4) starts the compensation of the slave subtree beginning from Ts_1 upon the compensation of the empty leaf node Tm_{112} using the following ECA rule.

- *Event*: change of state of Tm_{112}.
- *Condition*: (mode_sender = compensate) $\wedge$ (state_receiver = committed).
- *Action*: compensate receive node.

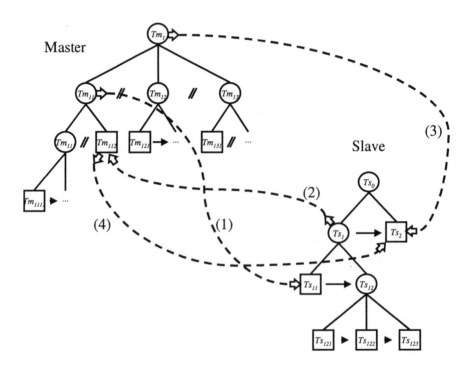

Fig. 8.9. Task delegation at the level of transaction trees

8.3.2 Task Coordination

The task coordination pattern is needed if several agents are developing a shared plan. The partial plans cannot be completely isolated from each other. Several milestones always exist between the single partial plans that link the various planning steps of different agent together. These links form primarily the task coordination pattern.

Example 8.4. Task coordination pattern

Already in Example 2.4, p. 14, we introduced the concept of task coordination by allocating three agents for scheduling the construction of the robot gripper. The three Execution Agents cannot allocate all the necessary production time slots completely independently from each other. At the latest, they must coordinate their actions at the assembling phase. For example, a synchronization point must be set between the Execution Agent of the chassis unit and the Execution Agent of the actuator for allocating a time slot for the production step of installing the actuator into the chassis.

For the normal operation mode, a pair of synchronization nodes is needed to implement this task coordination. This pair is marked by (1) in Fig. 8.10 and has the following ECA rule.

- *Event*: change of state of root node of the subtree scheduling the manufacturing of the actuator (T_a).
- *Condition*: state_sender = committed.
- *Action*: change the state of the receiver node to committed.

This ECA blocks the scheduling of the mounting of the actuator in the chassis unit until the Execution Agent of the actuator finishes scheduling the various manufacturing steps of the actuator. A typical problem arises when the synchronization node of the Execution Agent responsible for the chassis receives the commit message from the Execution Agent responsible for the manufacturing of the actuator and subsequently commits and starts the execution of the remaining subtree. At a later point, the actuator subtree is to be compensated due to a disturbance. This logically invalidates the status of the synchronization node and all subsequent nodes in the transaction tree of the chassis unit. To notify the Execution Agent of this compensation, another pair of synchronization is inserted on top of the same synchronization, but with the following ECA rule.

- *Event*: change of state of root node of the subtree scheduling the manufacturing of the actuator (T_a).
- *Condition*: (mode_sender = compensation) $\wedge$ (state_sender = committed).
- *Action*: change the mode of the receiver node to reassessment.

In this case, the ATM must start a *forward recovery* process as described in Sect. 6.3.3. It tries to *reassess* all subtransactions depending on the synchronization node (i.e., the subtree scheduling the mounting of the actuator into the chassis).

This disturbance has cascading effects on the Execution Agents of the same agent group. Due to their impact of the system performance, the implications of this disturbance are separately analyzed in the simulation study.

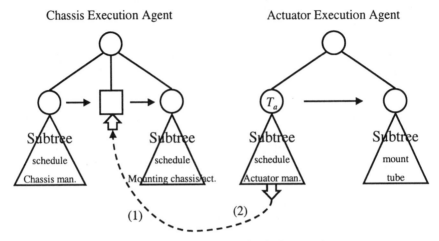

Fig. 8.10. Task coordination at the level of transaction trees

8.3.3 Termination Coordination

Due to several agent couplings mechanisms, including the above two coordination patterns, the commitment of the root node of a transaction tree does not directly lead to the termination of the whole tree. The main reasons is the presence of the synchronization nodes coupling the transaction trees at the various Execution Agents and preventing the independent termination of a single transaction. This means that the termination processes must be coordinated between these trees. Here, a procedure similar to the *2-Phase Commit* (2PC) protocol, applied for distributed transactions, is instantiated. A brief description of the 2PC protocol was presented in Sect. 4.4.2.

To emulate the 2PC protocol, one transaction tree must act as *coordinator* and is supplemented with the action nodes that collect the votes of the participants. These nodes form the children of the control node (T_c). The *participating* transaction trees are supplemented with control nodes to receive and execute the decision of the coordinator. These control nodes are illustrated in Fig. 8.11. As in the 2PC protocol, the coordination pattern could be made more complex to accommodate further disturbance in the operation of the protocol. Here, an explicit vote request is not needed. The participant sends its vote upon the completion of its original subtree (the one indicated by a triangle in Fig. 8.11). The pair of synchronization nodes marked by (1) sends the vote of the participant to the coordinator. The ECA rule is as follows.

- *Event*: change of state of root node of the original subtree (T_a).
- *Condition*: (state_sender = committed) ∨ (state_sender = aborted)
- *Action*: change the state of the receiver to the state of the sender.

Since the control node holding the P_i nodes is configured with the *AND* operator over the commitment of all its children, it exactly implements the voting principle of the 2PC protocol. If all vote *yes*, the control node commits and sends the commit message to all participants through the pair of synchronization nodes (2). They have the ECA rule:

- *Event*: change of state of root node of the original subtree (T_c).
- *Condition*: (state_sender = committed) ∨ (state_sender = aborted)
- *Action*: change the state of the receiver to the state of the sender.

If at least one participant votes *no*, the control node aborts and sends the abort message to all participants through the same pair of synchronization nodes.

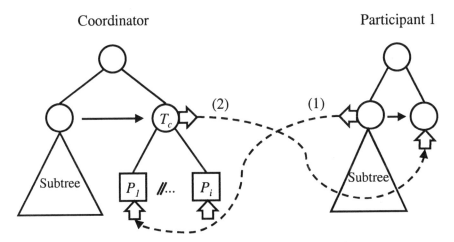

Fig. 8.11. Termination coordination at the level of transaction trees

8.4 Conclusion

In this last four chapters, we fully described our approach of having transactional agents to increase the robustness of MAS. Before moving to the next part of our work, it is worth making a quick checklist of the fulfilled requirements stated in Sect. 5.1.

The transaction model formally guarantees both the correct execution of agent actions and the recoverability of the system in the presence of disturbances. Guaranteeing robustness goes far beyond a mere syntactical aspect. The transaction model captures the semantic of the plan by modeling the various execution dependencies of agent actions. Using its powerful and yet flexible description, the model supports the various planning constructs. Through the use of synchronization nodes, the social aspect of MAS is fully supported. ECA rules are the building blocks for supporting the cooperation between agents executing a common plan. In order to face the potentially arising disturbances, inherent in a large and distributed IS, the model captures both the plan and the contingency behavior in one rigid structure. This allows the Execution Agents to provide the required robustness guarantees, increases the reactivity of the middleware, and couples planning and execution. The Execution Agent is very versatile and enjoys great autonomy in determining the appropriate behavior (either forward or backward recovery) to minimize the damage caused by the disturbance. On the implementation level, the Execution Agents fit well into the existing IT-landscape. No change in the internals of the underlying DBMS is needed, since the operations of the Execution Agent remains completely transparent. Moreover, there is no need for any centralized component to operate our system.

From this checklist, it is clear that we presented a solution that handles the robustness problem in MAS. However, our approach must be validated for the application in large-scale information systems, such as PPC applications. The performance of the Execution Agents middleware must be analyzed. By no means should the introduction of the middleware negatively affect the scalability of the MAS. *Simulation* is our means for this verification.

9 Simulation Study

The goal of this work is to increase the robustness of MAS by providing the necessary middleware to guarantee the robust execution of agent actions. Although robustness is a deciding factor in the application of MAS in large-scale IS applications, any robustness guaranteeing solution is not allowed to decrease the overall system performance or its scalability.

Before presenting our approach as a solution for MAS in large-scale IS applications, we need to evaluate its performance and scalability. Unfortunately, the MAS environment with all the variety of its input parameters and system settings is *too* complex to be modeled using simple analytical tools, such as mathematical models. That's why we design a simulation model and build an extensive simulator to evaluate the operation of MAS in an IS environment. The purpose of the simulation studies is *threefold*. The first purpose is to be able to give a quantitative assessment of the *performance* of the system before its actual deployment. Second, the *scalability* of the system is to be evaluated. Finally, the simulation study helps revealing a lot about the behavior of the transaction trees and hence the plans they implement under the operational workload. This largely enhances the *predictability* of the system, which is one of the major problems of MAS.

In this chapter, we describe the simulation model and define the performance indices employed in the evaluation before moving to the description of the actual simulation runs and the experimental results in the next chapter.

9.1 Simulation Model

First of all, we need to build our simulation environment. In our implementation prototype, we already have the Execution Agents with their core ATM module. The rest of the MAS architecture is not available and must be simulated. Simulation is essential, since there is no unique and complete system that can represent all possible MAS environments. And even if such system exists, we want to analyze our approach before the actual deployment of the system.

As illustrated in Fig. 9.1, we replace the levels above and underneath the Execution Agents with two simulated models. The level above the Execution Agents contains the *workload simulator*. This simulator represents the Planning Agents. It generates configurable plans that are submitted to the Execution Agents in form of transaction trees for execution. The *resource simulator* resides underneath the middleware layer of the Execution Agents. The role of this module is to simulate the execution of simple agent actions, i.e., the effect of ACID transactions on the

K. Nagi: Transactional Agents, LNCS 2249, pp. 151–159, 2001.
© Springer-Verlag Berlin Heidelberg 2001

database of the mini world. This level models the collective conflicts over resources [33]; in that case, the data objects. While the resource simulator reflects
failures due to conflicts in the underlying database, we need a third simulator,
namely the *disturbance simulator*, to model failures resulting from the coupling of
transaction trees. In the following subsections, we describe these simulators and
the transaction tree model executed by the Execution Agents.

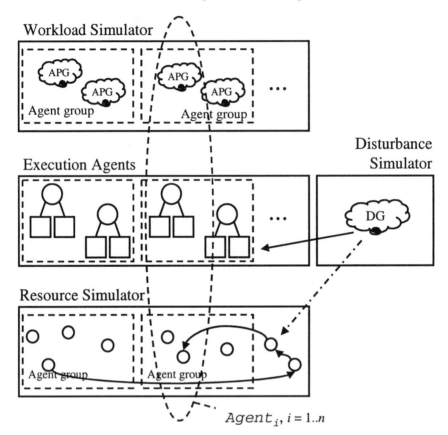

Fig. 9.1. The simulation environment

9.1.1 Workload Model

The workload for the Execution Agents is naturally the transaction trees they have
to execute. So, the workload model represents the Planning Agents that generate
these trees. The agent population is divided into agent groups. Each group contains a fixed number of agents that work on a shared plan. Each Planning Agent in
the group is represented by an *Agent Plan Generator* (APG) module. This module
generates a transaction tree and submits it to the corresponding Execution Agent.

When the Execution Agent finishes executing the transaction tree, it waits until all its counterparts in the agent group are also finished before requesting a new transaction tree from the APG. This behavior simulates the coordination pattern for termination coordination described in Sect. 8.3.3. In case the simulator is also configured for handling potential reassessment due to changes in the mini world, committed trees are transferred to the list of pending trees as illustrated in Fig. 9.2, until this phase comes to end. Meanwhile, the execution agent can process other transaction trees so long as no reassessment of a pending tree is needed.

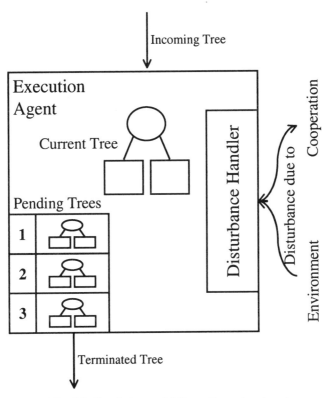

Fig. 9.2. Simulation model for an Execution Agent

Three parameters specify a transaction tree configuration as illustrated in Fig. 9.3.

- *Average Number of Children (C)*: is a uniformly distributed random variable between 1 and $2C$; determining the number of children of a control node.
- *Probability of Simple Transactions (S)*: is a Bernoulli trial with probability S that a child is an action node. Control nodes are generated with probability $(1-S)$ and lead to the generation of a further subtree.
- *Probability of Parallel Execution (P)*: is a Bernoulli trial with probability P that the children of a control node are executed in parallel. Otherwise, i.e., with

probability (1-*P*), the children of a control node are executed sequentially. We ignore the third choice of having alternative execution, since this setting results in a control node having one child, whose identity is determined at runtime instead at design time. The time for determining the shape of the tree is not relevant in the simulation study.

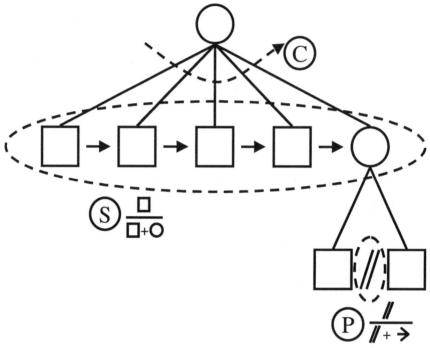

Fig. 9.3. Parameters for the transaction tree

These parameters are set arbitrarily and are used to model the workload of the original system to be simulated. To conduct a simulation study, system engineers have to assess typical values for these parameters. Since, in our study, we want to gain insight of the complex behavior of the system in general, we explore the workload space, in which all valid values of *P*, *C*, and *S* are used. By valid, it meant that the parameter settings must generate a finite tree. The condition for a finite transaction tree is that $(1 - S) \times (C + 0.5)$ must be smaller than 1. Otherwise, transaction trees with infinite depth could be generated. This restricts our feasible region to that narrow shaded area illustrated in Fig. 9.4.

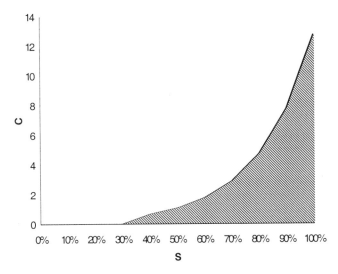

Fig. 9.4. Feasible region for simulation

We notice the absence of synchronization nodes in the generated transaction trees. During normal operation, they act only as a means for synchronization and show an effect similar to normal action nodes. In case of disturbances, the important role they play is modeled through the disturbance simulator as will be shown in Sect. 9.1.3 and through the implicit implementation of coordination patterns within the simulation model, such as the termination coordination.

Now that the transaction trees have been generated, the control parameters of their nodes must be set. In our simulation experiments, we adopt a persevering strategy to yield more concrete and quantitative results for our chosen performance indices. This means the following settings of control parameters of transaction tree nodes. All nodes must be compensated in case of backward recovery and all dependent action nodes must be reassessed in case of forward recovery. In other words, the guarding conditions always fail during the reassessment phase. In our presentation of the conducted experiments in Chap. 10, we provide the concrete values for further important control parameters of the transaction nodes.

9.1.2 Resource Model

The resource simulator models the collective conflicts over resources [33] by investigating the effect of the execution of simple agent actions. It simulates the operation of the underlying DBMS of the mini world. More precisely, it simulates the execution of the ACID transactions encapsulated in the simple agent actions. Therefore, we need to model the ACID transactions themselves and the concurrency control algorithms. We extract our model from standard literature in this domain, such as [14, 129, 130].

Execution time of database transactions, normally consisting of read and write operations, is represented by an exponential distribution with mean 15 seconds. In order to be independent of the concurrency control algorithm employed by the DBMS, such as the two-phase locking or the timestamp ordering algorithms, we use the most general representation for checking after the serializability of the executed history. For this, we construct a transaction *Serialization Graph* (SG) as described in Sect. 4.3.3, p. 44, to determine whether a transaction is to be *committed* or *aborted*. Each executing transaction is represented by a node in the graph. A directed edge indicates a conflict between two transactions. A conflict occurs if two transactions access the same data object and at least one operation is a write. The direction of the edge represents the order between the two conflicting operations. A transaction is aborted if its introduction results in a cycle in the serialization graph [8]. Edges are added with *three* probabilities:

- $P_{intra\text{-}agent}$ for nodes belonging to the same agents,
- a higher $P_{intra\text{-}agent\ group}$ for nodes belonging to the same agent group, and
- a highest $P_{inter\text{-}agent\ group}$ for nodes belonging to different agent groups.

This reflects an assumption about the planning algorithms. If properly designed, Planning Agents tend not to submit conflicting actions simultaneously. This applies to actions specified in plans belonging to the same agent group and to a greatest extent to actions belonging the same agent.

In our simulation experiments, $P_{intra\text{-}agent}$, $P_{intra\text{-}agent\ group}$, and $P_{inter\text{-}agent\ group}$ are set to 0.03, 0.06 and 0.09 respectively. Sources for these values as well as mean execution time are also taken from the literature in database modeling, where both the database and transaction sizes are reduced to a small size, while preserving the relationship between them. Fig. 9.5 illustrates a serialization graph. Each node has an *agent group identifier* (`AgGpID`), an *agent identifier* (`AgID`), and a *transaction identifier* (`TID`).

9.1.3 Disturbance Model

While the resource model reflects failures due to conflicts in the underlying database, the disturbance model describes failures resulting from two categories of dependencies. The first category results from changes in the real world during long running plan executions. A typical pattern of such execution is illustrated in our application scenario of Chap. 2. It consists of a phase of intensive actions, in which the necessary decisions are taken and registered in the database, followed by a quiet phase in which changes in the real world may not invalidate these decisions. At the end, another active phase takes place, in which these decisions are implemented in the real world [82]. This is exactly represented by the coupled execution of two transaction trees of the recovery example; presented in Sect. 6.3.4, p. 95. The second one is caused by the synchronization nodes and results from the coordinated execution of transaction tress of the Execution Agents in the same group. This corresponds to the task coordination pattern task described in Sect. 8.3.2.

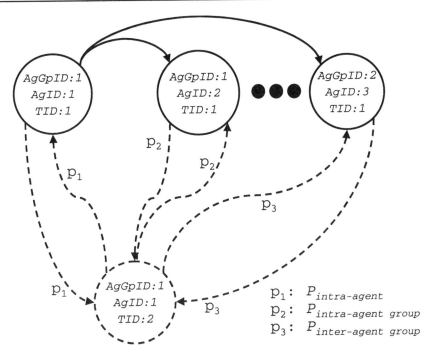

Fig. 9.5. Inserting a node (with *AgGpID*=1, *AgID*=1, and *TID*=2) into the serialization graph

In order to model the first category of disturbances, we built a Disturbance Generator (*DG*) module. In time intervals following an exponential distribution with mean $T_{Disturbance}$, it simulates disturbances occurring due to changes in the mini world. In our runs, we fix $T_{Disturbance}$ to 300 seconds, which has the same order of magnitude as the response time of a transaction tree. These disturbances launch the contingency behavior in the transaction tree and cause the reassessment of committed simple actions that are either part of the current transaction tree or part of the list of pending trees according to another Bernoulli trial with probability $P_{Disturbance}$. In this modus, a committed transaction tree has to remain pending for a certain time interval before being terminated. This time interval also follows an exponential distribution with mean $T_{lifetime}$. It simulates the follow-up process.

As for the second category of disturbances, an Execution Agent making a backward recovery of a subtree reports the number of affected simple actions to the disturbance simulator. The disturbance simulator, in turn, *simulates* ECA rules for synchronization nodes typically existing in coordinated transaction trees, explained in Sect. 8.3.2. It considers all committed simple actions at Execution Agents belonging to the same agent group for reassessment. Then, it introduces reassessment for each committed simple action according to a Bernoulli trial with a probability directly proportional to the ratio between the number of affected simple actions of the subtree and the total number of committed simple actions at all members of the agent group; the proportion constant being $F_{Coordination}$.

9.2 Performance Indices

It is clear that we cannot provide a unique performance index that combines all possible performance criteria, since the weighting constants are very application dependent. Therefore, we identify the most important indices and use them individually to analyze the performance of the system. In our analysis, we consider *five* basic performance indices. Nevertheless, other secondary indices can be directly deduced from the output dumps produced by the simulator. In this section, we describe these five indices.

The first index is the *throughput*. It accounts for the number of terminated actions per agent per second and is a direct measure for the performance and the scalability of the system.

$$Throughput = \frac{\sum \text{terminated simple actions}}{\text{Simulation time} \times \sum \text{agents in the simulation}} \text{(transaction/second.agent)} \quad (9.1)$$

Certainly a higher throughput is desired. In case of the increase in the number of agents in the system or the increase in the rate of occurrence of disturbances, a decrease in this performance measure is expected. Nevertheless, a good scalable system should cause no *thrashing* in the throughput.

The second index is the *response time* of the whole plan. In this index, we define the response time to be the time between the start of execution of the root node and the time of its termination or abandoning. In this index, we also account for the time wasted in aborted, compensated, reassessed, and abandoned actions. We also include time spent by the transaction tree waiting in the pending list of the Execution Agent in our calculation. In mathematical terms, the response time is defined al follows.

$$Response\ Time = \frac{\sum_{i=1}^{\substack{\text{number of transaction trees} \\ \text{generated in the simulation}}} (\text{End time of the root node}_i - \text{Start time of the root node}_i)}{\sum \text{transaction trees generated in the simulation}} \text{(seconds)} \quad (9.2)$$

A short response time is certainly desired.

Execution of *compensation* and *reassessment* actions has a very important economical meaning. For example, in our application scenario one gets only a percentage of the full price paid to the production unit in case of the cancellation of time slot allocation from the side of the product agent. Therefore, we represent the effect of these actions in the third performance measure. In many cases, one transaction specification can serve as compensation as well as reassessment. Due to the similarity of the effects of compensation and reassessment, we combine them into one index: the *compensation/reassessment factor*. This measure accounts for the ratio of successfully executed compensation or reassessment simple agent actions to the terminated/abandoned ones. A minimization of this ratio is certainly desired, since it implies fewer overhead and cost incurred during recovery.

Compensation/Reassessment factor

$$= \frac{\sum \text{compensated simple actions} + \sum \text{reassessed simple actions}}{\sum \text{terminated simple actions} + \sum \text{abandoned simple actions}} \quad (9.3)$$

The *abandonment factor* is the fourth performance index. It relates the number of abandoned simple agent actions to the total number of either terminated or abandoned ones. The index accounts for the incidences, in which the Execution Agent fails to execute a plan, exhausts all its retries, and returns control back to the Planning Agent. A low value of this metric is a good measure for achieving the design goal of separating planning from the details of execution and confirms the autonomy of the Execution Agent in executing its actions.

$$Abandonment\ factor = \frac{\sum \text{abandoned simple actions}}{\sum \text{terminated simple actions} + \sum \text{abadonned simple actions}} \quad (9.4)$$

The last performance index is the *abortion factor*. It calculates the ratio of aborted simple actions to the total number of terminated or abandoned ones. It accounts for work lost due to conflicting actions. Here also, a lower ratio is desired.

$$Abortion\ factor = \frac{\sum \text{aborted simple actions}}{\sum \text{terminated simple actions} + \sum \text{abadonned simple actions}} \quad (9.5)$$

9.3 Conclusion

In this chapter, we described the simulation model and the simulators built around the Execution Agents middleware. The model represents a configurable workload and the operation of the underlying DBMS of the mini world with the collective conflicts over data resources. The model also includes a disturbance simulator that generates fictitious failures occurring during the execution of coupled transaction trees.

With the above-defined five performance indices, we start describing our simulation experiments analyzing the system performance in the next chapter.

10 Simulation Results

With the simulator presented in Chap. 9, we are now well equipped for the evaluation of the operation of MAS in IS environments. The purpose of our simulation studies is:

- To give a quantitative assessment of the *performance* of the system before its actual deployment especially in face of disturbances,
- To evaluate the *scalability* of the Execution Agents middleware, and
- To gain insights about the behavior of the transaction trees leading to the enhancement of the *predictability* of the system.

In the simulation study, we first start our analysis with self-centered Planning Agents without considering any cooperation between them. We do not include any source of disturbance in the model apart from that coming from the databases of the mini world. The purpose of this set of experiments is to understand the behavior of the Execution Agents as *individuals* during the execution of isolated plans under various workload configurations and to evaluate the scalability of the system in general. Then, we carry our analysis one step further by allowing the Execution Agents to follow-up the execution of their actions to their actual completion in the *real* world instead of only writing them in the *mini* world. Here, we introduce the *first* category of disturbances simulated by the disturbance model, namely, the radical changes in the real world that invalidate the agent actions carried out against the databases of the mini world. The aim of these experiments is to quantitatively assess the damage caused by such disturbances by evaluating the cost of executing the contingency behavior, which brings the execution of agent actions to a well-defined and consistent state. Having done this, we move to the analysis of the *social aspect* of multi-agents. We model the behavior of groups of agents that cooperatively develop a shared plan and delegate its execution to their peer Execution Agents. These, in turn, coordinate the execution of the local transaction trees using of synchronization nodes as explained in Sect. 8.3.2. Here, the *second* category of disturbances simulated by the disturbance model comes in play. A typical disturbance invalidates the decision taken by an Execution Agent and causes the propagation of contingency behavior among the members of the same agent group. The aim of these experiments is also to quantitatively assess the damage caused by these disturbances. Finally, a concluding section ends the chapter.

K. Nagi: Transactional Agents, LNCS 2249, pp. 161–181, 2001.
© Springer-Verlag Berlin Heidelberg 2001

10.1 Scalability of Self-Centered Agents

In our simulation study, we analyze the performance of the Execution Agents middleware under various workload configurations. In this set of experiments, we first restrict ourselves to self-centered Planning Agents acting on the mini world without any cooperation between them [73]. In other words, this is the case of *antagonist* agents with *collective conflicts* over resources (in that case data objects of the mini world) [33]. Each Execution Agent executes its own transaction tree without doing any follow-up of the actual occurrence of these actions in the real world.

Here, the only source of disturbances is the database. It can reject an agent action if its execution results in a cycle in the serialization graph. In other words, the commit/abort decision, made by the resource simulator, plays the major role in the overall performance. Intuitively, the performance is dependent on the number of concurrently executing transactions and the job mix, i.e., the number of actions each agent is simultaneously having in the resource model. The aim of this set of experiments is to analyze the performance of the single agents and gain insights in their behavior, first as individuals, by trying to isolate each workload parameter and analyze the performance under its variation.

10.1.1 Parameter Settings

Since we are investigating self-centered Planning Agents, no agent groups are built and hence the input parameter $F_{Coordination}$ has no impact on the simulation runs. Moreover, since we do not include disturbances resulting from the follow-up process on this stage, we reset $T_{Disturbance}$ to ∞ and $T_{Lifetime}$ to 0. In other words, the only source of disturbance in the set of experiments is coming from the resource model due to aborted transactions. According to Sect. 6.3.2, this leads to the backward recovery in case a transaction node persistently aborts. However, from the description of forward recovery of Sect. 6.3.3, we are sure that recovery in the forward direction cannot occur since it can only result from retracted ECA messages. Since the Agents are self-centered in this set of experiments with no ECA rules, the transaction nodes will never operate in the reassessment mode. Following a persevering strategy, the control parameters of the transaction nodes are set as follows. All nodes, both action and control nodes, must be undone in case of failure of the parent node. The number of retries of action nodes is set to 5 in normal mode and to 2 in compensation mode. Compound nodes are also retried twice. In our runs, we fix the time interval between successive retries to 60 seconds for all node types in both operation modes.

In this set of experiments, we explore the workload space, in which all valid values of P, C, and S are used[11] (see the shaded region of Fig. 9.4). In each experiment, the number of agents is varied between 5 and 125. This way, the results of the experiments form large hypercubes. In the following subsections, we try to

---

[11] The exploration of the workload space is done using about 2600 experiments.

isolate each workload parameter and summarize the performance indices in a set of simple figures.

10.1.2 Effect of Increasing the Degree of Parallel Execution (*P*)

In this set of experiments, *S* and *C* are fixed to 100% and 3 respectively and the curves are plotted for *P* varying from 0% to 100%. All performance indices degrade *gracefully* with the increase in the number of agents. However, the rate depends on *P*. As illustrated in Fig. 10.1, the throughput of transaction trees, whose nodes are executed in parallel yields better results for under-populated settings. This situation is reversed with the increase in agents (more than 80 agents), in which it is better to submit agent actions sequentially. The explanation of this phenomenon is simple. The database has a certain capacity for executing transactions without coming into conflicts. For under-populated settings, this capacity is not yet reached; that is why nodes executing in parallel have a better chance of committing. This leads to the higher throughput (about 0.09 transaction per second per agent). As the agent population grows, the database reaches its critical capacity. It is then wiser to submit the action nodes in parallel to avoid overcrowding the database and hence a high abortion rate, which decreases the overall performance.

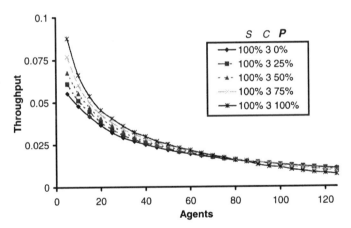

Fig. 10.1. Throughput under the variation of *P*

The response time, illustrated in Fig. 10.2, increases linearly with the increase in the population size. This is attributed to the time wasted in aborts, retries, and the eventually resulting compensations. Nevertheless, the slope of the increase remains the same for all values of *P*. This goes in line with the observation made about the throughput. For under-populated settings, parallel execution almost halves the response time of terminated transaction trees. For over-populated settings, the advantage slowly looses in importance and the reduction is only by 17%.

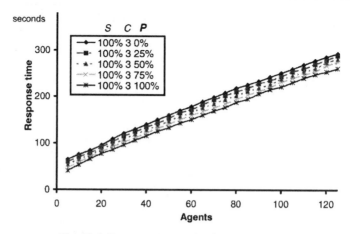

Fig. 10.2. Response time under the variation of *P*

Obviously, the key behind the degradation in the system performance is the number of concurrently executing transactions and the job mix in the resource model. They play the major role in aborting transactions. Taking a look at the abortion factor, in Fig. 10.3, we notice the rapid increase in the abortion factor in the case of *P* = 100% as the number of agents goes above 80 (marked by (1) in the figure). This indicates the point of reaching saturation in the resource model. For more sequential execution or lower population, this saturation point is not reached.

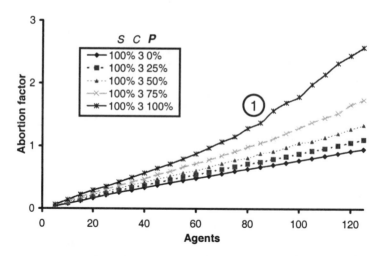

Fig. 10.3. Abortion factor under the variation of *P*

Since compensation is a direct result of repeated transaction aborts and the abandonment of transaction trees is a result of repeated aborts of the control nodes, the compensation factor, illustrated in Fig. 10.4, and the abandonment factor, illustrated in Fig. 10.5, develop the same tendency as the abortion factor.

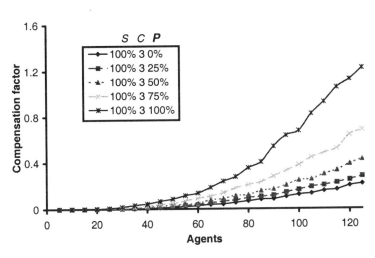

Fig. 10.4. Compensation factor under the variation of P

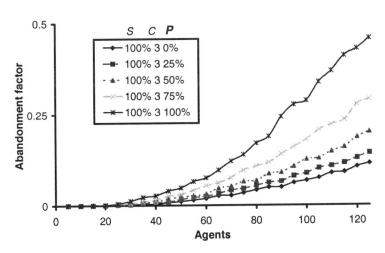

Fig. 10.5. Abandonment factor under the variation of P

In all the last three measures, we notice that the absolute values in case of large agent population are not very satisfactory. This is due to our choice of very high values for the resource model parameters leading to a rather dense serialization graph. Our purpose is to emphasize the effects of disturbance in the resource model. If we lower the values of $P_{intra\text{-}agent}$ and $P_{inter\text{-}agent\ group}$ to a reasonable 0.01 and 0.03, respectively, our experiments yield very good abortion factor, as illustrated in Fig. 10.6. The values for the compensation factor, Fig. 10.7, and the abandonment factor, Fig. 10.8, fall to negligible values.

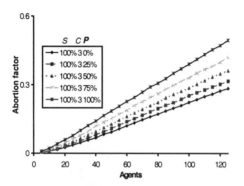

Fig. 10.6. Abortion factor under the variation of P using a sparse SG

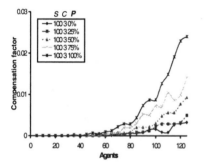

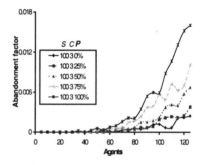

Fig. 10.7. Compensation factor under the variation of P using a sparse SG

Fig. 10.8. Abandonment factor under the variation of P using a sparse SG

10.1.3 Effect of Increasing the Average Number of Children (*C*)

In this set of experiments, both S and P are fixed to 100% and the scalability of the performance indices is plotted for C varying from 3 to 7. Unlike Sect. 10.1.2, changing the input parameter C results in different tree sizes. These settings represent an extremely heavy workload, especially the experiments with $S = 100\%$, $C = 7$, and $P = 100\%$, which we include in the analysis as an extreme region of the workload space.

The throughput, illustrated in Fig. 10.9, degrades gracefully with the increase in agents for reasonable values of C. For $C = 7$, throughput comes to a minimum value, in which only the subset of smaller transaction trees apparently terminates. In this set of experiments, the critical point of agent population is already at 40 agents as compared to 80 in the previous section.

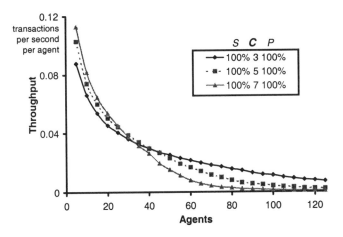

Fig. 10.9. Throughput under the variation of C

The response time, illustrated in Fig. 10.10, develops the same trends as the throughput. Remarkably, the response time tends to stabilize with the large increase in the number of agents in the system for the extreme value of $C = 7$. This increases our suspicion that, under these hard conditions, only the subset of smaller transaction trees terminates.

To confirm this suspicion, we need to investigate the abortion factor in Fig. 10.11. Whereas the slope of the abortion factor remains linear for small transaction trees with $C = 3$, the factor develops a parabolic behavior with $C = 5$. Luckily, this parabolic behavior tends to *stabilize* with the increase of the number of agent in system for $C \geq 5$. The only explanation confirms our suspicion of having only a subset of smaller transaction trees getting through the system. The *saturation* is due to the large number of retries and the long time between successive retries. They practically block the agents having very large transaction trees and, fortunately, let the others with smaller trees to execute their plans to termination. This can be clearly seen in the compensation factor, Fig. 10.12, and the abandonment factor, Fig. 10.13, which attains a completely unacceptable ratio of 0.95 and letting only 5% terminate when the number of agents reaches 125!

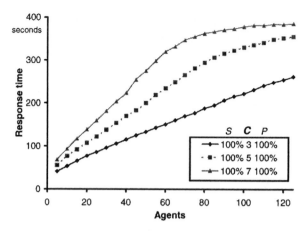

Fig. 10.10. Response time under the variation of *C*

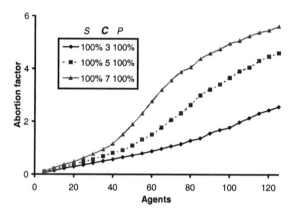

Fig. 10.11. Abortion factor under the variation of *C*

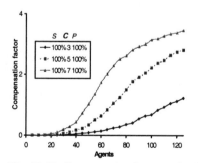

Fig. 10.12. Compensation factor under the variation of *C*

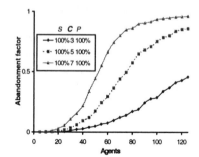

Fig. 10.13. Abandonment factor under the variation of *C*

Clearly, this unrealistic extreme setting is not acceptable for the performance of the system. Fortunately, this unacceptable performance rapidly improves if we allow for more sequential execution in the agent actions. This reflects the important role of input parameter P, i.e., the degree of parallel execution. We take two performance indices as example. Already at a value of $P = 25\%$, throughput curves, illustrated in Fig. 10.14, become the same for all values of C. The abandonment factor, illustrated in Fig. 10.15, drops from 0.95 to 0.35 at its worst case at the value $C = 7$! In other words, the sequential execution neutralizes the negative effect of having a large number of children in the control nodes.

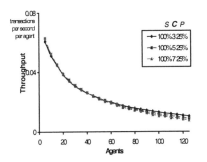
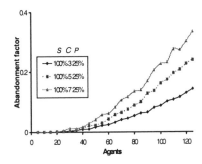

Fig. 10.14. Throughput under the variation of C with $P = 25\%$

Fig. 10.15. Abandonment factor under the variation of C with $P = 25\%$

10.1.4 Effect of Increasing the Tree Depth (*S*)

In this set of experiments, the values of C and P are fixed to 3 and 25% respectively and the curves are plotted for S varying from 100% to 80%. This leads to a variation of the average depth of action nodes from 2.0 to 4.6. and hence the average number of action nodes in a transaction trees from 3.5 to 9.9 nodes.

The throughput, illustrated in Fig. 10.16, degrades gracefully with the increase in the number of agents. From 5 up to 125 agents, it looses about 80% of its value. The throughput seems not be influenced with the increase of the depth of the transaction trees. For under populated settings, deeply nested trees have a slight advantage over flat trees. This situation is reversed as the population exceeds 75 agents.

The response time, illustrated in Fig. 10.17, increases linearly with the increase in the population size. The slope of the increase remains very acceptable for all values of S. Note that, due to the increase in the size of the transaction trees with the decrease in S, the response time of the *whole* transaction tree also increases with S. If we normalize the index by dividing it by the average number of action nodes in each tree configuration, the three curves overlap, including that of $S = 80\%$, which seemed relatively high at the first glance. This goes in harmony with the throughput results, which are hardly affected by the change in S.

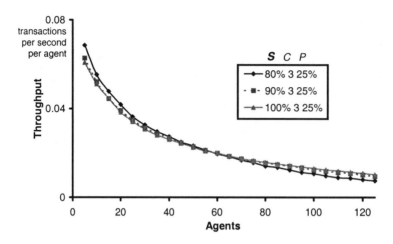

Fig. 10.16. Throughput under the variation of S

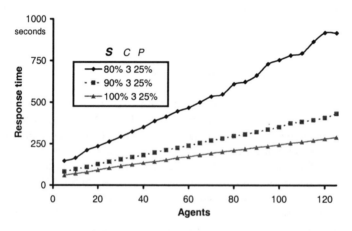

Fig. 10.17. Response time under the variation of S

The reason behind this insensitivity towards the value of S can be observed in the abortion factor of Fig. 10.18. Transaction aborts, which are the direct result of the conflicts in the resource model are hardly affected by the change in S. The increase in the abortion factor remains linear and the absolute values remains under control even for large agent populations. This speaks for the scalability of the system.

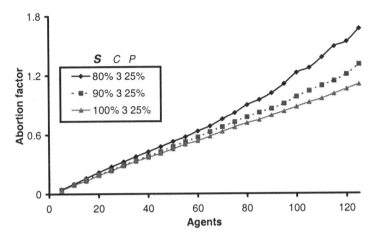

Fig. 10.18. Abortion factor under the variation of S

Similarly, the rest of the performance indices yield very good results. The compensation factor, illustrated in Fig. 10.19, and the abandonment factor, illustrated in Fig. 10.20, begin to leave their almost *zero* value only when the agent population gets above 40 agents. With 125 agents and $S = 90\%$, the compensation factor is under 0.45 and the abandonment factor remains under 0.15! These good values of the performance indices can even be ameliorated by increasing the number of retries in case of the transaction aborts.

10.1.5 Lessons Learnt

In the above-mentioned experiments, we analyze the performance of the agents, as *individuals*, with conflicts in the level of the mini world as the only source of disturbances. The simulation study reveals a lot about the behavior of the transaction trees and the plans they represent.

The performance indices are directly affected by the number of concurrently executing transactions and the job mix in the resource model. The most important parameter seems to be the degree of parallel execution P, since it strongly affects the job mix and the density of agent actions in the system. A precise estimation of the parameters controlling the serialization graph is also critical for getting representative values of the performance indices. MAS designers wanting to conduct such performance experiments can easily deduce the values of $P_{intra\text{-}agent}$ and $P_{inter\text{-}agent\ group}$ from the basic transaction parameters (e.g., average number of read and write operations in a transaction) using formulas found in [130].

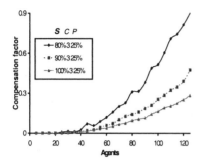

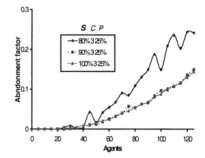

Fig. 10.19. Compensation factor under the variation of *S*

Fig. 10.20. Abandonment factor under the variation of *S*

For a growing number of agents under the various workload configurations, it is clear that the performance indices will be negatively affected with the large increase in the number of agents. Nevertheless, the good news is that there is no thrashing in any one of the indices. This means that the middleware of Execution Agents is *scalable*.

10.2 Long-Running Execution of Agent Plans

In the previous experiments, we analyzed the system performance for a growing number of antagonist agents with self-centered goals and competing on shared resources, (i.e., data objects stored in the databases of the mini world). Under the various workload configurations, we demonstrated the scalability of our system. Now, we can carry our analysis one step further by allowing the Execution Agents to follow-up the execution of their actions to their actual completion in the real world.

A typical pattern of such execution is illustrated in the application scenario of Chap. 2. It consists of a phase of intensive actions, in which the necessary decisions are taken and registered in the database, such as reserving the time slots in the Production Schedule Database. This phase is then followed by a quiet phase in which changes in the real world may not invalidate these decisions. At the end, another active phase takes place, in which these decisions are implemented in the real world, e.g., the actual drilling of hole in the chassis of the robot gripper. In case of disturbances due to radical changes in the real world that invalidate the already taken decisions, the Execution Agent must reassess these actions and recover (first in the forward direction) to reach a well-defined and consistent state of its plan. This is exactly represented by the coupled execution of two transaction trees of the recovery example; presented in Sect. 6.3.4, p. 95. The aim of this set

of experiments[12] is to quantitatively assess the damage caused by such disturbances [75].

10.2.1 Parameter Settings

In this set of experiments, we fix the size of the agent population to 60 agents.
Since we are only interested in disturbances resulting from changes in the mini
world, no agent groups are formed and $F_{Coordination}$ has no effect. Instead, we vary
the value of $T_{Lifetime}$ (the average time interval a committed transaction has to remain pending before termination) from 200 to 2800 seconds, which is about 10
times the value of $T_{Disturbance}$ (the average time interval between successive disturbances).

Guided by the experiments of Sect. 10.1, we choose a suitable configuration for
the transaction tree as a starting point. We set the values of P, C, and S to 100%, 5,
and 0% respectively. This results in generating flat transaction trees having a root
control node and 5.5 simple actions on the average that must be executed sequentially. The control parameters of the transaction nodes are set as follows. The
number or retries of action nodes is raised to 5 in order to avoid unnecessary
aborts of control nodes. Aborted control nodes are retried twice before abandoning
the execution of the transaction tree. We fix the time interval between successive
retries to 60 seconds for all node types in all operation modes. We repeat the experiments for increasing values of $P_{Disturbance}$, see Sect. 9.1.3. The performance indices are plotted in Fig. 10.21 through Fig. 10.25.

10.2.2 Results

First, we start with $P_{Disturbance} = 0\%$, representing the theoretical optimum, in
which the disturbances generated by the DG module of the disturbance simulator
do not effect either the active or the pending transaction trees. As expected, all
performance indices remain unchanged, except the response time, illustrated in
Fig. 10.22. It increases linearly with the increase in $T_{Lifetime}$, since the waiting time
in the pending queue is also included as part of the overall response time. This experiment serves as a basis of comparison.

Apart from this theoretical optimum, all performance indices deteriorate with
the increase in $T_{Lifetime}$. However, this degree of deterioration strongly depends on
the performance index and $P_{Disturbance}$. Agent throughput, illustrated in Fig. 10.21,
degrades heavily once $P_{Disturbance}$ gets above the zero level. With $P_{Disturbance} = 50\%$
and $T_{Lifetime} = 200$ seconds, the throughput is decreased by a factor of 2.6. This factor even becomes 7.7 at $T_{Lifetime} = 2800$ seconds. The good news is that the effect
of $T_{Lifetime}$ seems to weaken with the further increase in $T_{Lifetime}$. This can be observed in the decrease in the absolute value of the gradient of the plotted curves.
This would intuitively lead to a stabilization of the throughput value. On the other

---

[12] Approx. 1500 experiments

hand, the response time, illustrated in Fig. 10.22, seems to be less affected by the increase in $P_{Disturbance}$. The increase always remains linear and the increase in the slope of the curve is hardly remarkable.

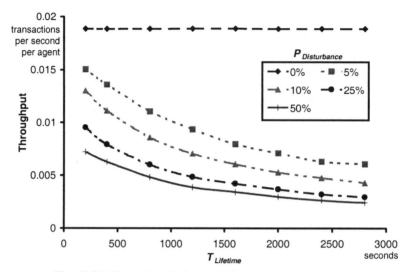

Fig. 10.21. Throughput for long-running execution experiments

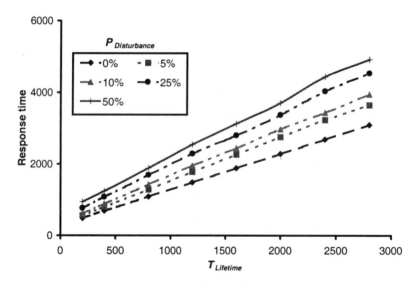

Fig. 10.22. Response time for long-running execution experiments

The deterioration of the other performance indices remains almost linear but seems to be more affected by the increase in $P_{Disturbance}$ than the response time. Both the slope and displacement of the curve representing the compensation/reassessment factor, illustrated in Fig. 10.23, are affected by the increase in $P_{Disturbance}$. Taking $P_{Disturbance} = 50\%$ as an example, the slope is more than doubled with the increase of $P_{Disturbance}$ from 5% to 50%. For the point $T_{lifetime} = 200$ seconds and $P_{Disturbance} = 50\%$, the factor jumps from 0.23 to 1.24. To some extent, the same also applies to the abortion factor illustrated in Fig. 10.25. However, for the abandonment ratio, illustrated in Fig. 10.24, only the slope seems to be affected. The displacement remains almost unchanged.

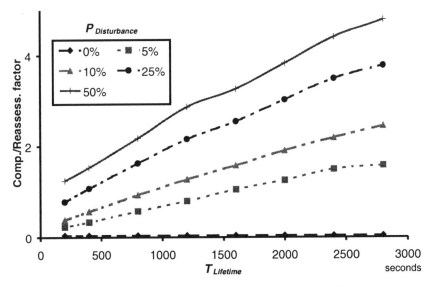

Fig. 10.23. Compensation/Reassessment factor for long-running execution experiments

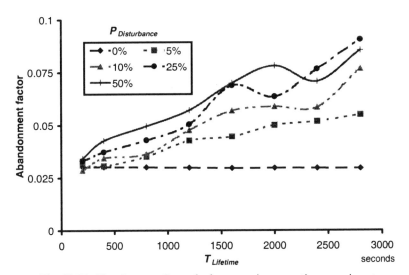

Fig. 10.24. Abandonment factor for long-running execution experiments

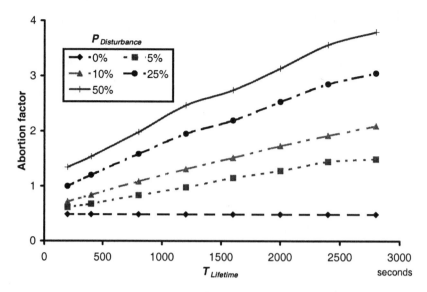

Fig. 10.25. Abortion factor for long-running execution experiments

10.2.3 Lessons Learnt

The results of the experiment confirm the intuitive fact that, in a dynamic environment, decision taken will not always remain valid especially if the time span between the decision taking process and the actual execution is too long. The good news is that for reasonable values of $P_{Disturbance}$, the system behavior is still acceptable. Moreover, as $P_{Disturbance}$ grows beyond 50%, the system shows an asymptotic behavior, which speaks for the stability of the system.

Since the value of $P_{Disturbance}$ and $T_{Disturbance}$ are relatively easy to estimate even before the actual deployment of MAS, system designers are encouraged to run such experiments under the expected workload in order to estimate how near to real-time their plans should be to yield acceptable performance.

10.3 Coordinated Execution of Agent Plans

Now, we leave the domain of antagonist agents and concentrate on social agents that cooperate in order to develop a shared plan. Having developed this plan among the group of Planning Agents, they delegate its execution to their peer Execution Agents, which must coordinate their execution of the local transaction trees. As discussed earlier, their means of doing that is to use synchronization nodes that implement the basic coordination patterns through the ECA rules. The implementation of these task coordination patterns is described in Sect. 8.3.2, p. 147.

A typical coordination problem arises when the synchronization node receives a commit message from its sender node and, as a result, commits. At a later point, the foreign subtree corresponding to the sender node is to be compensated due to a failure. This logically invalidates the status of the receiver node and all subsequent nodes in the tree. In this case, the Execution Agent starts a *forward recovery* process by trying to reassess all subtransactions depending on the receiver node. This disturbance is very dangerous, since it can have a *cascading* effect on the Execution Agents of the same agent group. The aim of this set of experiments[13] is to quantitatively assess the damage caused by such disturbances [75].

10.3.1 Parameter Settings

In this set of experiments, we fix the size of the agent population to 120 agents. Two main input parameters must be taken into consideration in investigating the effect of disturbance on the execution of coordination transaction trees. These parameters are:

- *The size of the agent group*, and
- *The degree of coupling of the transaction trees*.

Therefore, we change the size of the agent groups from 1 to 24; as can be seen along the x-axis of Fig. 10.26 through Fig. 10.30 and we repeat the experiments for increasing values of $F_{Coordination}$.

Here also, we choose the same configuration for the transaction tree as in Sect. 10.2. We set the values of P, C, and S to 100%, 5, and 0% respectively. Since we are no longer interested in disturbances resulting from the follow-up process, we reset $T_{Disturbance}$ to ∞ and $T_{Lifetime}$ to 0. The control parameters of the transaction nodes are set as follows. The number of retries of action nodes is set to 2 in normal, compensation, and reassessment modes. Control nodes are retried 5 times. This setting - although it negatively affects the performance indices - helps analyzing the effect of compensation of subtrees on the other Execution Agents of the same group, and hence the effect of propagating contingencies in coordinated transaction trees.

10.3.2 Results

First, we start with $F_{Coordination} = 0$, representing a theoretical optimum in which cooperating agents work without any negative side-effects between the members of the agent group. This setting outlines the positive effect of having several agents solving a problem. An improvement in all performance indices is observed. This is easily accounted for if we consider the job mix in the resource simulator. With the increase on the size of the agent group, directed edges of the transaction serialization graph tend to be added more with probability $P_{intra\text{-}agent\ group}$ than with

---

[13] more than 1000 experiments

probability $P_{inter\text{-}agent\ group}$. Since $P_{intra\text{-}agent\ group}$ is less than $P_{inter\text{-}agent\ group}$, this leads to fewer cycles in the serialization graph, and hence fewer conflicts, fewer aborts, fewer compensations and less abandoning of agent actions.

With the increase in $F_{Coordination}$, we notice a growing effect, namely, that of agents backing off their plans and affecting the execution of other coordinated transaction trees in the same agent group. This propagation of contingencies works against the positive effect of agent cooperation. This leads to the deterioration of all performance indices. Again, this can be intuitively explained. With the presence of such disturbances (represented by $F_{Coordination} > 0$), the larger the size of the agent group gets, the higher the chance of propagation of such contingencies gets. For the given setting of workload and resource parameters, all performance indices tend to achieve asymptotic values for $F_{Coordination}$ above 6. Precisely for $F_{Coordination} = 6$, the throughput, illustrated in Fig. 10.26, decreases by a factor of 250 as the group size increases from 1 to 24. The response time in Fig. 10.27 increases from 1000 to 5000 seconds. The Compensation/Reassessment factor, Fig. 10.28, the abandonment factor, Fig. 10.29, and the abortion factor, Fig. 10.30, are also badly affected. Clearly, this setting is an indication of a bad task allocation between the cooperating agents. In this case, distributed problem solving is not the right choice.

A point of equilibrium for $F_{Coordination}$, where both effects seem to equalize, is slightly different for each performance index. It is about 0.5 for both the throughput and the response time, 1 for both the compensation/reassessment and abortion factors, and 2 for the abandonment factor. Beyond these points, a more centralized problem solving approach yields better results.

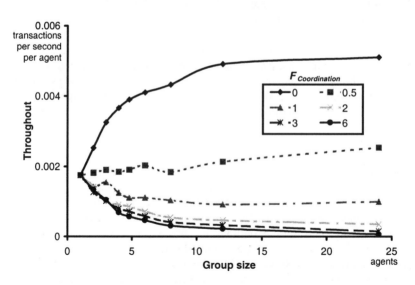

Fig. 10.26. Throughput for coordinated transaction trees

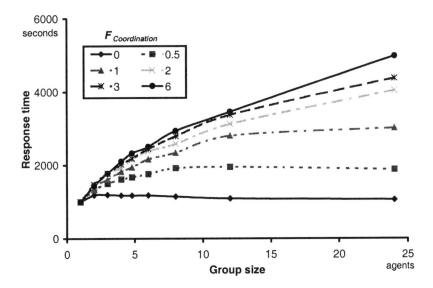

Fig. 10.27. Response time for coordinated transaction trees

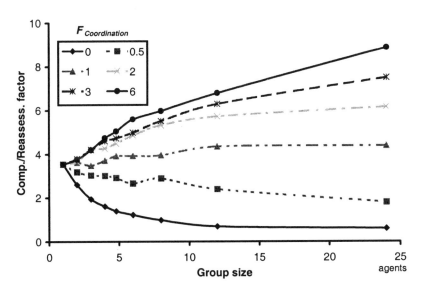

Fig. 10.28. Compensation/Reassessment factor for coordinated transaction trees

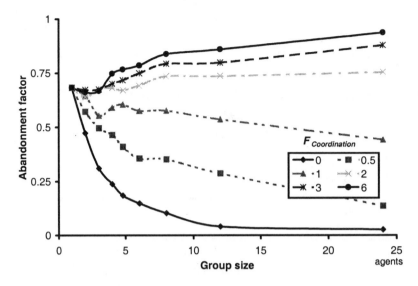

Fig. 10.29. Abandonment factor for coordinated transaction trees

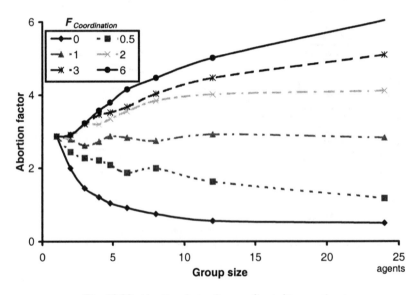

Fig. 10.30. Abortion factor for coordinated transaction trees

10.3.3 Lessons Learnt

The results of this experiment confirm the famous tradeoff between the gain in having several agents cooperatively working together on the same problem and the loss represented in the increasing overhead on coordinating their actions. The good news is that even under hard conditions, all performance indices tend to achieve asymptotic values in our system. MAS designers have to evaluate $F_{Coordination}$ typical for their workload. Using the results of this type of experiments, they should be able to determine the optimal group size that meets the required performance indices. Or in other words, given a group size, they can predict the MAS performance.

10.4 Conclusion

In this chapter, we analyzed the performance of our proposed solution using the simulation model presented in Chap. 9. By analyzing the system for a growing number of agents under the various workload configurations, we evaluate the scalability of our system.

Although almost all performance indices are negatively affected with the large increase in the number of Execution Agents in the system, no *thrashing* in any one of the indices is observed. This speaks for the *scalability* of the middleware. With the increase in the degree and frequency of external disturbances, an expected degradation of performance is observed in comparison to an ideal world without disturbances. Nevertheless, the system develops a very acceptable *asymptotic* behavior even under extremely high disturbances, which speaks for the *stability* of the system.

In general, the simulation results reveal a lot about the behavior of the transaction trees and the plans they implement. They allowed us to better understand the nature of the planning process and the effects of disturbances on the system.

In respect of system *predictability*, simulation proved itself to be a valuable tool for evaluating the overall quality of solutions provided by the MAS before the actual deployment. We encourage MAS designers to use our simulator to assess and hence fine-tune their systems before their actual development.

11 Summary and Future Work

11.1 Summary

The ever-growing complexity of modern distributed Information Systems and the difficulty to foresee all potentially arising disturbances holds out great potential for the application of MAS in this important domain. Despite many research efforts in the last decade, this technology is still in its infancy and is slow to find its way into large-scale information-rich applications such as ERP and PPC systems. The main technical challenge facing the introduction of MAS to such mission critical core applications is the lack of *robustness* in MAS.

In this thesis, a solution to the robustness problem is proposed. We aim at increasing the robustness of MAS applied in IS domains through *an underlying middleware*. The middleware provides *formal guarantees* on the robustness of the system by itself and independently from the original structure of the MAS architecture. It is clear that the middleware cannot encapsulate the whole semantic of the application. Therefore, the robustness provided by the middleware is defined in terms of guarantees given on a *technical* basis, which is guaranteeing the *correctness* and *recoverability* of the system. In view of this technical definition of robustness, we provide necessary guarantees on the robust execution of agent actions.

The basic idea behind our approach is to provide a structure that captures the execution dependencies of the plan of each agent. The structure is based on the *open-nested transaction model* introduced in the 80s in the database environments. We entrust the execution of the transaction model to fully decentralized *transactional* agents in middleware. These agents, called *Execution Agents*, are responsible for the robustness aspects. To keep them open for arbitrary agent frameworks, all the interactions between the Execution Agents and other components of a MAS architecture, such as the planning entities, the DBMS, etc., obey the emerging FIPA [37] standard.

Unfortunately, the standard open-nested transaction model cannot directly fit the MAS paradigm. Therefore, we extend the model to meet the requirement analysis stated in Chap. 5. The proposed model, presented in Chap. 6, is powerful enough to represent the agent plans and support the various planning approaches and methodologies mentioned in agent planning survey of Chap. 3. The real strength in our model is its capability of capturing both the *plan* and the *contingency* behavior of the plan in the face of disturbances within the definition of the transaction tree. In the face of disturbances, the Execution Agents automate several *patterns of behavior* for error handling, such as the automatic retrial of actions

K. Nagi: Transactional Agents, LNCS 2249, pp. 183–185, 2001.
© Springer-Verlag Berlin Heidelberg 2001

in case of simple failures, the automatic restoring of the Execution Agents after a software or hardware failure leading to their crash, and the automatic recovery in case of persisting failures or drastic changes in the IS invalidating parts of the already executed plans. Here, capturing the plan and the contingency behavior in one structure increases the autonomy of the Execution Agent in deciding the way to recover. The transaction model allows for both *forward* and *backward* recovery. The Execution Agents choose that direction to recovery which lowers the overhead endured by undoing committed work. Altogether with strong interaction protocols with the underlying DBMS of the underlying IS the implementation of the Execution Agent thus provides the required robustness guarantees as demonstrated in Chap. 7.

Moreover, the transaction model is also flexible to allow the evolution of the agent plans and their contingencies. As seen it Chap. 8, the Execution Agent can execute incomplete parts of the plan and allow its further refinement and reconfiguration during the execution. Supporting the social aspects of the MAS paradigm is completely new to the open-nested transaction model. In our proposed model, the support for cooperation between the agents is done through the synchronization nodes that couple the execution of independent transaction trees in different Execution Agents using their ECA rules. In Chap. 8, the implementation of various coordination patterns is shown using the synchronization nodes.

Before presenting our approach as a solution for MAS in large-scale IS applications, we wanted to be sure that it does not decrease the overall system performance or its *scalability*. Due the large complexity of MAS in an IS environment and the variety of its input parameters and system settings, we seek resort in *simulation*. For this purpose, a simulation model is designed, presented in Chap. 9. Equipped with an extensive simulator and a versatile set of performance indices, the performance of our proposed solution is analyzed in Chap. 10. The Execution Agents middleware is very *scalable* since no thrashing in any one of the performance indices is observed even under the large increase in the number of agents and under the various workloads and resource configurations. In face of a high frequency and degree of disturbances, the system develops very nice asymptotic behavior, which speaks for the *stability* of the system. An important advantage of the conducted simulation runs is that they reveal a lot about the behavior of the transaction trees and the plans they implement. They allow us to better understand the nature of the planning process and the effects of disturbances on the system, hence strongly increasing the *predictability* of MAS, whose lack has been always an inherent problem.

11.2 Future Work

Our research direction of providing robustness guaranteeing middleware for MAS is still in its infancy. In the course of our work, we came through several aspects worthy of further research and future work. In the following, we mention some of these aspects.

A basic requirement is that the Execution Agent middleware remains open for the joining and leaving of agents belonging to arbitrary architectures in an open agent marketplace. Although, we design the system to be compliant with the emerging FIPA standard, we still have a long way to go for our system to be part of the FIPA platform. To make the incorporation of the Execution Agents in the FIPA perfect, we need to define the transactional ontology of our transaction model as well as the interaction protocols, and not only the messages, as standard protocols within the FIPA standard.

Another area for possible research is developing further coordination patterns between the Execution Agents. In Chap. 8, we showed three basic coordination patterns. Further patterns can be developed by combining existing patterns. Certainly, an enrichment to the Action Repository is a library for storing coordination patterns. This way, the Planning Agents can use them as of-the-shelf ready-made components to define the coordination between their peer Execution Agents.

An interesting research point is extending the robustness guarantees from the execution of agent plans to the planning process itself. In Chap. 5, it is argued that restoring the whole internal status of the Planning Agent is neither *applicable* nor *desirable*. However, it is also argued that those parts of the planning processes needing robustness guarantees can be formulated as *internal actions*, which can be temporarily stored in the underlying database and handled by the Execution Agent as agent actions. Nevertheless, this is not always as simple as it seems to be. We clearly need to support the representation of intermediate formats to ease porting the formulation of the internal state of mind of the planning process to transaction trees. Petri-nets seem to be as a good candidate for this intermediate format.

On the level of performance analysis, our simulation study contributes a lot in gaining insights about the behavior of agents under various workload and resource configurations and degree of disturbances, which greatly improves the predictability of the MAS before its deployment. If we are going to promote our simulator as a standard tool for MAS designers, some work must be done to make it user-friendlier. A graphical interface to the simulator animating the simulated operation of the MAS would certainly enhance the understandability and increase the ability of MAS designers of analyzing the behavior of the individual agents, the MAS as a whole together the interaction with the underlying IS. Also a better presentation of the raw data resulting from the simulation runs would certainly shorten the analysis time and possibly lead to new observations about the behavior of the MAS.

Finally, a very challenging mission is to generalize our solution for non-database IS applications. For many reasons, the landscape of the underlying IS can be constituted of legacy systems, proprietary CAD/CIM systems, tailored ERP systems and self-implemented PPC systems, building isolated islands. Several research efforts, such as [100], analyze the requirements to make such subsystems have some of the desirable database functionality. Some efforts try to emulate the missing database functionality, such as guaranteeing the atomicity of their local operations or the possibility of defining compensation for their actions. Some research even tries to automate the generation of the compensation actions [83]. In the future, we can use these approaches to extend the applicability of our solution to operate on these special software applications.

Appendix I: Agent Implementation Prototype

In this appendix, we present a brief description of a prototype implementation of the proposed transactional agents middleware. In order to illustrate the functionality of the middleware, we implement a prototype of the Execution Agents. We also implement graphical user interfaces to emulate the functionality of the missing components of the MAS architecture and apply it in a highly simplified and abstracted version of the application scenario described in Chap. 2.

The appendix is organized as follows. First, we define the database scheme representing the mini world. Then, we describe the graphical tool to define agent action in the Action Repository. Another graphical tool is then described, which emulates the planning process. Using this tool, the user can develop transaction trees that are then submitted to the Execution Agent. The operation of the Execution Agent is wrapped by another graphical tool to show its internal operation to the user and allows him/her to introduce disturbance into the system.

I.1 The Mini World

Database relations implemented using ORACLE tables reflect the mini world of the manufacturing scenario given in Chap. 2. In the *Production Units Master Data*, several relations describe the production units in our enterprise. The most important relation in this category is the *MachineCapability*, which identifies the production steps that can be accomplished on each production unit. The definition of the *MachineCapability* relation is (ProductionUnitID, ProductionStepType).

The *Product Master Data* contains the production steps needed to manufacture the product and the construction dependencies between these steps. Since we only emulate the Planning Agent, we do not need to represent this information in an explicit relation. The information is implicitly considered while developing the plan using the Planning Agent emulator, described in Sect. I.3.

The *Production Schedule Data* is represented by a central relation, namely *ProductionSchedule*(Date, TimeSlot, ProductionUnitID, ProductAgentID, ProductionStepID, Price). This relation contains all time slots of all production units during the planning period with the identifier of the product agent and the production step that occupies the slot, together with the contracted price.

Since we do not actually implement the agent of the production units, we directly simulate disturbances occurring due to the failure in a production unit by manually freeing the corresponding time slots and notifying the affected Execution Agents instead of having an explicit relation for the *Production Control Data*.

K. Nagi: Transactional Agents, LNCS 2249, pp. 187–192, 2001.
© Springer-Verlag Berlin Heidelberg 2001

I.2 The Action Repository

The *Action Repository*, described in Sect. 5.6, contains all simple actions that can be attached to the leaf nodes of the transaction tree and that form the building blocks for the agent plan. The tool described in this section is used to define such actions. The tool whose GUI-interface is illustrated in Fig. I.1, is used to define new agent actions.

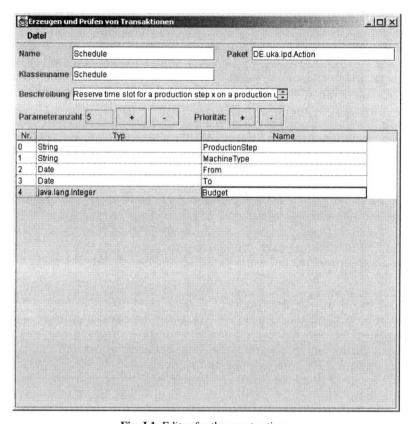

Fig. I.1. Editor for the agent actions

In this case, the necessary parameters, such as the class name, description, and execution parameters are supplied in the corresponding input masks. Then, a Java code skeleton is automatically generated and stored in the repository path. In Fig. I.2, a skeleton for the Schedule action is illustrated. It contains the predefined class properties and the methods used to read and write these properties.

```
import java.sql.*;
// insert your imports here

/**
 * Title:        ...<p>
 * Description:  ...<p>
 * Copyright:    Copyright (c) IPD<p>
 * Company:      IPD Uni Karlsruhe<p>
 * @author ...
 * @version 1.0
 */

public class Schedule extends ACID_Transaction
{
  // insert your private attributes here

  /**
   *
   */
  public Schedule() {
    super("Schedule",
          "Reserve a time slot for a production step x on a production unit of type y
           within the time period t1 and t2 with a maximum budget of a DM.",
          5);
  } // constructor

  public Class getParameterType(int index) {
    ...
  } // getParameterType

  public String getParameterName(int index) {
    ...
  } // getParameterName

  protected final boolean doActions(Connection con) throws SQLException {
    // need a connection
    if(con==null) return false;
    // insert your code here
      ...
  }
}
```

Fig. I.2. A Skeleton code for the Schedule action

Using this code skeleton, we implement a simple algorithm to allocate the time slots for the production steps. The algorithm gets the allocated time slots of the production steps depending on the production step in question from the *Production Schedule Data* and tries to find the next free time slot on a production unit that is capable of processing the step. This can be easily found from the *MachineCapability* relation. Conversely, the tool can load a *class* file containing an agent action and extract the metadata of the action from the compiled code. The user can thus edit this data and generate a new code skeleton.

I.3 The Planning Agent

The internal functioning and logic of the Planning Agent are not the focus of this thesis. Since we need the whole components of the MAS environment to demonstrate the operation of the Execution Agent, a simple graphical tool is implemented to let the user develop the agent plans thus emulating the functionality of Planning Agents.

The tool can *create* new plans, *store* them in XML files, and *change* the definition of existing plans by loading their XML file and graphically editing them. A snapshot of the tool is illustrated in Fig. I.3. In the left panel, the transaction tree is graphically presented by the tree structure. By clicking a node, its children are collapsed and its control parameters are displayed in the right panel, where editing is allowed. In Fig. I.3, the transaction tree of Fig. 6.2 is illustrated. The user can add control or action nodes by clicking the round buttons found in the upper left corner of the screen.

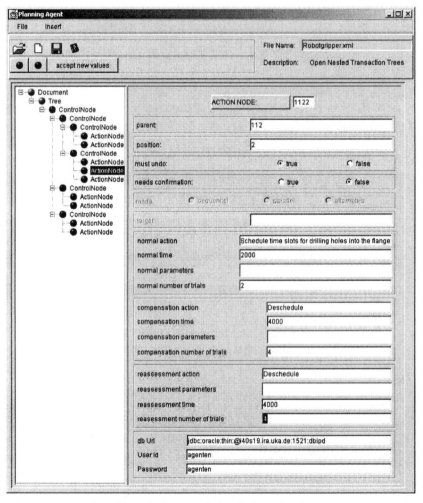

Fig. I.3. A GUI for emulating the Planning Agent

I.4 The Execution Agent

The main contribution of this thesis is the *Execution Agent*. We developed a full prototype of the Execution Agent that is capable of executing the transaction model and guaranteeing the robustness aspects, including the *correctness* as well as the *recovery* aspects.

A graphical user interface tool is implemented on top of the kernel of the Execution Agent, as illustrated in Fig. I.4. The tool wraps the original components of the Execution Agent; such as the ATM. Through the 'Erzeugen' button, the user is able to load a transaction tree by reading its XML definition. The transaction tree is then graphically displayed. By clicking the 'Starten' button, the execution of the transaction tree is started. Since the execution of the transaction tree lasts very few seconds, it is hardly possible for the user to follow the execution of the transaction tree. That is why, an 'Einzelschritt' button is introduced. By pressing this button, the execution of the transaction is carried out till the next state transition of any of the transaction nodes in the tree. Each color in the legend marks a different state of the control node. By observing the change in the color of the color nodes, the user has the chance to monitor the execution of the Execution Agent.

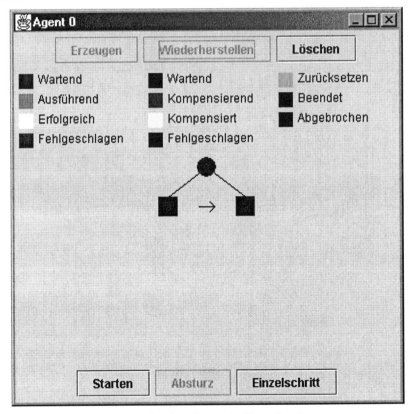

Fig. I.4. A GUI interface to the Execution Agent

This way, several Execution Agents can be started, all executing different transaction trees on the same database of the mini world. Using direct SQL commands, the user can directly introduce operational disturbances such as the failure of a certain production unit to the mini world and watch the reaction of the Execution Agent during their recovery in either direction.

To test the recoverability of the Execution Agent in case of software failures leading to its crash, two buttons 'Absturz' and 'Wiederherstelen' are introduced. The button 'Absturz' sends a *system.exit(0)* to the Java virtual machine that practically kills the Execution Agent instanteously without giving it a chance for a orderly shutdown. Pressing the 'Wiederherstelen' button calls the recovery algorithms described in Chap. 7, which restore the original state of the Execution Agent just before pressing the 'Absturz' button.

The coupling of the recovery mechanisms of the Execution Agent and the DBMS of the underlying mini world are implemented. In the current version of the prototype, solution 2 described in Sect. 7.2.6, p. 129, and solution 3 described in Sect. 7.2.7, p. 131, are implemented. For the later solution, we install another database for the mini world on DB/2 in order to use its system monitor features [56].

References

1. Alonso R, Garcia-Molina H, Salem (1987) Concurrency Control and Recovery for Global Procedures in Federated Database Systems. In: the quarterly Bulletin IEEE Technical Communications on database Engineering. Vol 10, issue 3, pp 5-11

2. Ambros-Ingerson J, Steel S (1988) Integrating Planning, Execution, and Monitoring. In: the Proceedings of the AAAI, pp 83-88

3. Austin J. How to do Things with Words. Clarendon, Oxford, UK, 1962

4. Bayardo R, Bohrrer W, Brice R, Cichocki A, Fowler J, Helal A, Kashyap V, Ksiezyk T, martin G, Nodine M, Rashid M, Rusinkiewicz M, Shea R, Unnikrisnan C, Unruh A, Woelk D (1997) InfoSleuth: Agent-Based Semantic Integration of Information in Open and dynamic Enviornments. In: Huhns M, Singh M (eds) Readings in Agents. Morgan Kaufmann, pp 205-216

5. Bellifemine F, Rimassa G, Poggi A (1999) JADE: A FIPA-Compliant Agent Framework. In: the Proceedings of the 4th International Conference and Exhibition on the Practical Application of Intelligent Agents and Multi-Agents, UK

6. Bernstein P (2000) Advanced Transaction Models. In: CSE593 Lecture on Transaction Processing University of Washington

7. Bernstein P, Newcomer E (1997) Principles of Transaction Processing. Morgan Kaufmann Publishers

8. Bernstein P, Hadzilacos V, Goodman N (1987) Concurrency Control and Recovery in Database Systems. Addison-Wesley

9. Bongaerts L (1998) Integration of Scheduling and Control in Holonic Manufacturing Systems. KU Leuven

10. Bratman M (1987) Intentions, Plans, and Practical Reason. Harvard University Press

11. Breitbart Y, Georgakopoulos D, Rusinkiewicz M, Silberschatz A (1991) On Rigorous Transaction Scheduling. In: the IEEE Transactions on Software Engineering, vol 17 issue 9, pp 954-960

12. Breitbart Y, Garcia-Molina H, Silberschatz A (1992). Overview of Multi-Database Transaction Management. In: the VLDB Journal, vol 1 issue 2, pp 181-239

13.   Burmeister B, Bussmann S, Haddadi A, Sundermeyer K (1998) Agent-Oriented Techniques for Traffic and Manufacturing Applications: Progress Report. In: Jennings N, Wooldridge M (eds). Agent Technology: Foundations, Applications, and Markets. Springer-Verlag

14.   Carey M, Franklin M, Livny M, Shekita E (1991). Data Caching Tradeoffs in Client-Server DBMS Architectures. In: the Proceedings of the ACM SIGMOD, pp 357-366

15.   Chauhan D, Baker A (1998) JAFMAS: A Multi-Agent Application Development System. In: the Proceedings of the 2nd International Conference on Autonomous Agents. ACM Press, pp 100-107

16.   Chen L, Sycara K (1998) WebMate: A Personal Agent for Browsing and Searching. In: the Proceedings of the 2nd International Conference on Autonomous Agents, ACM Press

17.   Christensen J (1994) Holonic Manufacturing Systems: Initial Architecture and Standard Directions. In: the Proceedings of the 1st European Conference on Holonic Manufacturing Systems

18.   Chrysanthis P, Ramamritham K (1990) ACTA: A Framework for Specifying and Reasoning about Transaction Structure and Behavior. In: the Proceedings of the ACM SIGMOD, pp 194-203

19.   Chrysanthis P, Ramamritham K (1991). ACTA: The SAGA Continues. In: Elmagarmid A (ed) Database Transaction Models for Advanced Applications. Morgan-Kaufmann

20.   Chrysanthis P, Ramamritham K (1997) A Formalism for Extended Transaction Models. In: the Proceedings of the International Conference on VLDB, pp 103-112

21.   Chrysanthis P, Ramamritham, K (1994) Synthesis of Extended Transaction Models using ACTA. In: the ACM Transactions on Database Systems, vol 19 number 3, pp 450-491

22.   Conry S, Kuwabara K, Lesser V, Meyer R (1991) Multistage Negotiation for Distributed Constraint Satisfaction. In: the IEEE Transactions on Systems, Man, and Cybernetics, vol 21 issue 6, pp 1462-1477

23.   DARPA I3 project "Intelligent Integration of Information". Web pages found under http://mole.dc.isx.com/I3/

24.   Davies C (1978) Data Processing Spheres of Control. IBM Systems Journal, vol 17 issue 2, pp 179-198

25.   German Research Foundation web pages under http://www.dfg.de

26.   Doucet A, Gançarski S, León C, Rukoz M (1999) Nested Transactions with Integrity Constraints. In: the Proceedings of the 8th International Workshop on Foundations of Models and Languages for Data and Objects: Transactions and database Dynamics

27. Du W, Elmagarmid A (1989) Quasi Serializability: A Correctness Criterion for Global Concurrency Control in InterBase. In: the Proceedings of the 15th International VLDB Conference, pp 347-355

28. Durfee E (2000) Distributed Problem Solving and Planning. In: Weiß G. (ed) Multi-Agent Systems: A Modern Approach to Distributed Artificial Intelligence. MIT Press

29. Elmagarmid A (1991) Database Transaction Models for Advanced Applications. Morgan-Kaufmann

30. Elmagarmid A, Leu Y, Liwin W, Rusinkiewicz (1990) A Multi-Database Transaction Model for InterBase. In: the Proceedings of the International Conference on VLDB, pp 507-518

31. Elmagarmid, A., Rusinkiewicz M., and Sheth A. Management of Heterogeneous and Autonomous Database Systems. Morgan-Kaufmann. 1999.

32. Fent A, wichert C, Freitag B (1999) Logical Update Queries as Open Nested Transactions. In: the Proceedings of the 8th International Workshop on Foundations of Models and Languages for Data and Objects: Transactions and database Dynamics

33. Ferber J (1999) Multi-Agent Systems: An Introduction to Distributed Artificial Intelligence. Addison-Wesley

34. Ferguson I (1992) Touring Machines: An Architecture for Dynamic, Rational, Mobile Agents. Ph.D. Thesis. Computer laboratory, University of Cambridge, UK

35. Fikes R, Nilsson N (1971) STRIPS: A New Approach to the Application of Theorem Proving to Problem Solving. In: the Proceedings of the 2nd International Joint Conference on Artificial Intelligence. London, UK, William Kaufmann

36. Finin T, Labrou Y, Mayfield J (1997). KQML as an Agent Communication Language. In: Bradshaw J (ed) Software Agents. MIT Press, pp 291-316

37. Foundation for Intelligent Physical Agents. Information and Specification available under http://www.fipa.org/.

38. Fischer K (1999) Agent-Based Design of Holonic Manufacturing Systems. In: the Journal of Robotics and Autonomous Systems. Elsevier Science B.V.

39. Fischer K, Müller J, Pischel M (1997) A Pragmatic BDI Architecture. In: Huhns M, Singh M (eds) Readings in Agents. Morgan Kaufmann

40. Franklin S, Graesser A (1996) Is it an Agent or just a Program? A Taxonomy for Autonomous Agents. In: the Proceedings of the 3rd International Workshop on Agents Theories, Architectures, and Languages. Springer-Verlag

41. Garcia-Molina H, Salem K (1987) Sagas. In: the Proceedings of the ACM SIGMOD, ACM Press, pp 249-259

42. Garcia-Molina H (1983) Using Semantic Knowledge for Transaction Processing in a Distributed Database. In: the ACM Transactions on Database Systems, vol 8 issue 2, pp 186-213

43. Garcia-Molina H, Gawlick D, Klein J, Kleissner K, Salem K (1990) Coordinating Multi-Transaction Activities. Technical Report CS-TR-247-90. Department of Computer Science, Princeton University

44. Garcia-Molina H, Gawlick D, Klein J, Kleissner K, Salem K (1991) Modeling Long-Running Activities as Nested Sagas. In: the IEEE Data Engineering Bulletin, vol 14 issue 1, pp 14-18

45. Georgakopoulos D (1990) Transaction Management in Multi-Database Systems. Ph.D. Thesis. Department of Computer science, University of Houston

46. Georgakopoulos D, Rusinkiewicz, Sheth A (1991) On Serializability of Multi-Database Transaction Through Forced Local Conflicts. In: the Proceedings of the 7th International Conference on Data Engineering, pp 314-323

47. Georgeff M, Lansky A (1990) Reactive Reasoning and Planning. In: Allen J, Hendler J, Tate A (eds) Readings in Planning. Morgan Kaufmann

48. Giampapa J, Paolucci M, Sycara K (2000) Agent Interoperation across Multi-Agent System Boundaries. In: the Proceedings of the 4th International Conference on Autonomous Agent. ACM Press

49. Gray J (1981) The transaction Concept: Virtues and Limitations. In: the Proceedings of the International Conference on VLDB

50. Gray J, Reuter A (1983) Transaction Processing: Concepts and Techniques. Morgan Kaufmann

51. Gruber T (1993) A Translation Approach to Portable Ontology Specifications. In: the International Journal of Knowledge Acquisition for Knowledge-Based systems, vol 5 issue 2

52. Hammer R (2000) Robustheitsmenchanismen für Multi-Agenten-Systeme. Studienarbeit (in German) Universität Karlsruhe

53. Hansmann KW (1994) Industrielles Management (in German). Oldenbourg-Verlag

54. Huhns M, Jacobs N, Ksiezyk, T, Shen W, Singh M, Canata P (1992) Enterprise Information Modeling and Model Integration in Carnot. In: the Proceedings of the 1st International Conference on Enterprise Integration Modeling. MIT Press

55. IBM Corp (1999) IBM DB2 Universal Database: System Event Monitors

56. IBM DB/2 web pages under htttp://www.ibm.com/software/

57. IBM MQSeries web pages under http://www.ibm.com/software/ts/mqseries/

58. Jennings N, Wooldridge M (1998) Applications of Intelligent Agents. In: Jennings N, Wooldridge M (eds) Agent Technology: Foundations, Application, and Markets. Springer-Verlag

59. Kernler H (1994) PPS der 3. Generation (in German). Hüthig Buch Verlag

60. Klusch M (1999) Intelligent Information Agents: Agent-Based Information Discovery and Management on the Internet. Springer-Verlag

61. Koestler A (1967) The Ghost in the Machine. Arkana Books. London, UK

62. Kühn E, Puntigam F, Elmagarmid A (1991) Transaction Specification in Multi-Database Systems Based on Parallel Logic Programming. In: the Proceedings of the 1st International Workshop on Interoperability in Multi-Database Systems (IMS91). Japan

63. Labrou Y (1996) Semantic for An Agent Communication Language. Ph.D. Thesis. UMBC

64. Landvater D, Gray C (1988) MRP Standard System. Oliver Wight Companies

65. Leu Y (1991) Flexible Transaction Management in the InterBase Project. Ph.D. thesis, Purdue University

66. Matheus C, Piatetsky-Shapiro G, McNeill D (1996) Selecting and Reporting what is interesting. In: Fayyad, U. et al. (eds) Advances in Knowledge Discovery and Data Mining. MIT Press

67. Mehrotra S, Rastogi R, Korth H, Silberschatz A (1991) Non-serializable Executions in Heterogeneous Distributed Database Systems. In: the Proceedings of the 1st International Conference on Parallel and Distributed Systems

68. Mehrotra S, Rastogi R., Korth H, Silberschatz A (1992) A Transaction Model for Multi-Database Systems. Technical Report TR-92-14, University of Texas at Austin

69. Moss E (1981) Nested Transactions: an Approach to Reliable Distributed Computing. Ph.D. thesis. Department of Electrical Engineering and Computer Science, MIT

70. Mulder M, Treur J, Fisher M (1997) Agent Modeling in METATEM and DESIRE. In: Singh M, Rao A, Wooldridge M (eds) Intelligent Agents IV: Agent Theories, Architectures, and Languages. Springer-Verlag

71. Müller J (1996) The Design of Intelligent Agents: A Layered Approach, vol 1177 of the LNAI series. Springer-Verlag

72. Nagi K (1999) Transactional Agents: A Robust Approach for Scheduling Orders in a Competitive Just-In-Time Manufacturing Environment. In: the Proceedings of the Workshop on MAS in Logistics and Economical Perspectives of Agent Conceptualization

73. Nagi K (2000) Scalability of a Transactional Infrastructure for Multi-Agent Systems. In: the Proceedings of the 1st Workshop on Infrastructure for Scalable Multi-Agent Systems at Autonomous Agents 2000

74. Nagi K (2001) Transactional Support for Multi-Agent Cooperation. In: the Proceedings of the 3rd DFG colloquium of the German Priority Research Program on "Intelligent Agents and Realistic Commercial Application Scenarios", Hameln

75. Nagi K (2001) Modeling and Simulation of Cooperative Multi-Agents in Transactional Database Environments. In: the Proceedings of the 2nd Workshop on Infrastructure for Scalable Multi-Agent Systems at Autonomous Agents 2001

76. Nagi K, Lockemann P (1999) An Implementation Model for Agents with Layered Architecture in a Transactional Database Environment. In: the Proceedings of the 1st International Bi-Conference Workshop on Agent-Oriented Information Systems (AOIS'99), Heidelberg

77. Newell A, Simon H (1972) Human Problem Solving. Prentice Hall

78. Newell A, Simon H (1976) Computer Science as Empirical Enquiry: Symbols and Search. In: the Communications of the ACM, vol 19 issue 3, pp 113-126

79. Nimis J (2001) Einbettung eines transaktionsgestützten Robustheitsdienstes in die FIPA-Plattform (in German). In: the Proceedings of the 3rd DFG colloquium of the German Priority Research Program on "Intelligent Agents and Realistic Commercial Application Scenarios", Hameln

80. Nimis J, Nagi K (2000) KRASH: Robuste Ausführung von Agentenplänen durch FIPA-konforme Transaktionsagent (in German). In: the Proceedings of the 2nd DFG colloquium of the German Priority Research Program on "Intelligent Agents and Realistic Commercial Application Scenarios", TU-Ilmenau

81. Nodine M (1993) Supporting Long-Running Tasks on an Evolving Multi-Database using Interactions and Events. In: the Proceedings of the 2nd International Conference on Parallel and Distributed Information systems, pp 125-132

82. Nodine M (1994) Interactions: Multi-Database Support for Planning Applications. Ph.D. thesis. Brown University

83. Nodine M, Zdonik S (1994) Automating Compensation in a Multi-database. In: the Proceedings of the 27th Hawaii International Conference on System Sciences

84. Nodine M, Nakos N, Zdonik S (1994) Specifying Flexible Tasks in a Multi-Database. In: the Proceedings of the 2nd International Conference on Cooperative Information Systems (CoopIS'94), Toronto

85. Nwana H, Ndumu D (1998) A Brief Introduction to Software Agent Technology. In: Jennings N, Wooldridge M (eds) Agent Technology: Foundations, Application, and Markets. Springer-Verlag

86. ORACLE 8i web site under http://www.oracle.com

87. The Object Transaction Service, Version 1.1 (1994) OMG Document orbos/ 97-12-17

88. Van Dyke Parunak H (1987) Manufacturing Experience with the Contract Net. In: Huhn M (ed) Distributed Artificial Intelligence. Pitman

89. Van Dyke Parunak H (1998) Practical and Industrial Application of Agent-Based Systems

90. Van Dyke Parunak H (1998) The AARIA Agent Architecture. In: the Proceedings of the ICAA Workshop on agent-Based Manufacturing

91. Patil R, Fikes R, Patel-Schneider P, McKay D, Finin T, Gruber T, Neches R (1997) The DARPA Knowledge Sharing Effort: Progress Report. In: Huhns M, Singh M (eds) Readings in Agents. Morgan Kaufmann

92. Poslad S, Buckle P, Hadingham R (2000) The FIPA-OS Agent Platform: Open Source for Open Standards. In: the Proceedings of the 5th International Conference and Exhibition on the Practical Application of Intelligent Agents and Multi-Agents, UK, pp 355-368

93. Rao A, Georgeff M (1991) Modeling Rational Agents within a BDI Architecture. Technical Report 14. Australian AI Institute, Carlton, Australia

94. Rao A, Georgeff M (1992) An Abstract Architecture for Rational Agents. In: the Proceedings of the 3rd International Conference on Principles of Knowledge Representation and Reasoning (KR'92), pp 439-449, Morgan Kaufmann

95. Reuter A (1989) ConTracts: A Means for Extending Control Beyond Transaction Boundaries. In: the Proceedings of the 3rd International Workshop on High Performance Transaction Systems, Asilomar

96. Rohwedder, E (1999) Using SQLJ-A tutorial. In: the 25th International Conference on Very Large Data Bases (VLDB), Edinburgh

97. Russell S, Norvig P (1995) Artificial Intelligence: A Modern Approach, Prentince Hall

98. Sahib M, Karoui R, Sedillot S (1999) Open-Nested Transactions: A Support for Increasing Performance and Multi-tier Applications. In: the Proceedings of the 8th International Workshop on Foundations of Models and Languages for Data and Objects: Transactions and database Dynamics, Dagstuhl

99. Scheer AW (1994) Wirtschaftsinformatik (in German). Heidelberg. Springer-Verlag

100. Schuldt H, Schek HJ, Alonso G (1999) Transactional Coordination Agents for Composite Systems. In: the Proceedings of the International Database Engineering and Applications Symposium (IDEAS'99), Canada

101. Shaw M (1988) Dynamic Scheduling in Cellular Manufacturing Systems: A Framework for Networked Decision Making. In: the Journal of Manufacturing Systems, vol 7 issue 2, pp 83-94

102. Shehory O, Sycara K (2000) The RETSINA Communicator. In: the Proceedings of the 2nd International Conference on Autonomous Agents. ACM Press

103. Sheth A, Larson J (1990) Federated Database Systems for Managing Distributed, Heterogonous, and Autonomous, Databases. In: the ACM Computing Surveys, vol 22 issue 3, pp 183-236

104. Shoham Y (1993) Agent-Orient Programming. In: Artificial Intelligence, vol 60 issue 1, pp 1-92

105. Singh M, Huhns M (1999) Social Abstractions for Information Agents. In: Klusch M (ed) Intelligent Information Agents: Agent-Based Information Discovery and Management on the Internet. Springer-Verlag

106. Smith R (1980) The Contract Net Protocol: High Level Communication and Control in a Distributed Problem Solver. In: the IEEE Transactions on Computers, vol C-29

107. Steinaecker Jv. Logistikorientierte Produktionsplanung und -steuerung: Gegenstand, Konzepte und Kritik (in German). Web page under http://www.lis.iao.fhg.de/steinaec/veroeffe/pps/pps.htm

108. Sycara K (1999) In-Context Information Management through Adaptive Collaboration of Intelligent Agents. In: Klusch M (ed) Intelligent Information Agents: Agent-Based Information Discovery and Management on the Internet. Springer-Verlag

109. Sycara K, Liu J (1994) Distributed Meeting Scheduling. In: the Proceedings of the 16th Annual Conference of the Cognitive Society, Atlanta, August 13-16

110. Sycara K, Pannu A (1998) The RETSINA Multi-agent System: Towards Integrating Planning, Execution, and Information Gathering. In: Proceedings of the 2nd International Conference on Autonomous Agents. ACM Press

111. Sycara K, Decker K, Zeng D (1998) Intelligent Agents in Portfolio Management. In: Jennings N, Wooldridge M (eds) Agent Technology: Foundations, Applications, and Markets, pp 267-282

112. Tal A, Alonso R (1994) Commit Protocols for Externalized Commit in Heterogeneous Database Systems. In: the Journal on Distributed and Parallel Databases, vol 2 issue 2

113. Thumm R (1983) Funktionspläne zur Modellbildung von Materialflußsystemen (in German). In Bahke E (ed) Wissenschaftliche Berichte des Institutes für Fördertechnik der Universität Karlsruhe, Germany

114. Encina web pages at the IBM Transarc lab: http://www.transarc.ibm.com/

115. Ullman J (1982) Principles of Database Systems. Rockville, MD: Computer Science Press

116. Vossen G, Groß-Hardt M (1993) Grundlaged der Transaktionsverarbeitung (in German). Addison-Wesley

117. Wächter H, Reuter A (1991) The ConTract Model. In: Elmagarmid A (ed) Database Transaction Models for Advanced Applications. Morgan Kaufmann

118. Wagner G (2000) The AOIS Glossary on the Agent-Orientation in Information Systems, found under http://www.aois.org

119. Weikum G, Schek H (1991) Concepts and Applications of Multi-Level Transactions and Open Nested Transactions. In: Elmagarmid A (ed) Database transaction Models for advanced Applications. Morgan Kaufmann

120. Wichert CA, Fent A, Freitag B (1998) How to Execute ULTRA Transactions. Technical Report MIP-9812. Fakultät für Mathematik und Informatik, Univertät Passau

121. Wiederhold G (1997) Mediators in the Architecture of Future Information Systems. In: Huhns M, Singh M (eds) Readings in Agents. Morgan Kaufmann

122. Wilkins D, Myers K (1995) A Common Knowledge Representation for Plan Generation and Reactive Execution. In the Journal of Logic and Computation, vol 5 issue 6, pp 731-761

123. Wöhe G (1990) Einführung in die allgemeine Betriebswirtschaftslehre (in German). Verlag Vahlen, München

124. Wolski A, Veijalainen J (1991) 2PC Agent Method: Achieving Serializability in Presence of Failures in a Heterogeneous Multi-Database. In: Databases: Theory, design and Applications, pp 268-287

125. Wooldridge M (2000) Intelligent Agents. In: Weiß G (ed) Multi-Agent Systems: A Modern Approach to Distributed Artificial Intelligence. MIT Press

126. Wooldridge M, Jennings N (1995) Agent Theories, Architectures, and Languages: a Survey. In: Wooldridge M, Jennings N. (eds) Intelligent Agents. Springer-Verlag

127. Wörn H, Lockemann P (1999) Robuster Betrieb und simulationsgestützte Optimierung von Multi-Agenten-Systemen in Produktion und Logistik (in German) Accepted Research Proposal to the German Research Foundation

128. Distributed Transaction Processing (1991) The XA Specification, X/Open CAE. Specification. ISBN 1- 872630-24-3. C193. X/Open Company Ltd. Apex Plaza, Forbury Rd., Reading, Berkshire, RG11AX, UK

129. Yu P, Heiss H, Dias D (1991) Modeling and Analysis of a Timestamp History Based Certification Protocol for Concurrency Control. In: the IEEE Transactions on Knowledge and Data engineering, vol 3 issue 4, pp 525-537

130. Yu P, Dias D, Lavenberg S (1993) On the analytical modeling of database concurrency control. In the Journal of the ACM, vol 40, number 4

131. The Zeus project. Home pages under http://www.labs.bt.com/projects/agents/zeus/

Subject Index

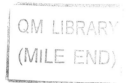

Lecture Notes in Computer Science

For information about Vols. 1–2175
please contact your bookseller or Springer-Verlag

Vol. 2213: M.J. van Sinderen, L.J.M. Nieuwenhuis (Eds.), Protocols for Multimedia Systems. Proceedings, 2001. XII, 239 pages. 2001.

Vol. 2214: O. Boldt, H. Jürgensen (Eds.), Automata Implementation. Proceedings, 1999. VIII, 183 pages. 2001.

Vol. 2215: N. Kobayashi, B.C. Pierce (Eds.), Theoretical Aspects of Computer Software. Proceedings, 2001. XV, 561 pages. 2001.

Vol. 2216: E.S. Al-Shaer, G. Pacifici (Eds.), Management of Multimedia on the Internet. Proceedings, 2001. XIV, 373 pages. 2001.

Vol. 2217: T. Gomi (Ed.), Evolutionary Robotics. Proceedings, 2001. XI, 139 pages. 2001.

Vol. 2218: R. Guerraoui (Ed.), Middleware 2001. Proceedings, 2001. XIII, 395 pages. 2001.

Vol. 2219: S.T. Taft, R.A. Duff, R.L. Brukardt, E. Ploedereder (Eds.), Consolidated Ada Reference Manual. XXV, 560 pages. 2001.

Vol. 2220: C. Johnson (Ed.), Interactive Systems. Proceedings, 2001. XII, 219 pages. 2001.

Vol. 2221: D.G. Feitelson, L. Rudolph (Eds.), Job Scheduling Strategies for Parallel Processing. Proceedings, 2001. VII, 207 pages. 2001.

Vol. 2223: P. Eades, T. Takaoka (Eds.), Algorithms and Computation. Proceedings, 2001. XIV, 780 pages. 2001.

Vol. 2224: H.S. Kunii, S. Jajodia, A. Sølvberg (Eds.), Conceptual Modeling – ER 2001. Proceedings, 2001. XIX, 614 pages. 2001.

Vol. 2225: N. Abe, R. Khardon, T. Zeugmann (Eds.), Algorithmic Learning Theory. Proceedings, 2001. XI, 379 pages. 2001. (Subseries LNAI).

Vol. 2226: K.P. Jantke, A. Shinohara (Eds.), Discovery Science. Proceedings, 2001. XII, 494 pages. 2001. (Subseries LNAI).

Vol. 2227: S. Boztaş, I.E. Shparlinski (Eds.), Applied Algebra, Algebraic Algorithms and Error-Correcting Codes. Proceedings, 2001. XII, 398 pages. 2001.

Vol. 2228: B. Monien, V.K. Prasanna, S. Vajapeyam (Eds.), High Performance Computing – HiPC 2001. Proceedings, 2001. XVIII, 438 pages. 2001.

Vol. 2229: S. Qing, T. Okamoto, J. Zhou (Eds.), Information and Communications Security. Proceedings, 2001. XIV, 504 pages. 2001.

Vol. 2230: T. Katila, I.E. Magnin, P. Clarysse, J. Montagnat, J. Nenonen (Eds.), Functional Imaging and Modeling of the Heart. Proceedings, 2001. XI, 158 pages. 2001.

Vol. 2232: L. Fiege, G. Mühl, U. Wilhelm (Eds.), Electronic Commerce. Proceedings, 2001. X, 233 pages. 2001.

Vol. 2233: J. Crowcroft, M. Hofmann (Eds.), Networked Group Communication. Proceedings, 2001. X, 205 pages. 2001.

Vol. 2234: L. Pacholski, P. Ružička (Eds.), SOFSEM 2001: Theory and Practice of Informatics. Proceedings, 2001. XI, 347 pages. 2001.

Vol. 2235: C.S. Calude, G. Păun, G. Rozenberg, A. Salomaa (Eds.), Multiset Processing. VIII, 359 pages. 2001.

Vol. 2237: P. Codognet (Ed.), Logic Programming. Proceedings, 2001. XI, 365 pages. 2001.

Vol. 2239: T. Walsh (Ed.), Principles and Practice of Constraint Programming – CP 2001. Proceedings, 2001. XIV, 788 pages. 2001.

Vol. 2240: G.P. Picco (Ed.), Mobile Agents. Proceedings, 2001. XIII, 277 pages. 2001.

Vol. 2241: M. Jünger, D. Naddef (Eds.), Computational Combinatorial Optimization. IX, 305 pages. 2001.

Vol. 2242: C.A. Lee (Ed.), Grid Computing – GRID 2001. Proceedings, 2001. XII, 185 pages. 2001.

Vol. 2244: D. Bjørner, M. Broy, A.V. Zamulin (Eds.), Perspectives of System Informatics. Proceedings, 2001. XIII, 548 pages. 2001.

Vol. 2245: R. Hariharan, M. Mukund, V. Vinay (Eds.), FST TCS 2001: Foundations of Software Technology and Theoretical Computer Science. Proceedings, 2001. XI, 347 pages. 2001.

Vol. 2246: R. Falcone, M. Singh, Y.-H. Tan (Eds.), Trust in Cyber-societies. VIII, 195 pages. 2001. (Subseries LNAI).

Vol. 2247: C. P. Rangan, C. Ding (Eds.), Progress in Cryptology – INDOCRYPT 2001. Proceedings, 2001. XIII, 351 pages. 2001.

Vol. 2248: C. Boyd (Ed.), Advances in Cryptology – ASIACRYPT 2001. Proceedings, 2001. XI, 603 pages. 2001.

Vol. 2249: K. Nagi, Transactional Agents. XVI, 205 pages. 2001.

Vol. 2250: R. Nieuwenhuis, A. Voronkov (Eds.), Logic for Programming, Artificial Intelligence, and Reasoning. Proceedings, 2001. XV, 738 pages. 2001. (Subseries LNAI).

Vol. 2251: Y.Y. Tang, V. Wickerhauser, P.C. Yuen, C.Li (Eds.), Wavelet Analysis and Its Applications. Proceedings, 2001. XIII, 450 pages. 2001.

Vol. 2252: J. Liu, P.C. Yuen, C. Li, J. Ng, T. Ishida (Eds.), Active Media Technology. Proceedings, 2001. XII, 402 pages. 2001.

Vol. 2253: T. Terano, T. Nishida, A. Namatame, S. Tsumoto, Y. Ohsawa, T. Washio (Eds.), New Frontiers in Artificial Intelligence. Proceedings, 2001. XXVII, 553 pages. 2001. (Subseries LNAI).

Vol. 2254: M.R. Little, L. Nigay (Eds.), Engineering for Human-Computer Interaction. Proceedings, 2001. XI, 359 pages. 2001.

Vol. 2256: M. Stumptner, D. Corbett, M. Brooks (Eds.), AI 2001: Advances in Artificial Intelligence. Proceedings, 2001. XII, 666 pages. 2001. (Subseries LNAI).

Vol. 2258: P. Brazdil, A. Jorge (Eds.), Progress in Artificial Intelligence. Proceedings, 2001. XII, 418 pages. 2001. (Subseries LNAI).

Vol. 2259: S. Vaudenay, A.M. Youssef (Eds.), Selected Areas in Cryptography. Proceedings, 2001. XI, 359 pages. 2001.

Vol. 2260: B. Honary (Ed.), Cryptography and Coding. Proceedings, 2001. IX, 416 pages. 2001.

Vol. 2264: K. Steinhöfel (Ed.), Stochastic Algorithms: Foundations and Applications. Proceedings, 2001. VIII, 203 pages. 2001.